Stories Of New Jersey

ITS SIGNIFICANT PLACES, PEOPLE AND ACTIVITIES

Compiled and Written by the
Federal Writers' Project of
the Works Progress Admin-
istration for the State of
New Jersey

Profusely Illustrated

M. BARROWS AND COMPANY

1938   NEW YORK

974.9
Fed

Sponsored by The New Jersey Association of Teachers of Social Studies

New Jersey Guild Associates, Inc., Co-operating Sponsor

SOLE DISTRIBUTORS

RADEMAEKERS

NEWARK   NEW JERSEY

PRINTED IN THE UNITED STATES OF AMERICA
BY J. J. LITTLE AND IVES COMPANY, NEW YORK

PREFACE

This volume of Stories of New Jersey is the result of a two-year experiment carried on by the Federal Writers' Project in New Jersey. In November 1936, after consultation with several educators, the Project began issuing to the schools and libraries of the State periodical pamphlets dealing with significant aspects of New Jersey life.

The first issue of 3,000 copies was sent to those school principals who had indicated an interest in the service. The demand for additional copies was so great and the reputation of the service grew so rapidly that the issue had to be increased to 10,000 copies, which is the maximum possible by the reproduction method used. Thirty *Stories* were distributed during 1936-37, and twenty during 1937-38.

The service was designed to stimulate the interest of New Jersey school children in the affairs of the State and to supply the schools with data, not otherwise available, to supplement the curriculum of the social study courses. There has been no attempt to follow a particular course of study or to deal with any one period or activity.

In response to requests from students, teachers, librarians and historians, urging that this material be put in more permanent form, some of the original bulletins have been reprinted here. Several new *Stories* have been substituted for those which seemed to have less value as reference material. As the work continues new material will

iii

be presented with the hope that there will eventually be accessible a collection of useful New Jersey material.

In an effort to avoid error we have indebted ourselves to many experts, too numerous to list here. We are especially grateful to The New Jersey Association of Teachers of Social Studies for their encouragement in the preparation of this volume and for their support in sponsoring it.

IRENE FUHLBRUEGGE, *State Director*

VIOLA HUTCHINSON ⎱
SAMUEL EPSTEIN   ⎰ *Assistant State Directors*

FOREWORD

The most interesting and charming pamphlets written and distributed by the Federal Writers' Project in New Jersey during the years 1936, 1937 and 1938 were welcomed so enthusiastically by the schools and libraries of our State that The New Jersey Association of Teachers of the Social Studies moved to promote publication in a more permanent form. These stories of historic spots, personages, and unusual industries of New Jersey, presented in a single volume, afford valuable supplementary reading material for use in our schools. For these reasons The New Jersey Association of Teachers of Social Studies is very happy to join with The New Jersey Guild Associates in sponsoring this volume.

The Federal Writers' Project in New Jersey deserves great credit for rendering this unique service to our State. To them, alone, all honor is due for the painstaking care with which the facts have been gathered, the articles written, and the stories edited. Both admiration and gratitude for this achievement prompts The New Jersey Association of Teachers of Social Studies to state that its sole contribution to this volume has been that of urging for it a wide circulation and a useful life.

THE NEW JERSEY ASSOCIATION
OF TEACHERS OF SOCIAL STUDIES

WORKS PROGRESS ADMINISTRATION

HARRY L. HOPKINS, *Administrator*
ELLEN S. WOODWARD, *Assistant Administrator*
HENRY G. ALSBERG, *Director Federal Writers' Project*

CONTENTS

ILLUSTRATIONS

All photographs not otherwise credited are by the
New Jersey Writers' Project staff photographers

PLACES

Ringwood Manor

RINGWOOD MANOR STATE PARK

Ringwood Manor, a fine old estate that resembles an outdoor museum, is the newest New Jersey State park. Within the 78-room mansion and scattered indiscriminately about the grounds is an amazing collection of relics, art objects and knicknacks. A great iron cogwheel leans against a tree; a huge mortar planted on the front lawn is aimed toward the adjoining lake; stretching along a terrace are 24 enormous links of the great iron chain that was stretched across the Hudson to protect West Point from British warships; and throughout the formal gardens are newel posts and iron gates, marble columns and statuary, ancient millstones and the bleached skulls of long-dead cattle in which birds find convenient nesting places.

Ringwood Manor lies between the wooded slopes of a rugged little valley at the northern end of Wanaque Reservoir, only a mile from the New York State boundary and about 10 miles southwest of Suffern, New York. The Manor House and about 100 acres of land were given to the State in 1937 by Erskine Hewitt, the last owner of an estate once occupied by early iron manufacturers.

The iron mined in the nearby hills was converted at the Ringwood forges into munitions and field equipment for Washington's army, and the plant continued in operation long after modern methods of smelting and forging had carried iron manufacture to other regions. Until 1931 Ringwood was the center of an active community. The pretentious house and gardens, the many relics and objects of art gathered from all parts of the world reflect the importance of the owners and the wealth they took from an estate that once covered 15,000 acres in the Ramapo hills.

On the path before the house are crushing stones and grindstones found in the vicinity. They indicate that the section was an Indian camp site. About 1739 Cornelius Board, a Welsh miner then living at Little Falls, learned from the Indians that there was iron ore in the Pompton mountains. They led him to the head of the Ringwood River, a branch of the Pequannock, and there he built a small furnace. In May of the following year Board sold the furnace and 16 acres for £63 to the Ogden family, residents of Newark, who had been surveying the iron fields of northern New Jersey and had bought up several water-power sites along the Pequannock River.

It was the Ogdens who gave the northern New Jersey iron industry its start. They built a splendid house and several smaller dwellings and carried on an active trade in forged iron which was shipped by mules to points on the Hackensack and Passaic Rivers, where it could be transferred to boats.

Word of this promising enterprise came to the ears of Peter Hasenclever, a shrewd German promoter. He went to London and persuaded people influential in court circles to buy shares in a company that was to develop resources in the new world. It is said Queen Charlotte and some of her maids of honor subscribed. The new concern was called the American Iron Company, and Hasenclever was sent to America as resident manager.

In the *New York Mercury* of March 5, 1764, appeared an advertisement offering for sale the Ogden properties

on the Ringwood River. This Hasenclever bought for
£5,000, together with additional lands at Long Pond, in
all 15,000 acres.

He imported several hundred workmen from Germany
and Ireland; rebuilt the Ogden residence; put up cabins
for the workmen, storehouses, a gristmill, a sawmill and
a stamping mill and constructed dams to provide water
power. The mines and forges prospered, and so did Hasenclever.

The company was also interested in iron properties in
New York State along the Mohawk River, where 50,000
acres had been acquired. In two years Hasenclever had
spent £54,600, which was £14,400 more than had been
pledged; but no money had found its way back to the
stockholders. Hasenclever's management of the company's
affairs was brought into question, and he returned to England to find that his associate there was bankrupt and had
allowed the concern to become seriously involved. After
restoring his credit abroad, Hasenclever returned to America in 1768, but in his absence the American interests had
likewise fallen into danger.

At Hasenclever's request, Governor William Franklin
appointed a commission of four appraisers to investigate
the management of the Ringwood, Long Pond and Charlotteburg properties. Their report upheld Hasenclever's
conduct; they argued that he needed only more time to
put the American Iron Company on a paying basis. Nevertheless, Hasenclever could obtain no further credit, and he
returned to London bankrupt in 1769. A photostatic copy
of the book recounting the proceedings against the German promoter is in the Ringwood Manor House. He de-
fended himself in *The Remarkable Case of Peter
Hasenclever*, published in 1773, but it was 1787 before

his rights were secured in the Chancery Court of London. By that time Hasenclever had recouped his losses and become a successful merchant in Landeshut, Germany.

After Hasenclever's return to England John Jacob Faesch, one of the great early ironmasters and an associate of Hasenclever, was left in charge. Then, in 1771, the management of the Ringwood properties was turned over to Robert Erskine, a young Scottish engineer. He was left to carry on the work as best he could, for the financial condition of the company was very unstable. There is a tradition that the investors who were closest to King George III persuaded him to sign the tax on tea to make up to them for their losses. Thus Ringwood, which was to play an important part in the Revolution, may have been an indirect cause of the war.

When the Revolution broke out Erskine at once sided with the colonists and sold his products to the patriots. Because he was one of the few engineers in the country, Washington appointed him Geographer and Surveyor General to the Revolutionary Armies. Erskine made most of the military maps, including those for the Jersey campaigns. In the New York Historical Society there are 114 of the 129 maps in Erskine's own handwriting; several are in the possession of J. P. Morgan; the remainder are in Washington. These maps are models of accuracy and execution.

The master of Ringwood and his forges were so important to the Colonial cause that extreme precautions were taken to protect them. The names were not mentioned in military dispatches, lest the messages fall into the hands of British spies.

Ringwood's position on the main road halfway between West Point and Morristown made it a convenient place for conferences between Washington and his generals. It is said that many of Washington's letters dated from "headquarters" were written in this secluded valley.

The road to Ringwood was carefully guarded, and a battery was planted on the mountain at Suffern. Erskine organized and drilled a company of men ready to march against any attack. Several times the English troops got as far as Mahwah, just over the mountains. Once a raiding party reached Ringwood and set fire to the house. Mrs. Erskine escaped in her nightgown, her watch safely hidden in her slipper. Fortunately the raiders had found their way first to the wine cellar. While they dallied there, American troops arrived, and the invaders were driven off.

Erskine administered the industry so efficiently that he was called the "Lord of Ringwood." He built a dam at Tuxedo and dug a ditch to carry the waters of Lake Tuxedo to increase the water power. He also built a dam at Greenwood Lake. Day and night the forges were turning out ammunition for the patriots.

There are a number of entries in Washington's expense accounts, such as items for washing and for shoeing of horses, that refer to stops at Ringwood. Washington was at Ringwood when he sent orders for the suppression of the Pompton mutiny. General Howe's report of this uprising was written in the house. When the war ended there was a great victory dinner at the Manor, attended by Washington and guests from as far as New York. Impressed by the beauty of the country, Washington is said to have suggested that Ringwood would be ideal for a great recreation ground. He foresaw that New York would become the largest city in the country, if not in the world. Thirty-five miles away, New York was then a two days' journey; the time required now is less than two hours.

On that tragic day, October 2, 1780, on which the young Major André was executed at Tappan, Robert Erskine died as a result of exposure while on a surveying expedition. Though some of Washington's staff were present, the general did not witness the execution of the young English spy. The shutters of headquarters at Tappan were closed, and it is possible that the saddened Commander in Chief was traveling through the northern hills to the home of his devoted friend.

In 1782 Washington returned to Ringwood and planted an elm beside the brick crypt in which Erskine was buried. The grave may be seen today. Beside it is that of Erskine's secretary, Robert Monteith.

After Erskine's death his widow and her second husband, Robert Lettis Hooper, an army officer, managed the property for three years. In 1783 all the iron was offered for sale, and the place was closed.

It was not until 1807 that the Ringwood mines and forges were again active. The property was purchased by Martin Ryerson, who ran the industry successfully for 30 years. Under his three sons who followed him the business dwindled, due partly to the opening of the Pennsylvania fields and to the improvement in methods of iron manufacture.

During the management of the elder Ryerson, Ringwood forges furnished munitions for the War of 1812. Standing on the lawn in front of the house today is one of the main deck guns of the frigate *Constitution*, forged here. A grove of trees flanking the terrace in front of the house was planted by Mrs. Ryerson to commemorate the Peace of Ghent that ended the conflict.

REVOLUTIONARY RELICS AT RINGWOOD MANOR

By 1853 the fortunes of Ringwood were at a low ebb. Peter Cooper, the great industrialist and philanthropist, loaned the Ryersons money to build up the tottering structure; but in the end he was forced to purchase it. The management of the iron properties was turned over to Abram S. Hewitt, who in partnership with Peter Cooper's son, Edward, owned the Trenton Iron Company. Ringwood promised a valuable source of supply for the firm of Cooper and Hewitt, which became one of the most important concerns in the iron-mining industry. After Abram Hewitt married his partner's sister Ringwood was chosen as their summer home.

As the mines brought wealth to the Hewitt family, the house and gardens were enlarged and embellished. There is no trace in the present mansion of the simple Colonial lines of Robert Erskine's house, partly destroyed by the British raiding party. Each owner has altered it according to his tastes and needs. Finally the whole has been covered with stucco.

The gardens have been laid out with walks, rose arbors, terraces and ponds; adorned with statues, ornamental gates, Chinese vases, Italian marbles and French fountains; and sprinkled with relics of Colonial and early American history. In the garden there are columns from the old New York Life Insurance Building. In the tower of the house hangs the bell from the old furnace which summoned the workmen in times of danger. The windows of the glass piazza were formerly part of the Cooper Union Art School in New York City.

Museums, expositions and private collectors have drawn on the storehouse of treasures preserved by the proprietors of Ringwood. At the Centennial Exposition in Philadelphia in 1876 there was shown a complete Revolutionary kitchen, with utensils, spit crane and spiders, all furnished by Mr. Hewitt. These were never returned.

The stables are unusually elaborate, with paneled cypress walls. When Henry Ford founded his American Village at Dearborn, Michigan, Ringwood supplied him with five carloads of relics, including carriages and sleighs dating from 1757, many of which were made to order by Brewster. These old vehicles had been standing unused in the stables.

The mines finally closed in 1931, and will probably not be reopened. Although the nearby hills are still rich in iron ore, it is no longer profitable to extract it. Upwards of 500 men, many of them descendants of those who came here in the early days of the industry, were thrown out of work when the mines were shut down. Many of these are Jackson Whites, a mountain folk who have lived in the Ramapo Mountains since the Revolutionary War. They have depended for subsistence on the mines, and still speak of the "Company" with awe, while "The Family" means only the Hewitts. In the early years, before Peter Cooper's time, money was practically unknown to the workmen. All of their trading was done at the company store—still in existence—where they were credited with supplies in exchange for their services.

Ringwood Manor State Park is under the jurisdiction of the Department of Conservation and Development. Here, within easy distance of the metropolitan area, are woodlands almost completely unspoiled, and relics that recall a great period in the Nation's development.

OLD OXFORD FURNACE

New Jersey has fallen heir to Oxford Furnace. Once it was a thriving iron smelter, pouring forth smoke and gushing streams of white hot molten iron to be made into horseshoes, nails and stoves for the colonists and cannon balls to fight the Indians, French and British.

The ruins of the old furnace are on the slope of Scott's Mountain, in the village of Oxford, about a block from State Highway 30. It was built in 1742 by Jonathan Robeson, in what was then the wilds of Morris (now Warren) County, and for 140 years it served New Jersey well.

Oxford Furnace was placed to take advantage of a vein of ore containing 60% of iron. Some of the shafts, at the outset, were sunk close to the furnace, but later considerable ore was taken from the Kisbaugh Mine, situated several miles north near Great Meadows and the Pequest River.

There were other mines three-quarters of a mile south. Among these was Car Wheel Mine, named for an industry established in 1840 when railroads were being built. Its founders were the Scranton brothers, George and Selden, for whom the city of Scranton, Pennsylvania, was named. They found the Oxford pig iron well adapted to their needs and operated the furnace many years.

Oxford ore was recommended as the best for making steel, since it also contained carbon. Britain, however, did not encourage the more finished forms of industry here, and the Governor reported only one steel plant in the

OXFORD FURNACE AS IT LOOKS TODAY. AT THE EXTREME LEFT CAN BE SEEN THE REMAINS OF THE OLD FURNACE. THE BUILDING IN THE CENTER WAS THE STAMPING MILL, AND THE CHURCH AT THE EXTREME RIGHT WAS ONCE THE GRISTMILL

Province in 1768. The smelting of crude pig iron, which could be taken to England for making into hardware, was not forbidden, however.

Iron is rarely found in the earth in a pure state. It is scattered in veins and fragments throughout rocks. The method of extracting the iron from the rock has not changed since the early days of the Oxford Furnace. Modern machinery, however, with large furnaces and electric power, has made it possible to extract or smelt hundreds of tons of pure iron a day, while in the early days two or three tons were considered good.

Smelting iron consists merely in applying intense heat to the ore. This melts both the iron and the rock. The iron, being heavier, runs to the bottom, while the liquid rock floats to the top. The molten iron is drawn off through holes in the bottom of the furnace, while the rock and other impurities are carried off through another vent. This waste matter is called slag.

Some of the cannon balls made at Oxford for the French and Indian Wars, 1754-1763, have been found among the cinder heaps. Another product of this period was chimney firebacks. These were cast in molds in several patterns. One bears the British coat of arms with the lion and the unicorn and the date 1746. Another shows a Colonial couple preparing to dance. Some of these firebacks have been found in old houses in Northern New Jersey. Most of Oxford's iron, however, was in the shape of "pigs" or rough cast blocks that were pounded into other forms at New Jersey forges.

The furnace also shipped its pigs to Philadelphia, where some of them became ballast for ships. The iron was carried in oxcarts about four miles to the Delaware River below Belvidere. Here at Foul Rift the iron was placed aboard Durham boats for the two-day voyage to Philadelphia.

The Durham boat, invented by Robert Durham, was designed to carry goods through the Delaware River rapids. Flat bottomed with sharp ends, some of them were 66 feet long, 6 feet wide and 3 feet deep, capable of carrying 15 tons. The first one was built in 1740, and so many others followed that at one time there were several hundred on the river, employing over 2,000 men. A crew of six was required to propel and steer them by oars or poles, though they used sails at times.

Throughout the Revolution Oxford was safely sheltered by Washington's line of defense along the Watchung Ridge, 30 miles to the southeast, and continued to supply the Continental Army with cannon balls.

Production at the Oxford Furnace, which had risen to three tons of pig iron a day, declined about 1807. Two years later it was bought by Morris Robeson, grandson of Jonathan Robeson. The sides of Scott's Mountain and other hills around the works became bare of trees. Its 4,000 acres of woodland were exhausted. Soon the ironmaster had to close the furnace for lack of fuel, "go out of blast," as the workers sadly said. For 20 years it was idle or produced only chimney backs and stoves. Many of the forges that had used its pig iron fell into ruins.

Building of canals brought about a change for the better in New Jersey industry, including iron. When the Morris Canal was opened in 1831 and the Pennsylvania canal system was completed, they brought the new fuel, Pennsylvania coal, to New Jersey. Oxford then sprang into new life. About this time William Henry, manager of the works, invented the "hot blast." This was a method of heating the air before it was forced through the fire. Aided by larger bellows, this increased production to four tons and more a day. It was necessary to enlarge the furnace, and soon the output reached 10 tons a day. The pig iron was hauled to the Morris Canal a few miles distant and thence aboard boats to the Delaware, to Philadelphia by the Pennsylvania Canal, and to many towns in New Jersey.

Another peak of prosperity came to Oxford in the Civil War, when iron was in great demand. The Scranton brothers rebuilt the works to a capacity of 12,000 tons a year. They also erected a foundry, a rolling mill and a nail factory that turned out 240,000 kegs a year.

The activity of the Civil War period was short lived. Soon afterward the iron fields of Western Pennsylvania and Indiana began production. New Jersey operators could not compete with these new fields that had the advantage of a nearby fuel supply from the soft-coal mines. Oxford was "blown out" for the last time in 1882. Since then the crumbling stones and bricks have served only as a memento.

But the historic ruins are not the only reminders of a prosperous industry. Behind the furnace stands a long stone barn that housed the mules that once strained to pull the little ore trucks up the ramp to the stamping mill. Behind the barn is a pile of slag; mountain would perhaps be a better word, for the pile towers more than 50 feet above the houses at its base and stretches for nearly a mile to the north. Slag was considered a waste product once, but now it is used for road construction. So immense is this slag deposit that although thousands of truckloads have been carted away, there is hardly a visible effect on the pile.

Of the furnace itself, only 25 feet remain of what was once a 38-foot, pyramid-shaped stack. It stands close to the foot of the hill, largely concealed by the engine house and boilerhouse, later additions. The lower half of the engine house was originally the stamping mill, where the ore was crushed before being smelted. It stands beside a raceway that carried water from Furnace Creek to turn the water wheel that ran the stamping mill as well as the big leather bellows that blew air into the furnace.

High on a hill overlooking the furnace is the three-story house that was built in 1754 by the Shippen brothers, Joseph and William, who then owned the controlling interest in the furnace. Joseph was known as "Gentleman Joe," because of the many distinguished guests from New York and Philadelphia whom he entertained in the little village. Though the house has been remodeled from time to time, the original walls of native stone remain intact. Its broad front is partly hidden by glass-enclosed porches. This house went with the furnace, and the many owners and lessees used it in turn.

Near the house is the three-story gristmill that ground flour for the workers and feed for the animals that hauled ore and fuel. For the past 25 years the gristmill has been used as a Methodist Church. At the peak, where once hung a pulley to hoist grain, now hangs the church bell, without cover, like those of the Spanish missions of California.

Some of the older residents of the neighborhood still tell stories of the days when Oxford was a booming mining town. One of these, a lurid Hallowe'en story, relates the visit about 60 years ago of the ghost of Jerry Mack. Jerry had been found dead at the furnace one February day. Although the cause of his death was a mystery, people soon ceased wondering about it. Jerry Mack was forgotten. But Jerry had not forgotten his former associates. One windy night just before Hallowe'en three workers at the furnace heard a voice above the wind calling over and over, "doomed to wander, doomed to wander." There was a rustling at the stack house door, and as the workmen looked up, there stood Jerry's ghost carrying an umbrella and dressed in a long-tailed coat. Without waiting for a second look, all three dived through the window and, without stopping, fled for their homes three miles away. Jerry then wandered about and scared the wits out of three more workmen. The next morning the whole town was terror stricken. There was an investigation, but nothing could shake the six men from their story. They had seen Jerry Mack; and what was more, not one of them would ever set foot near the furnace again.

In fact, they all left town a few days later, taking their families and household goods with them.

The Warren Pipe and Foundry Co. of Belvidere, last owner of Oxford Furnace, decided that the historic value of the furnace should be perpetuated. The company has given the ruins and some land to the State, which plans to restore and preserve it for the benefit of future Americans. The restoration will be under the direction of the New Jersey Historic Sites Commission.

ROCKAWAY RIVER: A GATEWAY TO
THE IRON REGION

Although it is one of New Jersey's smaller rivers, the Rockaway was once important as the gateway to the vast magnetic iron deposits of Morris County. Its fingerlike branches penetrate the northern hills beyond the Watchung ridges, where hundreds of shafts were sunk when New Jersey provided most of the iron for America. Most of these mines were abandoned as the industry shifted to richer deposits in other States.

Forges and furnaces set up in this region by the early colonists produced iron household utensils and ammunition for the Revolutionary Army. These Colonial industries are only memories now. But the brooks and springs that feed the Rockaway as it twists among the hills, draining an area of about 200 square miles, are still tinged with iron from the hidden veins in the rocky ridges.

Tumbling down its mountain stairway, the stream falls more than 1,000 feet to its mouth, pausing long enough to form a number of lakes on the way. The largest of these is the Jersey City Reservoir, covering 120 acres south of Boonton. Throughout the region are numerous natural lakes fed or drained by the Rockaway branches. Other lakes have been created by damming the streams for water power.

The North American Glacier dug out the beds of some of the lakes about 100,000 years ago. Others were created as the glacier pushed masses of gravel and boulders into

THE ROCKAWAY FALLS AT BOONTON

water courses. Behind these barriers the water piled up until it overflowed. In recent years the lakes, the river and the brooks have created a vacation land for thousands from cities and towns. Commercially, the river is still a source of power for modern mills at a few points along its banks.

Green Pond Mountain separates the East Branch from the West Branch of the river until they join a short distance above Wharton. The West Branch rises 1,200 feet above sea level in tiny Lake Madonna on Sparta Mountain, southwest of Oak Ridge Reservoir and remote from any large town. Lake Madonna is 40 miles from the mouth of the river.

Falling steadily through rocky country, draining ten lakes, the river emerges from Lake Swannanoa in the northwest corner of Morris County and flows southward through Longwood Valley. Almost all of the lakes in this region served early industry.

Rockaway seems to be the white man's shortening of

the Indian name of the river, *roga weighwero,* which means "running out of a deep gorge." It is an especially fitting title for the East Branch. This stream flows from Green Pond, a lake two and one-half miles long at the foot of the mountain, where for more than a mile a granite cliff rises 150 feet over the lake. Leaving the lake, the brook races through a boulder-strewn ravine between steep rock walls and drops 300 feet in less than four miles in a series of cataracts and waterfalls. Halfway between Green Pond and Lake Denmark the water drops sheerly from the summit of Green Pond Mountain to the brook almost 100 feet below. An old road paralleling the stream is passable only on foot or horseback. Swollen by rain or melting snows in spring, the stream overflows its banks and runs over the road.

This region today contributes far more to the war strength of America than it did during the Revolution. At forest-lined Lake Denmark the Navy has a large ammunition storehouse, and down the stream a mile and one-half, at Picatinny Arsenal on Lake Picatinny, the Army makes ammunition for military forces in the New York area. These munitions depots are on the sites of Colonial iron centers.

In Rockaway Borough, where a dam furnishes water power for the old Rockaway gristmill, the river turns sharply north for about eight miles to the Powerville Dam. This stretch of quiet water, shaded by trees whose branches often meet overhead, is popular with canoeists and fishermen. The New Jersey Fish and Game Commission stocks the stream with thousands of trout each year.

South of the river around Denville are Arrowhead Lake, Rainbow Lake, Indian Lake and Lake Estline, with log cabins and summer bungalows on their shores. From the north, Deer Pond, Lake Valhalla, Surprise Lake, Ideal Lake, Fayson Lake and Dixon's Pond feed the Rockaway. All are popular with summer visitors. East of the river between Denville and Boonton is a group of five lakes around which has developed the modern commuters' town of Mountain Lakes.

From Powerville the river continues southeastward over a steep rocky course and plunges down 22-foot Boonton Falls into a rugged gorge, one of the outstanding scenic features of Morris County. The bridge into Boonton at the foot of the gorge is lined with fishermen during the season. Southeast of the town the river flows into Boonton Reservoir, which covers the site of old Boonetown, an important iron town before 1834.

As it emerges from the northeast corner of the reservoir, the river bends northward for a short stretch and then turns abruptly southeast through a stretch of flat meadowland to join Whippany River between Pine Brook and Hanover Neck.

For many years authorities have considered building a two-mile dam at this point to form a lake which would cover 25 square miles of now worthless meadow, drained by the Whippany and Rockaway Rivers. This project would destroy more than 5,000 acres of mosquito-breeding ground and prevent floods in the Passaic Valley.

Historians say that the first iron produced in New Jersey (other than bog iron from the southern swamps) was probably forged in the Rockaway region. From the Indians the colonists learned of the prized "black stone" from which the red men had made sturdy hatchets. Scouts from the Newark colony first found the source of this iron ore near Succasunna in Morris County. The discovery was almost equal to finding money, because every piece of land bought from the Indians was paid for partly in iron tools, hatchets, knives and hoes. These had to be imported from England at high prices.

As early as 1685 or 1700 a party of Newark and Elizabeth pioneers, skilled ironworkers among them, set out for the Passaic River frontier. On the west side of the Passaic near the mouth of the Rockaway, they cleared a tract extending to the Whippany River. Close to the present village of Whippany they built a forge known for many years as Old Forges. These men followed the streams up into the hills to find the "black stone," which was carried by pack horses back to the forge.

Today bats live in the scores of old mine shafts on the range of hills spreading southwest from Wharton and the Rockaway River. One of these, the Dickerson Mine, was bought by Mahlon Dickerson, Governor of New Jersey. Its ore contained 82% of iron.

The prospectors covered the whole basin of the river and its branches and reached beyond to Ringwood and Charlotteburg. As the veins of ore were discovered, more and more forges and furnaces were built. Despite the opposition of English ironmasters who tried to crush the infant enterprise, the colonists developed an industry that enabled them to achieve independence of Europe. At one time northern New Jersey had 80 forges and furnaces.

Denmark, where the United States Naval Ammunition Depot is situated, is the site of the Burnt Meadow Forge, established in 1750. It was owned by Col. Jacob Ford, commander of the militia who kept the enemy away from the numerous forges scattered through the Morris County hills, all of which were furnishing munitions to the Revolutionary Army.

Most productive of the Morris County mines was the

ROCKAWAY RIVER
BASIN

COMPILED BY
FEDERAL WRITERS' PROJECT, W.P.A.
NEW JERSEY

SCALE OF MILES

Hibernia group, which continued to operate long after the Civil War. Close to the village of Hibernia, about five miles north of Rockaway Borough, these mines and the Hibernia Furnace, built 1763, were bought during the Revolution by William Alexander, one of Washington's generals, who was called Lord Stirling. He soon had skilled men at work molding small cannon for the Continental Army. In the museum at Washington's Headquarters in Morristown is an iron pig bearing the mark "Hibernia" on one side.

When the Morris Canal was opened in 1831, Hibernia's iron was taken on oxcarts to Dover, and there loaded on canal boats. Dover soon became an important center of trade on the canal. It had two forges making chain cables for clipper ships; three rolling mills, one built in 1792, and a foundry where sugar and fish kettles, ten-plate stoves, salt pans and other useful things were made of cast iron. Dover is still working iron at its rolling mill, run by the Rockaway River's power.

The folk for miles around drove into Dover for shopping during the canal era, and the older boys and girls attended its academy, which was also the church on Sunday. Some of these boys and girls lived long enough to hear the song written about 30 years ago:

> Put on your old gray bonnet
> With the blue ribbons on it;
> While I hitch old Dobbin to the shay.
> And through the fields of clover
> We'll drive up to Dover
> On our golden wedding day.

COLONIAL HOUSES OF NEW JERSEY

It is over 300 years since the first Dutch settlers came from New Amsterdam to northern New Jersey to trade with the Indians. Many of the houses built since 1664, when they began to establish permanent homes, are still standing, reminders of the thrifty, comfort-loving farmers who brought European civilization to the New Jersey wilderness. The ownership of slaves supplied ample labor to build the houses of local sandstone and a mortar made of river mud mixed with straw or hogs' hair. The walls, about 1½ feet thick, helped to keep the interior warm in winter and cool in summer.

The great eaves that project above the front door are the most noticeable characteristic of these North Jersey Dutch houses, which were almost invariably built to face south. Ingeniously designed for comfort, the eaves served as an awning in the summer, and yet permitted the winter sun, hanging low in the south, to shine in the front windows and door.

The early houses had just two rooms and an attic reached by a ladder. To save space there was no hall between the rooms, and, for privacy, there was no connecting door, but separate front entrances. Beside each door was one great window, and sometimes a second smaller window was placed in the rear wall. So few windows were used because glass was expensive and not effective as an insulator.

Usually the single fireplace, built in the west wall of

The Old Demarest House at River Edge

the house, was wide enough to take big logs and high enough for the large cranes that held the heavy iron kettles in which Dutch housewives prepared the family meals. There was always a cellar, reached by outside steps beside the front doors. Beams for the rafters and the joints under the wide plank floors were roughly squared and adzed from trees growing on the land.

Typical of this style is the tiny old David Demarest house in River Edge, built about 1680. The roof is pitched from the ridge and curves out to cover the eaves overhanging the twin doors and two large south windows. Though this type of pitched roof was used occasionally, the Dutch generally preferred the gambrel roof, which slopes gently from the ridge, then breaks steeply down to the eaves. The flatter portion provided more space in the attic without increasing the size of the building and was often used on larger houses with a central hall and stairway. The attic could then be utilized for comfortable bedrooms.

One of the best examples of the latter form, and much larger than the Demarest house, is the Terhune house in Hackensack, built about 1708. The gambrel roof ends in long eaves extending over a south porch, built many years later. The unusual width of the house made the roof very high, providing not only a second floor but also a considerable attic above. The outside stonework, rougher and cruder than in the later houses, has been whitewashed, giving the old stone an aged, crusty texture beneath the ivy vines. The door in the central hall halfway up the steep, narrow stairway to the attic was kept closed during the winter, a customary arrangement in houses of this type.

As families grew, an addition much larger than the original house was sometimes built, and the old house became the kitchen wing. Occasionally a second small wing was added to the opposite end of the new addition to form a central house with balanced side wings. The Hopper house on Polifly Road in Hackensack grew this way. The central portion, built in 1808, is much newer than the kitchen wing.

Toward the end of the 18th century the eaves were extended still further, and small columns were placed beneath them to form a porch. This was sometimes done on both front and rear.

The Dutch houses built after 1800 show the influence of settlers from New England, who introduced English Georgian details which appear in the enframements of doorways, delicate fanlights, transoms and side lights and molded cornices.

Some of the houses were built of wood instead of stone and the frame walls filled with brick like the Vreeland house in Leonia, the finest example of the fully developed Dutch Colonial style in New Jersey. The frame part was built about 1836 as an addition to the small stone wing to the east, which was kept for service quarters. The front and rear porches are purely Dutch, but the beautiful leaded glass fanlight and narrow side lights framing the doorway, the gables adorned with oval windows and the carving of the woodwork around the doors and windows show the strong English influence.

The charm of the Dutch Colonial lies in its impression of coziness, comfort and gentility. The soft curve in the roof line where it meets the walls and the deep shadow of the overhanging eaves, low over the first floor windows, seem to reflect something of the personal home life of the interior. The style has been much copied in modern house design, but it is not often that the simple grace of the old houses is successfully reproduced.

There is a marked difference between the styles of the northern and southern New Jersey Colonial houses. The Swedes settled in this section before the middle of the 17th century, but were soon mastered by the Dutch. There are no purely Swedish houses standing today, but the Swedes who remained in the section exerted a marked influence on the architecture introduced by their Dutch conquerors.

Taking advantage of the clay and sand soil of southern New Jersey, the pioneers built their homes of brick made from the native clay. The earliest houses were small one-story buildings with gambrel roofs, such as the office of Thomas Revel, in Burlington, built in 1685. The high, steep roofs of the South Jersey houses gave so much extra

HANCOCK HOUSE, HANCOCK'S BRIDGE, SALEM COUNTY

space in the attic that it became a real second floor. For ventilation and light the Dutch often placed two dormer windows at the front. Only a few of these very old little houses remain as they were; to most of them the Swedes added a full second floor where the attic used to be. In many cases the shape of the original gambrel roof line can be traced in the brickwork of the gables.

The Dutch used either white or a dull blue-gray brick to decorate the exterior, and almost always they placed their initials and the date of building in the gables. The Swedes imitated the use of patterns, at first with simple checkerboard or diamond designs, but later they tried very intricate patterns, such as the one on the Dickinson house at Alloway.

In South Jersey the great overhangs built by the Bergen County Dutch were replaced by "pent eaves," small projections of roof between the first and second stories to protect the windows and doorway from rain and snow. Sometimes the eaves were built along the sides of the house as well as the front. It is not known where pent eaves originated, but they were common in parts of Europe and in England at the time.

The Hancock house at Hancock's Bridge, site of a massacre of American soldiers during the Revolution, has two patterns, the checkerboard and zigzag, worked into its walls with glazed brick. Now owned by the State and preserved as a Colonial museum, the two-story house is one of the best examples of South Jersey Colonial architecture.

MORRISTOWN NATIONAL HISTORICAL PARK

On February 27, 1933, when only four days remained before the expiration of the Seventy-second Congress, Representative Percy H. Stewart of Plainfield, New Jersey, rose to make a special request of the House of Representatives. He asked to have the rules of the House suspended so that his colleagues might discuss his bill for the establishment of a national historical park at Morristown.

Speaker John Nance Garner granted the permission, and the clerk then read the bill that had been passed by the Senate two and a half weeks earlier. When the reading had been completed, Mr. Stewart rose to speak for the measure:

Mr. Speaker, this bill provides for the creation of a national historical park by setting aside certain areas at and in the vicinity of Morristown, N. J. Mr. Lloyd W. Smith proposes to donate to the Federal Government approximately 1,000 acres of land, and the city of Morristown has by a referendum of citizens, voted to turn over about 300 acres of land to the Federal Government. These two gifts comprise the camp ground occupied by the Revolutionary Army during the winter of 1779 and 1780, and the Revolutionary cemetery. In addition, the Washington Association of New Jersey proposes to donate the famous Ford

WASHINGTON'S HEADQUARTERS, MORRISTOWN

House, used by General Washington and his staff as headquarters during the time the army was in camp at Morristown. This donation is to include also the many priceless treasures which have been collected by the Washington Association. . . . .

The New Jersey Congressman continued for about five or six of the ten minutes allotted to him, describing the historical significance of the proposed park and dwelling on New Jersey's importance in the Revolutionary War. Amidst applause from the Congressmen he closed with the hope that there would "not be a single vote in opposition to accepting this splendid patriotic gift."

Representatives were immediately on their feet with questions. Mr. Stewart assured Representative Blanton of Texas that thousands had already visited the Ford House and informed Mr. Hill of Alabama that no battles had been fought on the site of the park. Representative Watson of Pennsylvania came to the support of the Congressman from his neighboring State. "Morristown is so closely allied with Washington . . ." he said, "that we should not turn down the gentleman's proposition."

"I thank the gentleman," said Mr. Stewart.

Representative Carl Michener of Michigan leaped into the discussion with a flat statement that he intended to oppose the bill because he felt the park would be too costly to the Federal Government. To this Representative Cochran of Missouri replied, "As a matter of fact this is about the first bill that has been introduced which gives the government something for nothing. The government is receiving property worth $1,000,000 for only $7,500 a year for maintenance."

Mr. Michener's opposition grew more pointed. He insisted that if the house passed the Morristown bill it should also accept a proposition to take over the Everglades in Florida, which "some people call the alligator park bill." Another New Jersey Congressman, Charles A. Eaton, quickly inquired:

Do I understand the gist of the argument of the gentleman from Michigan is that the sacred ground occupied by Washington and the fathers of this Republic is on a level with alligators and snakes of the Everglades?

After a vigorous protest that he did not mean to make such a comparison, Mr. Michener retired from the floor and left Representative Blanton to carry on. Mr. Blanton agreed that the park might prove a huge financial burden to the Government and added that Morristown did not compare with Mount Vernon as a shrine "of the great Father of our country."

Representative Eaton then returned to the conflict to insist that Morristown did rank as a shrine with Mount Vernon, pointing out that it had been called "The Valley Forge of New Jersey." It ought to be preserved," he argued, "as a sacred shrine by and for our people to the end of time."

Mr. Eaton's plea terminated the debate. The question was put to the House by Speaker Garner, and the bill was quickly passed with a better than 2-1 majority. On March 2, just one day before his administration ended, President Herbert Hoover signed the bill which created the Nation's first national historical park.

Four months later, on July 4, 10,000 people gathered in the natural amphitheater on the grounds of Washington's Morristown headquarters for the formal dedication of the park. In a graceful message President Franklin D. Roosevelt recognized Morristown's proud claims by referring to the city as "in fact, if not in name, the capital of the future republic" and by characterizing the Ford House as "our first White House." As the Federal Government's official representative, Secretary of the Interior Harold L. Ickes received the deeds to the historic lands from the mayor of Morristown and made the principal address of the ceremony.

After expressing his pleasure to be in the hills of Morristown, "at once so beautiful and so historic," the Secretary praised Washington's genius "in selecting these hills as his military headquarters, difficult of access as they were to the foe, yet for the Revolutionary commander within easy striking distance of two vital cities, New York and Philadelphia." In conclusion, he observed that this same strategic location would make Morristown National Historical Park a patriotic shrine easily accessible to a sixth of the Nation's population.

At the time of the dedication of the Morristown Park, there were 21 other national parks. Of these only a few had historic associations comparable to those of Morristown, and none approached it in size. The Morristown National Historical Park is really three historical parks in one. Each unit has its full share of Revolutionary significance: the Ford Mansion as Washington's headquarters; Fort Nonsense as the refuge of the Continental soldiers guarding military stores; and Jockey Hollow three miles southwest as the site of the encampment of more than 12,000 soldiers of the Continental Army. Taken together, the three divisions tell the story of one of New Jersey's outstanding contributions to the success of the colonies in their struggle for independence.

Ever since Washington's occupancy of the Ford House in the desperate winter of 1779-80, the lovely Colonial mansion has been the historical heart of Morristown. Its setting on an expanse of sloping lawn on which stand towering trees has doubtless changed little from the day when the house was built in 1774 by Colonel Jacob Ford, a wealthy iron and powder manufacturer. It was then the most pretentious residence in Morristown, a village of 300 people.

For generations the beautiful door of the Ford House has been thrown open to those who would come close to the cares and responsibilities, the joys and triumphs experienced by Washington and his staff. Furnishings and decorations have been acquired to suggest the atmosphere of the Revolutionary period. Delicate Colonial furniture makes the spacious central hall appear much as it did when Martha Washington ordered it cleared for one of the many balls she gave to keep up the morale of the Continental Army.

The dignity with which the house bears its age of eight score and four befits the statement that "under its roof have gathered more characters known to the military history of our Revolution than under any one roof in America." Visitors from abroad, like Kosciusko and Pulaski from Poland, Baron von Steuben from Prussia, the Chevalier de la Luzerne from France and Don Juan de Miralles from Spain, brought hope of foreign aid that occasioned rejoicing and celebration in the generous Virginia way of the Washingtons. No event was more jubilantly observed than Lafayette's arrival in 1780 with word that the King of France was sending a fleet of ships and 6,000 troops to the aid of the colonies.

Washington's fellow American generals, Greene, Wayne and Light Horse Harry Lee, however, brought mostly discouraging news of the progress of the war. Equally depressing were the constant accounts of bickerings with the Congress and State Legislatures over support of the army. Perhaps the bitterest experience for Washington at Morristown was the report of Benedict Arnold's treason at West Point. It was the climax of a tragedy in which an important scene had been played at the New Jersey headquarters.

At the Dickerson Tavern on the village green Arnold had been tried early in 1780 on charges of abuse of power brought by Pennsylvania officials. The military court did not pronounce him guilty, but recommended a reprimand from the Commander in Chief. Washington reluctantly complied, but tried to soften Arnold's mortification by offering him command of West Point. Arnold's treachery was the general's thanks.

The gay temperament of two of the youngest members on Washington's staff, Alexander Hamilton and Lafayette, often helped to relieve the heavy gloom. The French nobleman's witty tongue and zestful spirit could always be counted on to enliven an evening, and Hamilton's successful courtship of General Philip Schuyler's daughter, Betsy, brought a youthful buoyancy to the atmosphere.

Both Hamilton and Lafayette lived for a time in the Ford House with Washington and his family and others. Despite the size of the mansion, it was taxed beyond its facilities, and Washington wrote to Greene:

> I have been at my present quarters since the 1st day of December and have not a Kitchen to cook a Dinner, . . . Nor is there a place at this moment in which a servant can lodge, with the smallest degree of comfort. Eighteen belonging to my family, and all of Mrs. Ford's are crowded together in her Kitchen, and scarce one of them able to speak for the colds they have caught.

Mrs. Ford was one of the few of Washington's hostesses who refused to accept payment for her hospitality. The general, however, insisted on plastering the house at his own expense. When Washington moved in, he instructed Mrs. Ford to make an inventory of her possessions. At the time of his departure she reported that her belongings were intact, save for the absence of a silver tablespoon. After the war, Washington replaced this with a spoon from his service at Mount Vernon, inscribed with the initials "G.W."

Directly behind the Ford House is the Historical Museum of Morristown, recently built by the Department of the Interior. Its valuable collection of Washington material, nearly all acquired by the Washington Association of New Jersey, includes a Gilbert Stuart portrait of the general; a diorama depicting the mutiny of the regiment of the Pennsylvania Line; a 104-pound link of the great iron chain stretched across the Hudson to prevent the British fleet from reaching West Point; and some weapons captured from the British at the Battle of Princeton. It is intended to place all the historical articles from the Ford House in this museum and to furnish the house completely as a typical eighteenth century mansion. Among the exhibits which are still on view in the house itself are the piano used by Nellie Custis, Washington's adopted daughter, and the china and silverware with which Washington and Lafayette were served.

About two miles from the headquarters stands Fort Nonsense. Originally built in 1777 during Washington's first winter in Morristown, it gradually crumbled away and was rebuilt in 1937 by the National Park Service, aided by the Civilian Conservation Corps. Although the Watchung Mountains seemed to provide a measure of protection, the Continental Army was constantly on the watch for British attacks. The high ridge on which Fort Nonsense was situated strategically commanded a pass through the mountains and was probably used as the site of a beacon to summon the militia in times of danger.

In its natural state the hill was probably adequate for the purposes of the army. Washington, however, ordered a fort built there, possibly to afford greater protection to the town, its valuable stores of munitions and important iron works. The soldiers contended that the job was designed only to keep them busy and dubbed the project "Fort Nonsense."

The original fort was constructed of earth. The hill was cut in a series of terraces, upon each of which soldiers took their stand. The fort was rebuilt from a study of military manuals of the Revolutionary period.

Difficult as conditions were at the Ford House through the frigid winter of 1779-80, Washington himself would have been the first to agree that the greatest measure of suffering was experienced three miles beyond the town, at Jockey Hollow. In what is now an inviting tract of forest overgrown with hardwoods and wildflowers, 12,000 American soldiers camped under the most trying circumstances. At the headquarters the housekeeper was once obliged to sell large quantities of salt to provide food for the general, but of his men at Jockey Hollow Washington wrote that they sometimes went "five or six days together without bread" and that at one time they "ate every kind of horse food but hay."

Winter struck at the encampment before they could build proper huts, and an epidemic of smallpox carried off hundreds of men. Portions of the barrack huts remain, and Jockey Hollow Cemetery holds the graves of about a hundred men who died here. Across from the cemetery has been built a military hospital which is an exact reproduction of the one used by the Continentals. Up the hill from the hospital stands the rebuilt hut of the officers of the Pennsylvania Division. Reconstruction of other authentic huts is planned by the National Park Service, which administers Morristown National Historical Park.

The most famous event associated with Jockey Hollow occurred the winter following that which Washington spent in Morristown. On January 1, 1781, 2,000 veteran

Courtesy Wide World Photos

Revolutionary Hospital, Jockey Hollow

troops of the Pennsylvania Line mutinied against the authority of the Continental Congress. Poorly fed and clothed, unpaid for 12 months, the men were convinced that their officers had deceived them on the terms of enlistment. Their patience snapped when they learned that new recruits were being offered the handsome bounty of three half-joes ($26.43).

The mutineers seized ammunition and provisions and appropriated horses from the stables of their commander, General Anthony Wayne. In a brief skirmish they killed Captain Adam Bettin, who had attempted to restrain them. Wayne tried to placate them, but he was warned that he would be put to death if he fired his pistol. He was also assured that the men would obey his orders should the British attack.

Meanwhile British spies offered the men a considerable sum to fight for England. The soldiers were as furious at this reflection on their loyalty to their country as they had been at their commanding officers. They quickly turned over the British agents to Wayne, who promptly executed them.

With two colonels, the general accompanied the men to Princeton, where he presented Washington with a written list of their complaints. A council of war was called by the Commander in Chief, and the mutiny was settled by discharging many of the men from the service. The mutineers had intended to go to Philadelphia to confront Congress with their demands, but they accepted this peaceable solution.

Closely associated with events in the Pennsylvania Line mutiny is the Wick House, which stands farther down the road running through most of Jockey Hollow. Captain Henry Wick of the New Jersey militia lived here, but it was his daughter, Temperance, who made tradition for the farmhouse. According to the legend, two mutinous soldiers attempted to commandeer Tempe's horse when they met her on the road. She pretended to submit, and the soldiers let loose their hold on the horse's bridle.

Instantly, Tempe brought her whip down on the horse's flanks, and he galloped up the hill. When she reached the farmhouse, the girl led her horse into the kitchen, through the parlor and to a bedroom in the northwest corner of the house. She closed the wooden shutter and spread the featherbed on the floor so that the horse's stamping would be muffled. When the soldiers arrived, they searched the barn and adjoining woods, but fortunately never thought that the animal might be in the house. According to another version of the story, Tempe rode the horse straight into the house without stopping to dismount. Regardless of the authenticity of the Tempe legend, the house itself retains more of its original appearance than any other Jockey Hollow building standing during the war. Partial restoration was made by the Civilian Conservation Corps.

About 175 CCC boys are carrying on the work of reconstruction and improvement of the huts and landmarks under the supervision of the National Park Service. Other field work has been accomplished through the Works Progress Administration and Public Works Administration. Washington's Headquarters and the Historical Museum may be visited daily except Sunday from 9 to 5 o'clock. Fort Nonsense and Jockey Hollow are open every day from 9 o'clock until dark. Free lecture and guide service may be obtained by making advance arrangements with the superintendent of the park.

PATERSON, THE "FEDERAL CITY"

Paterson, the city of mills and factories, owes its beginnings to the dreams of one of the fathers of the country, the brilliant first Secretary of the Treasury, Alexander Hamilton. The realization of the dream was somewhat delayed, and perhaps has fallen short of the hopes of the founder; but Paterson has, nevertheless, followed the pattern laid out for it in the early days of the country's history.

Though the Revolution had left America politically independent of Great Britain, leading minds soon realized that the new country must secure her industrial independence as well. To stimulate pride in home manufactures, the newspapers took pains to attract the public's attention to the fact that when Washington was inaugurated he was wearing a suit of broadcloth of the finest American manufacture.

The new world had been looked upon as a producer of precious metals, pelts and raw materials for the mother country to turn into manufactured articles. These the colonists had to buy at advanced prices. They were prevented from making woolen, cotton or linen cloth for sale, and they were not allowed to build furnaces to convert the native iron into steel.

Alexander Hamilton was greatly impressed with the Great Falls of the Passaic River in northern New Jersey. He foresaw it as the site of a great manufacturing center to supply the needs of the country. Here was the water

THE PASSAIC RIVER FALLS

power to turn the mill wheels and a navigable river to carry the manufactured goods to the market centers.

The Revolution over, in the midst of the thousand and one details of organization of the Government that occupied him, Hamilton proceeded to put his pet idea into motion. His plan was to form a large stock company which would engage in all sorts of manufacturing and would encourage other enterprises as well. Although he was convinced that the Great Falls of the Passaic was the logical site for a manufacturing center, he kept that part of his plan to himself. In the newspapers of New York and Pennsylvania, as well as in those of New Jersey, articles appeared designed to interest moneyed citizens in a "Federal City" to be placed at some favorable spot accessible to the cities along the seaboard.

There were a number of influential men who saw at

once the wisdom of the plan, and gradually the idea began to take hold of the imagination of the people at large. It was the first organization of its kind in the world and, because of its novelty, was received doubtfully by some and enthusiastically by others. Among the first to give support to the plan was the new Governor of New Jersey, William Paterson.

Several meetings were held to consider plans of organization and location. New Brunswick was one of the sites suggested. It had the advantage of a location on a broad river and it was, in addition, the birthplace of Governor Paterson. Newark was another suggested site. But, in the end, Hamilton had his way. The Great Falls of the Passaic were called into service to furnish the needed power, and the smooth-flowing Passaic River, the transportation —essentials of the plan.

Under a charter signed November 22, 1791, the Society for Establishing Useful Manufactures was organized. The city was named Paterson, in honor of the Governor of New Jersey who signed the charter. With the backing of Hamilton and Paterson to give them assurance, people from all parts of the country hastened to buy shares in the new company at $100 each. The list of the first subscribers contains the names of men prominent in the business and political affairs of the new country. The State of New Jersey assisted with a subscription of $10,000 and, in addition, authorized a lottery to raise money for the enterprise. The practice of raising money through lotteries for public purposes, charities, churches, improvements, etc., which was more or less customary during Colonial days, had been abused in several instances; and it was only in special cases that the governing body permitted this method of raising money.

The organizers of the "S. U. M.," as the company came to be called, were so certain that the whole country would benefit by its activities that they introduced into the charter some startling provisions which have since become a burden to the City of Paterson. For instance, the property of the Society was to be exempt from all taxes for ten years, and, thereafter, from all but State taxes. Later, when the S. U. M. gave up its manufacturing activities and leased its land to private organizations, the city, because of the original charter, was prevented from collecting taxes on the property.

The Society bought about 700 acres of land above and below the falls and began digging a raceway. The French engineer, Pierre L'Enfant, who had been engaged to lay out the National Capital, was called into service. He conceived the plan of a magnificent city laid out in splendid avenues and reached by a fine highway from Newark. The newspapers of the day spoke in enthusiastic terms of the fine prospects of the "National Manufactory," where they fondly believed would be produced all the cotton, cassimeres, wallpapers, books, felt and straw hats, shoes, carriages, pottery, bricks, pots, pans and buttons needed in the United States. But L'Enfant's plans were more magnificent than practical, and Peter Colt, treasurer of the State of Connecticut, was chosen in his place.

A stone mill, four stories high, about 55 by 80 feet, was erected. There was nothing in the country like it, with its 768 spindles for spinning cotton. It would be an insignificant mill now, but it promised great things in those days.

It is impossible to realize today the difficulties in the way of this pioneer manufacturing enterprise. Most of the machinery had to be imported, as well as the workmen to set it up and operate it. Moreover, the money to finance the venture did not come in so quickly as anticipated. Of the $1,000,000 capital authorized, only about $60,000 was subscribed. William Duer, the governor of the Society, whose wealth and business experience had been counted on to set the new venture on its feet, lost all his money in a sudden panic in New York and was sent to jail for debt. Foreign manufacturers flooded the market with goods the Society had planned to produce. An agent sent abroad with $50,000 to purchase supplies made off with the money; this was the final blow.

Alexander Hamilton was too much absorbed with affairs of government to give as much time as was necessary to the scheme. With his financial genius and energy he might have been able to carry the plan through successfully, but he had to leave the S. U. M. to fend for itself.

The Society limped along ineffectually until it finally decided, in 1796, to give up the business of manufacturing. Private concerns were invited to take up its land holdings, and the once hopeful Society of Useful Manufactures became nothing more than a glorified landlord.

Paterson of today is not the "Federal City" of which Alexander Hamilton dreamed; but it has moved along consistently as a manufacturing center with a long list of products to its credit, three of which never entered into even the far-seeing calculations of Hamilton—silk, locomotives and airplane motors.

NEW JERSEY'S FIRST SUMMER RESORT

Cape May, at the southernmost point of New Jersey, where the State dips its toe into the Atlantic Ocean, is the oldest of its many seashore resorts. The Indians discovered it and liked it long before the shot of a musket broke the quiet of the forest or before the ring of a woodsman's axe was heard in the land.

Cape May became a vacation resort for the Lenapes. They wore paths to it with their moccasined feet, fished along the shore, and dug for clams and oysters all summer. When it was time to return to the fields to harvest their maize, the red-skinned summer visitors dried oysters, clams and fish to take back with them for use in the winter.

The first white man to enter Delaware Bay passing the cape, was Henry Hudson, who sailed up the coast in 1609 in his bark, the *Half Moon*. Hudson claimed the land in the name of the States-General of the Netherlands. Fourteen years later the Dutch West India Company sent out Captain Cornelius Jacobsen Mey to establish settlements. Arriving in Delaware Bay in the *Glad Tidings* in 1623, Mey gave his own name to the cape.

Peter Hyssen, the Dutch captain of a whaling ship, purchased the land from the Indians before 1640. He paid for it in the usual way with copper kettles, knives, beads and other trinkets. His tract was four miles wide and four miles long.

There were many whales off the New Jersey coast in

SUMMER VISITORS AT CAPE MAY IN THE 1880's

the early days, and whalers found the cape a convenient place to bring their catches and cut them up. Besides the Dutch whalers, there were others from Long Island and Connecticut who put up sheds at Cape May as early as 1640. There was no permanent settlement until 1685.

These early settlers were peaceful Quakers, tending rigidly to their farms and their simple home life. Even when pirates like Captain Kidd and Blackbeard Teach came to fill their empty water casks from Lilly Pond they were not disturbed. Kidd, a privateer out of New York, turned pirate and was pursued by the King's officers. He was captured and hanged in London from the yardarm of his ship. His captors complained that they had received no cooperation from the Cape May people because the Quakers there disliked "gaols" (jails), and refused to help in sending anyone to jail. Many of them had suffered imprisonment in England because of their religious beliefs.

A report by Colonel Quary to the British Lords of Trade in 1699 shows that Captain Kidd did use Cape May as a hide-out. The report says:

> I have, by the assistance of Col. Basse, apprehended four more the pyrates at Cape May. Hee (Kidd) hath been here (Cape May) about ten days and the people frequently goes on board him. Hee is in a sloop with about fourty men and a vast treasure.

For years many people have dug in the sands in hope of finding the famous Kidd treasure. Nothing, however, has been found except those sparkling but worthless stones known as Cape May diamonds. These are colorless Crystals of quartz found in granite, gneiss and other rocks and also in most sands and gravels. They were produced in the furnaces of an ancient geological age when these rocks were heated to a melting point. Glass is made from the sand underlying this region.

During the Revolution, British men-of-war would land boats and raid Cape May for cattle and fill their water barrels from Lilly Pond. The inhabitants were so angry over these raids that they sacrificed their own fresh water supply by digging a ditch from the ocean to the pond, making the water brackish and unfit to drink. This discouraged the enemy from coming.

After the Revolution, aristocratic Philadelphians sailing on Delaware Bay began landing at the small fishing village on the Cape and came to like it. It was an ideal place for bathing. The water was not too deep, and the beach was firm, with a gentle slope. The settlers finally realized that there was money to be made in providing

food and lodging for the visitors. In 1801 Postmaster
Ellis Hughes put the following advertisement in the
Philadelphia Daily Aurora:

> The subscriber has prepared himself for entertaining
> company who use sea bathing, and he is accom-
> modated with extensive house-room, with fish, oysters,
> crabs, and good liquors. Care will be taken of gentle-
> men's horses. Carriages may be driven along the
> margin of the ocean for miles, and the wheels will
> scarcely make an impression upon the sand. The
> slope of the shore is so regular that persons may wade
> a great distance. It is the most delightful spot that
> the citizens may retire to in the hot season. A stage
> starts from Cooper's Ferry [Camden] on Thursday
> in every week and arrives at Cape Island on Friday;
> it starts from Cape Island on Friday and Tuesday
> each week and arrives in Philadelphia the following
> day.

The ambitious postmaster also called attention to the
view of the lighthouse, the many ships that came there,
and the cool ocean breezes. He gave the routes for those
traveling in their own carriages, and mentioned that there
were boats for those who wished to travel by water. Eager
vacationists sailed slowly down the Delaware, or drove
along the bad, sandy road from Camden in dearborns
(four-wheeled carriages).

The accommodations to which the postmaster referred
in the advertisement consisted of a huge barnlike building
with one room, called the Atlantic Hotel. At night, a
large sheet divided it in half. The men slept on one side
and the women on the other. Later it was improved and
became the resort of many prominent and wealthy men.

Commodore Stephen Decatur came there season after season for 16 years.

The hotel prospered. The year after the historic advertisement, boats ran regularly from Philadelphia to Cape May. In 1818 Congress Hall, another hotel, was built. By 1830 there were six boarding houses, three of them very large, to accommodate the increasing summer population.

Bathing suits in those days were strange collections of old clothes which were carried to the Cape in carpetbags. Shoes and stockings were worn to protect feet from pebbles and shells. Later a regular bathing suit was designed with long sleeves, skirts, pantaloons with ruffles, and drawstrings at the neck, wrists and ankles.

By 1850 Cape May was on its way to becoming the leading summer resort in the country. A steamboat made the trip from Philadelphia in half a day. Each spring the natives set out the pier at which the boat tied up, and each fall they took it apart and stored it because of the winter storms.

Among the famous politicians who came to the resort at about this time was Henry Clay. He was so popular that at one time a group of women admirers chased him along the beach and cut off locks of his hair as souvenirs.

The building of the West Jersey Railroad from Philadelphia to Cape May in 1866 spread the Cape's name far and wide. Congressmen, bankers, wealthy manufacturers and noted writers came here. Society leaders from Washington, Richmond and Baltimore made the place a fashion center. Five Presidents of the United States—Pierce, Buchanan, Lincoln, Grant and Harrison—were entertained in the large hotels.

Days were spent pleasantly in bathing, sunning on the

beach, and driving on the firm sands at low tide. In the evenings there were dancing, gambling and other amusements. The resort later offered such attractions as the Annapolis Naval Academy Band, and the Marine Band with John Philip Sousa.

By 1900, with the development of other resorts along the coast, Cape May began to lose its popularity. In 1903 Henry Ford came to the cape with several other men who were interested in racing to try out his experimental car in a race on the three-mile stretch of smooth beach. A touring car was brought along to assist in starting Ford's auto. The contest was not won by the Ford entry.

Ford had to sell the touring car later in order to get enough money to return to Detroit with the racing car. Daniel Focer was the buyer, and Ford appointed him the agent for the new Ford car. The agency is operating today, and the old touring car stands on the display floor among the streamlined modern models.

Cape May is no longer the famous resort it was; however, the old homes and stately hotels are standing, and people who like its beauty and quiet still return year after year.

CRADLE OF THE TELEGRAPH

On Speedwell Avenue in Morristown, New Jersey, stands an undistinguished two-and-one-half-story frame building, once a part of the famous Speedwell Iron Works. Now situated on the grounds of a private residence, its age has been disguised by a new shingle roof and clapboard siding, and the original basement is half concealed in a banked lawn. Here was born one hundred years ago an industry that has transformed the commerce of the world.

Samuel Finley Breese Morse came to Morristown in 1837 to work with Alfred Vail on a problem which had challenged scientists for almost a century. Alfred, son of Stephen Vail, proprietor of the Speedwell Iron Works, was an earnest young mechanic. Morse was no young man; behind him lay two years of persistent experimentation with the telegraph. And behind this was the memory of the checkered career as a portrait painter, satisfaction with the high praise of critics, disappointment with the low sums of patrons. At 46 Morse was well equipped with the persevering spirit so often necessary to scientific accomplishment.

Just how much Morse knew about the field in which he was soon to become famous is an unsettled question. An artist turned inventor practically overnight, he could have spent years catching up on what had been accomplished in the complicated science of telegraphy. He would have had to go all the way back to the first proposal for communication by electricity in a letter published in 1753 in the *Scots Magazine* of Edinburgh, signed only with the mysterious initials, "C.M."

Twenty-one years later George Louis Le Sage exhibited at Geneva the first telegraph instrument on record. This device required a separate wire for each letter of the alphabet. At the receiving end was a row of tiny lettered pith balls, suspended on silk threads at the terminals of the wires. As the current was sent through their respective wires the balls would swing, enabling the receiver to spell out words and sentences. In the years that followed, experiment with the telegraph spread all over the continent and to England, where in 1824 William Sturgeon developed the electromagnet, the direct inspiration of Morse's work on the telegraph.

Returning from Europe in 1832 on the packet *Sully*, Morse listened to a fellow passenger, Dr. Charles T. Jackson, describe experiments showing the property of electricity to travel over any length of wire instantaneously. Jackson commented that the presence of the current in any part of the line could be ascertained by the spark, or by an electromagnet. The electromagnet that Jackson described consisted of soft iron bent in the shape of a horseshoe, around the limbs of which was wound a copper wire in a loose coil. With a flash of understanding that went to the heart of the problem of achieving an electric telegraph, Morse remarked, "If the presence of electricity can be made visible in any part of the circuit, I see no reason why intelligence may not be transmitted instantaneously by electricity." That statement was the birth of today's telegraph.

After discouraging efforts to secure painting commissions, in 1835 Morse became a professor in the Fine Arts

Department of the University of the City of New York, now New York University. Relatively free from financial worry, he set to work to develop the idea suggested by Jackson's information on the electromagnet. Whether Morse knew that a number of crude instruments had already accomplished instantaneous transmission is another doubtful matter. It is far more important that he grasped the problem immediately and that he labored until he brought telegraphy from the stage of theories and rude experimental apparatus to that of practical use.

From the time that Morse began to apply his understanding to the task of developing the telegraph, his work became crisscrossed with that of three other scientists, Dr. Leonard Gale, Dr. Joseph Henry and Alfred Vail. Although their just share in the great work can probably never be determined accurately, all undoubtedly contributed significantly to the final triumph. Technical difficulties with an instrument made in 1836 sent Morse first to Dr. Gale, a colleague on the faculty of the university. Gale gave him important advice on the best type of battery for his purposes and suggested increasing the number of turns of wire on the electromagnet, thereby making the magnet stronger.

This latter advice was based on the work of Dr. Henry. Henry had indeed all but forestalled Morse in the invention of an electric telegraph. While a professor at Albany Academy in 1831, he hung a mile of copper wire around the walls of a large classroom and placed a battery and one of his powerful magnets at each end of the circuit. When the magnet was excited by impulses from the battery, it caused a rod, which had been in contact with it, to move and strike a bell. A year later Henry accepted a position at the College of New Jersey, now Princeton, where in 1836 he built a telegraphic circuit between two campus buildings. He was more interested in the purely scientific aspect of his invention and did not develop it beyond signaling.

In September 1837 at New York University, in a room hung with 1,700 feet of wire, Morse actually sent a message. His apparatus differed greatly from that which became the parent of present-day instruments. The simple plan of sending letters and numerals by pressing down a key by hand did not occur to the inventor until later. This early apparatus was much more complicated. Each time electricity passed through it, an electromagnet at the receiving end attracted a soft iron bar to which a pencil was fastened. When the current was shut off, a spring pulled the iron bar and pencil back to the original position. The pencil was thus moved back and forth over a strip of paper, which traveled along beneath it, and made a series of V-shaped marks which could be translated into letters and words.

To make and break the circuit at the sending end in some regular way Morse used pieces of metal with an edge notched in different combinations to represent characters. Pieces of this "type" were set in a form to spell out words. The sending lever, which operated like a seesaw, closed and opened the circuit alternately. At one end of the lever was a spike pointing downward. As the "type" was pushed along beneath this spike, the points pushed the spike upwards, so that the opposite end of the seesaw descended to close the circuit. In the spaces between the "type" points, the contact would be broken. The series of contacts activated the magnet at the receiving end, and the pencil recorded the symbols. The zigzag line was in effect

THE VAIL BARN, CRADLE OF THE TELEGRAPH

a crude forerunner of the dot and dash system later employed.

For the experiment at New York University Morse selected the word "successful." It was an apt choice, for in the company which witnessed the demonstration was Alfred Vail, who was so impressed that he desired to have a share in the enterprise. He persuaded his father, Judge Stephen Vail, and his brother, George, to advance $2,000 to cover the expense of perfecting the instrument.

Vail and Morse entered into a contract under the terms of which Vail was to give his services, $2,000 in cash and the use of his father's shop in return for one-quarter of the American royalties and one-half of the foreign interest. Vail retired to his shop in the yard of his father's iron works and applied himself to working out mechanical improvements on Morse's instrument.

Judge Vail was now in the telegraph business, and, businessman that he was, he expected results. His own skepticism at his son's enthusiasm was heightened by the jests of his friends and, worse still, by the evasive attitude of the inventors themselves.

About four months after the contract had been signed, a very short time in the development of an invention, but doubtless a very long time to dubious Judge Vail, Morse and his son invited him to a demonstration at the Speedwell shop. They also asked people from the iron works and the surrounding districts.

Morse, at this time, considered that the most efficient method of communication was by using numerals, each of which referred to a word in a specially numbered dictionary. The dictionary was prepared; the apparatus was in order; three miles of copper wire had been looped about the walls of the room. When the group assembled on January 6, 1838, the judge handed his son a message on a slip of paper, saying, "If you can send this and Professor Morse can read it at the other end, I shall be convinced." Alfred Vail must have stiffened when he read his father's sentence—"A patient waiter is no loser." A moment or two passed while he assembled the numbers for the message; then there was only the scratching of Morse's pen at the other end of the wire. When he had finished writing, he handed the message to the judge, correct. Jubilation at the success of the experiment broke the tenseness of the atmosphere, and Judge Vail, now convinced, immediately urged that the inventors ask Congress to establish a Government line.

Although they were not able to flash the news instantly to the *Morristown Journal*, shortly afterward Vail and

Morse had the satisfaction of reading the following account of their work in that paper:

It is with some degree of pride, we confess, that it falls to our lot first to announce the complete success of this wonderful piece of mechanism, and that hundreds of our citizens were the first to witness its surprising results. No place could have been found more suitable to pursue the course of experiments necessary to perfecting the details of machinery than the quiet retirement of the Speedwell works, replete as they are with every kind of convenience which capital and mechanical skill can supply. . . . Others may have suggested the possibility of conveying intelligence by electricity, but this is the first instance of its actual transmission and permanent record.

Despite such an enthusiastic reception and Judge Vail's haste to commercialize their success, the scientists continued to improve their instrument. Only 18 days after the Morristown demonstration, they held another trial at New York University at which letters of the alphabet replaced the old numerals so that the dots and dashes actually spelled out words. According to the *New York Journal of Commerce*, this improvement increased the number of words that could be transmitted in a minute from ten to twenty.

In a short time, however, Morse and Vail discarded type altogether and substituted the key and keyboard which have remained permanent features of the telegraph ever since. The sending instrument which they devised was a simple affair. A spring raised a metal knob over another metal knob attached to a board. When the top knob was pressed down to make contact with the lower one, the circuit was completed.

Alfred Vail pushed on to perfect the recording of the dots and dashes. After considerable experiment with pens, pencils and other markers, he finally adopted a blunt steel stylus which marked the telegraphic symbols on a sheet of paper. Years later, when the question of the true invention of the telegraph was being dragged through the courts, Vail explained that by the terms of his contract with Morse he could not obtain a patent for the device.

To convince the public of the practical possibilities of the telegraph it was necessary to give a demonstration covering two distant points. It was not enough to send a message from one room to another or even from one house to another. It had to be shown that a message could be sent over a wire, no matter how great its length.

Again and again Congress was petitioned for a subsidy to permit building a telegraph line between Baltimore and Washington, but each time it was presented the bill died in committee. The public seemed utterly indifferent to the whole idea. Talking over wires! It was absurd!

On February 23, 1843, the bill was again introduced. It passed the House by 6 votes, but it had only a slim chance in the Senate, due to the pressure of business. Morse asked two Senators if they thought the Senate would consider his bill before its adjournment, but they gave him no grounds for encouragement. He went to his room wholly discouraged.

The next morning as Morse was sitting at breakfast Annie Ellsworth, the daughter of the Commissioner of Patents, called on him. When he expressed surprise at the early call, she said, "I have come to congratulate you."

"Indeed, for what?"

"On the passage of your bill."

Her father had waited in the Senate gallery till the end of the session, when, to everyone's surprise, $30,000 had been appropriated for the construction of the line between Washington and Baltimore. Morse was so elated that he promised the young woman to let her choose the first message.

Work was started at once. There were no precedents to go by. Every move was a pioneer step. Two-thirds of the appropriation was exhausted in using underground wires, but this method was found unworkable, because of faulty insulation. Fighting against the loss of time and money, they hung the wire between tall poles, using the necks of bottles for insulation at the poles. This idea was contributed by Ezra Cornell, mechanic, inventor, promoter and businessman who later founded the great university that bears his name.

On May 24, 1844, the day of the demonstration, Morse sat at the transmitter in the Supreme Court Room of the Capitol; Vail waited at the receiving end in Baltimore. Annie Ellsworth handed Morse the message, "What Hath God Wrought?" which he ticked out on the key. In a few moments the receiver clicked out the same message. The telegraph was a success.

Morse offered his invention to the Government for $100,000, but it was refused. However, $8,000 was voted to maintain the 40-mile line already constructed. The inventors and a promoter then organized the Magnetic Telegraph Company with a line from Philadelphia to New York. In 1846 Vail and Morse leased the Washington-Baltimore line from the Government and shortly afterward acquired it outright for the Magnetic system.

Congress had definitely taken itself out of the telegraph business.

Even before this there had been competition from other lines. As companies increased, patents were infringed on, and Morse and his partners were obliged to spend much time defending their claims. An unfortunate side light on this litigation was the frequent presence of Dr. Joseph Henry as a witness against Morse. Henry had been offended in 1845 when Vail's book on the telegraph had failed to take into account the importance of his use of the electromagnet in transmitting signals.

The Morse company joined with other telegraph companies, but in 1859 they were absorbed by the American Telegraph Company. The era of swift expansion across the continent was at hand; and the telegraph was ready to play its part in the development of the Nation.

A CONFEDERATE SHRINE IN NEW JERSEY

The heroes of the Civil War are honored on two memorial days in New Jersey. May 30 is dedicated to the soldiers who fought for the Union, and April 26 to the soldiers who fought for the Confederacy.

At Finn's Point National Cemetery, adjoining the Fort Mott reservation, about five miles from Salem, the Federal Government, in 1912, erected an 85-foot monument. On 12 tablets at the base are inscribed the names of 2,436 soldiers of the Confederacy who died during a cholera epidemic in Fort Delaware, where they were being held as military prisoners.

Every April 26 a group of the Confederate Daughters of America journey to this spot to place wreaths at the monument in tribute to the men who were brought here for burial from the island fort where they had died miserably of neglect and disease, far from their homes.

The cemetery, enclosed by a gray stone wall, with its orderly rows of gravestones, its well-kept lawns and fine trees, is an impressively peaceful spot. A fringe of native brush and scrub oaks is kept as a bird refuge. The songs of birds and the wind in the trees are the only sounds that penetrate the quiet. Leading inward from the entrance gates are two rows of bronze plates, on each one of which is inscribed a verse of Theodore O'Hara's famous poem, *The Bivouac of the Dead*.

FINN'S POINT CEMETERY

One verse of the poem sounds a solemn note:

Rest on, embalmed and sainted dead!
Dear as the blood ye gave
No impious footstep here shall tread
The herbage of your grave:
Nor shall your glory be forgot
While Fame her record keeps,
Or honor points the hallowed spot
Where Valor proudly sleeps.

At one end of the cemetery a smaller monument honors the 165 Union soldiers, of the Fort Delaware garrison, who died in the same epidemic. Now that the scars of war are healed, the Union soldiers are also honored by a wreath placed there by the descendants of their former enemies. Over the graves of all, the Stars and Stripes flutters constantly in the breeze.

Fort Delaware, today the central link in the chain of forts near the mouth of Delaware River, was designed to protect the city of Philadelphia. It was completed in 1859 —just in time for the Civil War. Pea Patch Island, on which the fort is situated, lies about midway in the Delaware River between the Delaware and New Jersey shores.

There is a legend dating back to Colonial times that a ship laden with peas was grounded on a sandbar at this point. The roots grew, accumulating drift and sediment until an island of about 178 acres appeared on the surface of the water. Parts of the island are actually about three feet below water level, and a sea wall has been built to keep out the tide.

By 1861 about 1,000 prisoners were interned on the swampy little island with its grim granite fort. Some prominent citizens of Salem County and Delaware who had given evidence of their sympathy with the Southern cause were among the first to be confined there. In 1862 the place began to fill with war prisoners, and by the end of 1863, 12,000 prisoners, most of whom were taken at Gettysburg, were crowded together in a place that could accommodate only 4,000 with safety. Rude wooden barracks were constructed to house the wretched men. Barbed wire and alert sentries discouraged them from rash attempts to escape; those who managed to elude the guards and get to the mainland were helped to reach their own lines by means of an underground railway system that had been set up in Salem and in southern Delaware.

Fort Delaware was to the South what Andersonville and Libbey were to the North. It was a cesspool of misery, dirt, lice, rats and disease. Dr. S. Weir Mitchell, who

later became famous as a specialist in nervous diseases and
a writer of historical romances, was at this time Federal
Inspector of Prisons. In a letter written to his sister he
describes the conditions of the island. Part of his letter
is as follows:

> Tomorrow I go to Fort Delaware to inspect that
> inferno of detained rebels. A thousand ill, twelve
> thousand on an island that should hold four thou-
> sand, the general level three feet below the water
> mark; twenty deaths a day of dysentery, and the liv-
> ing having more life on them than in them. Occa-
> sional lack of water,—and thus a Christian nation
> treats the captives of its sword.

> The thermometer is ninety. Not that I care. It may
> go until it requires a balloon to get any higher, and
> not reach my boiling point.

Unruly prisoners were thrown into dungeons built into
the solid masonry of the fort. These dungeons were totally
dark and ventilated only by an airshaft too narrow to
admit a small man.

The only water supply was the rain that washed off
the flat roofs of the fort, drained along gutters and then
filtered through sand. When this supply failed, water was
brought from Brandywine Creek in Delaware and dumped
into cisterns without any attempt at filtering.

When the number of dead exceeded the capacity of the
cemetery on the little island, the government decided to
bury them on the Jersey shore at Finn's Point, on what is
now the Fort Mott reservation. A government tug, the
Osceola, chugged back and forth across the mile of water
transporting loads of bodies. Long ditches were dug and

the dead were dumped in—2,436 of them—without even the questionable glory of being shot down on the battle-field.

A government launch from Fort Mott takes visitors to Pea Patch Island, where the old granite fort, surrounded by its 40-foot moat, looks much as it did in those dark days of the Civil War. Many of the old cannon balls, some weighing as much as 107 pounds, are still in evidence.

On the ground floor is one of the bastion rooms set aside for a bakery; the old-fashioned brick oven built into the walls can still be seen. It could not have supplied much more bread than the officers needed for themselves.

During the late 1880's and '90's young people from Salem held dances in the guardrooms and prison rooms on the second floor. But from the time of the Spanish-American War no civilian has been allowed on the island without special permission from the War Department.

PRESIDENT GROVER CLEVELAND

GROVER CLEVELAND'S BIRTHPLACE

Grover Cleveland never came back to the little white house in Caldwell, New Jersey, where he was born. Caught in the swirl of American politics, he moved forward until at last he sat in another white house on Pennsylvania Avenue in the Nation's capital. But his friends and admirers appreciated the significance of the modest dwelling set in a broad green lawn in the shadow of a red brick church, on busy Bloomfield Avenue.

The former President had been dead two years when it was first planned to make a memorial of the house in

BIRTHPLACE OF GROVER CLEVELAND, CALDWELL, N. J.

which he had been born. Built in 1833, it was still being used as the manse of the First Presbyterian Church when in 1910 a number of prominent Democrats of Caldwell, Verona, Essex Fells and Roseland met to discuss taking over the house as a permanent political club. In the face of opposition from the trustees of the church, the plan collapsed, but the following year it was agreed to sell the birthplace to the Cleveland Memorial Association for $18,000, even though there was loud dissent from those who wanted the church to retain ownership. The resolution passed, 15 to 2, and the sale was consummated March 9, 1912.

Dr. John H. Finley, then president of the College of the City of New York and at present associate editor of the *New York Times*, Cleveland H. Dodge and George W. Perkins were to act as trustees of the property until the Cleveland Birthplace Association had legal status. Also interested in the patriotic venture were Thomas A. Buckner, then vice president of the New York Life Insurance Co., and President Day of the Equitable Life Assurance Co.

On March 18, 1913, the 76th anniversary of Grover Cleveland's birth, the home was dedicated before one of the largest crowds ever assembled in Caldwell. Mrs. Thomas Jex Preston Jr., widow of the President, his children, Esther, Marion and Richard, and several members of the Cleveland cabinet attended. Dr. Finley presided. The streets and houses of the borough were hung with flags and bunting, and a band paraded on Bloomfield Avenue to the schoolhouse where the pupils were waiting to be dismissed to march to the exercises.

In 1915 William H. Van Wart, secretary of the Association, suggested that the United States take over the manse, as it was always called, and preserve it as a national memorial. The following year President Woodrow Wilson, who had spoken from its steps in 1910 during his gubernatorial campaign, brought the plan to Congress. The Association was willing to offer the home free of all encumbrances if Congress would make it a public memorial and provide for its upkeep. The annual cost of maintenance, it was computed, was no more than $500. When the Attorney General gave it as his opinion that such a purchase was impossible, the idea was abandoned.

Even though George M. Canfield, who had subscribed $10,000 originally, left a $20,000 endowment in his will, the Association was having difficulty in maintaining the property, which by 1930 was valued at $100,000. There were other isolated instances of philanthropy, but by 1933 it was clear that the Association could not support the home. It was Dr. Finley who then asked: "Should not the State of New Jersey show her pride in her only native son who, of his own choice, came back to her after serving as Governor of a sister state and twice President of the United States, by making his birthplace a State memorial?"

The legislature considered the question, and on June 13, 1933, the State Senate voted to take the house as a gift from the Grover Cleveland Birthplace Association. But since the State cannot accept property encumbered by debts, a $5,000 mortgage held up formal acceptance of the manse. Finally, on February 13, 1934, Governor A. Harry Moore named a board of 20 trustees, serving without pay, to maintain the Cleveland birthplace for the State. Among the trustees were Dr. Finley, Newton D. Baker, former Secretary of War, Adolph Ochs, Richard F. Cleveland, Louis Annin Ames and Edward D. Duffield. The transfer ceremonies took place October 6, 1934. Under the Works Progress Administration a $10,000 program of renovation was inaugurated.

Additions had been made to the house from time to time after the Clevelands moved away, but when it was decided to make a memorial of the manse the house was restored as nearly as possible to its original form. Except for minor details, the eight-room dwelling remains as it was when the infant who was to become President slept in the borrowed maple cradle in the small room on the first floor. The flooring, of planks of random width, is almost intact; the original bannister railing, bent from one piece of wood, is still pinned to the walls by wooden pegs. The door and the windows and the white enamel doorknob are just as they were. On the black door lock is the broadwinged figure of the American eagle, symbolic, perhaps, of the destiny of the child who was born here.

Charles E. Welsh, curator of the home, estimates that about 250 visitors come each month to walk about the grounds and look at the exhibits. These include, in addition to Cleveland's cradle and his White House chair, the desk he used while mayor of Buffalo, the lawbooks over which he pored, the preacher's license given to his father by the New York Presbytery, the family Bible and numerous religious tomes Richard Cleveland must have used for his Sunday sermons. Carefully preserved in a box is a piece of the wedding cake served to guests at the White House when Cleveland married Frances Folsom.

On the walls of the home are many pictures of the President, the members of his family and his many close friends. The variety of his correspondence attests his attraction, which overrode the boundaries of politics or creed. Joseph Jefferson, who created the rôle of Rip Van Winkle on the stage, and Richard Watson Gilder, poet and editor, wrote affectionate letters. The letters of Richard Croker, who wrote to Congressmen begging that they attempt to influence the President's policies, are strong testimonials of Cleveland's steadfast political honesty.

Grover Cleveland was born in the manse on March 18, 1837, three years after his father, the Reverend Richard Falley Cleveland, had come to occupy the pulpit of Caldwell's First Presbyterian Church. The minister and his wife, Ann, named their fifth child for Steven Grover, Richard Cleveland's predecessor. The family lived in Caldwell, with an income of never more than $600 a year, until 1841, when a call came from Fayetteville, New York.

The Clevelands led a difficult life at Fayetteville. The

family soon grew to eleven, and the meager salary of a country preacher, however augmented by donations from kindly parishioners, had to be stretched a long way. When the boy was 14, circumstances compelled him to give up his education and take a job clerking in a store. For 22 months he slept in a cold room above the store, tormented by rats that overran the banks of the canal and burrowed in the earth beneath the shabby houses. He rose early and worked very late for a dollar a day and "keep."

Then the family's financial situation improved, and Grover was able to quit his job. But his father died shortly after, and rather than burden his family with additional expenses Cleveland left home for New York, where he found a job as bookkeeper in a school for the blind. This did not last long, and he looked to the West for a brighter future.

On his way to the city of Cleveland, which bears the name of one of his kinsmen, he stopped off at Buffalo to see an uncle. This man persuaded him to remain in Buffalo and placed him with an important law firm, where the boy began training for his profession.

In 1859 he was admitted to the bar, and by 1863 he had become assistant district attorney of Erie County. When the Civil War broke out he was called in the draft, but because he was virtually the sole support of his family he borrowed $300 to buy an exemption. Cleveland became sheriff of Erie County in 1870, and 11 years later was elected mayor of Buffalo, pledged to cleanse the city of the remnants of a once-powerful ring of grafters. Tammany Hall opposed him in the campaign for Governor of New York in 1883, but he was elected after a bitterly fought campaign and began a relentless war against corruption in government.

The Democratic convention in the following year was a hard-fought and turbulent affair. The announcement of Cleveland's candidacy was greeted by a mixture of cat-calls and cheers. But the poor reception was not indicative of the final result. In 1884, a scant three years after becoming mayor of Buffalo, Grover Cleveland was elected President of the United States.

His administration was marked by serious labor troubles, and in his message to Congress on April 22, 1886, Cleveland indicated how deeply concerned he was with the quarrels of labor and capital. There was no department of labor at the time in the Cabinet, although a Bureau of Labor, with limited powers, was already in existence. Cleveland advocated that the work of this bureau be expanded by the appointment of a permanent commission to arbitrate labor disputes. This agency, he hoped, would function better than a board chosen only after a controversy had begun. The present National Labor Relations Board represents the development of Grover Cleveland's vision.

In 1888 Cleveland was defeated for reelection by Benjamin Harrison, but his popularity had by no means waned, for in 1892 he was returned to the Presidency, the only man so rewarded in our history. After a second term of splendid service to the Nation, he retired to Princeton. Cleveland died there June 24, 1908, at "Westland," the estate that he had named for former Dean West of Princeton University.

The Grover Cleveland Birthplace trustees have planned a publicity campaign to acquaint visitors with the first home of a great President. A sign at the entrance to the Borough of Caldwell directs tourists to the house. When the task of gathering more relics has been completed, the trustees hope to publish a booklet describing the manse more fully.

The simple white house with its four gables and lattice-work, the trim lawn, the bucket well that stands in the yard—ali these are the mementoes of the beginning of an American career.

ANIMAL QUARANTINE

Years ago the spread of tuberculosis and foot-and-mouth disease among farm animals caused the loss of millions of dollars yearly. In order to safeguard the home cattle from infectious diseases brought in from abroad, the United States passed a law in 1884 providing for an inspection and quarantine service for animals.

As soon as the animal quarantine legislation was passed the Department of Agriculture set about establishing quarantine stations where imported animals could be held while undergoing observation and inspection. One of these, for the Port of Baltimore, was at Turner in Maryland; another, somewhat larger, for the Port of New York was first established at Garfield, New Jersey, and later moved to its present site at Clifton, where a 50-acre reservation has been set aside as a sort of Ellis Island for imported animals. They are held here from 15 to 30 days to determine whether they are carrying disease. When a ship enters an American harbor the passengers must pass through a routine quarantine inspection and the captain must testify that there is no contagious disease among the passengers or crew; but where there are animals in the cargo the procedure is more rigorous.

All such animals as sheep, goats, cattle, horses, camels, giraffes—those that graze or chew the cud—must be passed by a veterinarian before the owner is allowed to take them to his home. If, however, an animal comes into the country with papers certifying to its good health, and the certificate is countersigned by a United States Government official, the animal may be admitted without quarantine. Dogs, cats and similar pets have not been subject to quarantine regulation for many years.

Animals that must be submitted to quarantine are taken from the steamer and shipped directly to the Clifton Quarantine Station by the Newark branch of the Erie Railroad. They must remain until the superintendent is satisfied that they do not carry any infectious disease. The length of the term of quarantine varies with different kinds of animals. Sheep, goats, deer and antelope are usually released after 15 days, while cattle stay for an average of 30 days.

Since most of the animals are brought in for breeding purposes, they are of the highest class and must be given the finest care and food. Often their new owners stay at the station with them during the quarantine period to keep an eye on them.

On the reservation are 19 polished-brick barns and two of wood, each with its own spacious, fenced-in paddock. The barns are of the latest design and are kept scrupulously clean and well ventilated. Each barn is about 35 feet long and 25 feet wide. There are accommodations for about 600 cattle. Separated from the barns and paddocks by a steel-wire fence is the residential section, where are the houses of the superintendent of the station and the chief mechanic. These white frame houses are pleasantly surrounded by several acres of well-kept lawn, trees and shrubbery.

Only the employees of the owner are allowed to handle the animals. These men must remain at the station during the quarantine period, attending to the feeding, watering and cleansing just as if they were in the home barn. The workers of one owner are not permitted to enter the barns and paddocks of another owner. All expenses, except water and light, which are provided by the government, must be met by the different owners.

Every day the superintendent in charge of the quarantine inspects the visitors. The government employs four workmen to keep the barns in good order and fumigated after each consignment has left. These men are not allowed to enter a barn that is occupied. When a workman has completed fumigation of a barn, he has to be fumigated himself before proceeding to the next barn. These four workmen are also charged with keeping pasture lands in proper state. The superintendent, in addition to supervising the farm, has to spend a good deal of time at the Port of New York examining the animals as they arrive to make sure that they meet the high standards set by the United States Government. There is today an embargo against the importation of livestock from about 50 countries where hoof-and-mouth disease is prevalent.

Occasionally the cows, sheep and deer have some strange-looking fellow guests. Frank Buck of "Bring 'Em Back Alive" fame, before turning over the jungle animals which he imports for zoos and parks, has to submit them to the regular quarantine. A newly arrived giraffe may raise a proud nose above the fence that separates him from the humble sheep, goats or cows in an adjoining paddock; but for all his distinguished foreign air he must submit to the same laws that govern the common everyday animals of the field and farm. Most of the cattle come from the Channel Islands, Jersey and Guernsey, for these are the most desirable for breeding purposes.

One is apt to find visitors from odd corners of the earth feeding on New Jersey grass at the Clifton Station.

Recently 34 musk oxen from Greenland on their way to Africa were guests. From Singapore came three mouse deer. These tiny animals less than a foot high and weighing less than 15 pounds were shipped to California as household pets.

LIVING LANDMARKS

Older and more beautiful than the granite columns and bronze tablets by which New Jersey honors famous men and events are a number of fine old trees that have withstood storm and blight for centuries. Some of these, because of their historic associations, are being cared for today by patriotic societies, governmental agencies or private individuals.

Of these testaments to New Jersey's passing history, oaks and sycamores are most plentiful. Both are hardwood species and noted for long life. The oak grows slowly. The sycamore—sometimes called the buttonwood—sets a faster pace; by some authorities it is considered the most massive of our native deciduous trees. It resembles the plane tree, and is distinguished by its burrlike blossoms and the periodic peeling of its bark, which leaves streaked patches of white. The sycamore prefers low ground, and is most commonly found in southern New Jersey.

Close to the bank of the Delaware River in the city of Burlington there stands a sycamore whose age is estimated at 250 years. Though it has been filled with cement and has lost many of its branches, the old tree maintains a sturdy grip on life. It measures 20.3 feet in circumference at breast height. Once the river flowed directly beneath the tree, which has given weight to the tradition that it served as a mooring mast for the ship *Shield* that brought early settlers to Burlington in the autumn of 1678. For this reason it is often referred to as the Shield Tree. After Burlington became the seat of government of West Jersey the sycamore shaded the lawn at the home of William Franklin, last Royal Governor of the Province, and the son of Benjamin Franklin.

In 1765 the board of trustees of the College of New Jersey (now Princeton University) ordered the planting of a row of sycamores before the residence of the president of the college. This was the year in which England passed the Stamp Act. For this reason the Princeton sycamores have been associated with the War of Independence, and are often called the Stamp Act Trees. Two of the trees still stand near the house occupied by the dean of the faculty. They are 90 feet in height and have diameters of 3 feet.

In front of the old Baptist meeting house in Hopewell, on land donated by John Hart, a signer of the Declaration of Independence, stands another great sycamore. Under its branches Colonel Jacob Houghton, a Revolutionary patriot, rallied Jersey farmers with news of the Battle of Lexington, ending his stirring address with the cry, "Men of New Jersey, the redcoats are murdering our brethren of New England! Who follows me to Boston?" Every man, tradition states, answered, "I!" This fine old tree now shades the quiet burying ground where Hart and Houghton both rest.

At Shrewsbury are two sycamores of great beauty that have been preserved for their historic importance. They stand about 100 feet apart in an island in the center of Shrewsbury Avenue nearly opposite Old Christ Church. The larger and, presumably, the older of the two trees bears a bronze plaque which reads:

THIS SYCAMORE
PLANTED BY THE EARLY COLONISTS
IN THE ROYAL PROVINCE OF NEW
JERSEY MARKED THE DELAWARE TRAIL
USED BY THE INDIANS AND LATER
BY WASHINGTON'S TROOPS ON THE
BURLINGTON PATH

BURLINGTON SYCAMORE

Memorialized by
Monmouth Chapter D.A.R.
June 28, 1935

A plaque on the other tree designates it as one of the 13 sycamores which, according to tradition, were placed to commemorate the original 13 colonies. Though several unmarked sycamores stand along the side of the avenue, it has not been possible to establish the location of the remainder of the traditional 13 trees.

In 1930 the board of freeholders undertook to cut down the trees because they were a traffic hazard. The women of the town, aroused, sent a messenger to Freehold to get an injunction that would stop the destruction. Men were already at work, but the women delayed them by feeding them cakes and ice cream—even passing refreshments to those in the uppermost branches until word came to stop the work. The trees are now in the care of patriotic societies of Monmouth County.

Probably the most famous tree in New Jersey is the Salem Oak, a 400-year-old veteran which stands in the Friends' Burial Ground in Salem. For more than a century the Society of Friends has kept faithful guard over the tree and has carefully gathered its acorns to fill the many requests that have come in from all parts of this country and abroad. In 10 years $2,000 has been spent in surgery and care.

Measurements made in 1933 gave the height as 73 feet; circumference 5 feet from the ground, 19.5 feet; spread, 10,516 square feet. Beneath its branches John Fenwick is supposed to have made his treaty with the Indians in 1675 when he purchased extensive lands for the Quaker colony which he established. This treaty, made six years previous to Penn's famous treaty, was the first made by a white man with the Indians that was not broken.

Equaling the Salem Oak in beauty, age and size is a great lightning-scarred white oak on farm land owned by Daniel Gaskill, at the end of First Avenue, in Mantua, Gloucester County. It is said that the Indians gathered under it for their councils, a tradition strengthened by the knowledge that they used the banks of Mantua Creek for

SALEM OAK

a rendezvous. There is no historical event associated with this tree, nor has it enjoyed the care given the Salem Oak. Some of its powerful branches might be trimmed of dead wood, but the dense foliage testifies to a sound heart. Summer and winter it is a picture of symmetry and beauty. It has a breast high circumference of 19 feet and 9 inches and looks like a miniature forest balanced on a single stem.

There is a white oak on the Hartshorne estate in the Navesink Highlands, not far from the Shrewsbury River, which was in its second or third century when Richard Hartshorne in 1671 bought the land from the Indians. In 1778 a 12-mile line of British soldiers, burdened with supplies, retreated from Monmouth Battlefield to ships anchored off Sandy Hook. An English officer—tradition says it was Sir Henry Clinton—saluted Richard Hartshorne, and complimented him on his holdings in the Highlands. Hartshorne is said to have answered firmly, "I intend to hold them, sir." His descendants still possess the land on which the oak stands.

In the Presbyterian Churchyard at Basking Ridge, Somerset County, stands a white oak reputed to be 400 years old. Its great branches, extending almost 140 feet, are strengthened by many wire cables, iron rods and braces to help it withstand the effects of age. In its shadow the British attacked General Charles Lee in 1776, taking him prisoner; around its trunk, it is said, they tethered their horses while raiding in the vicinity in 1781.

Another white oak called the "Shoe Tree," in the quiet town of Belvidere, is revered because it recalls a homely custom of our fathers rather than an important historical event. Its name derives from a tradition that the early settlers used to stop beneath it, before going across the road to church, to put on their shoes, which they had carried in their hands up to this point. When some years ago the street was widened the townspeople insisted that the tree be left standing in the center of the road, even though it caused inconvenience to traffic. At an age of 250 or 300 years the old landmark is still in excellent condition.

These old trees sometimes live in the cities, surrounded by tall buildings. In Military Park, Newark, there is an Oriental plane estimated as being 175 years old, a witness possibly of Washington's retreat from New York in 1776. Still in excellent condition, it towers over the shrubbery of the park, unperturbed by the hurrying traffic and the crowded department stores which face it.

On a farm now known as "Poet's Dream," just south of Matawan, at Freneau, there is a grove of locust trees near the grave of Philip Freneau, the poet of the Revolution.

The trees were a century old when young Philip played in their shade on his father's 100-acre farm, which was called Mount Pleasant Hall. Later he walked under the locusts with Eleanor Forman, who became his wife; many of his poems were supposedly written in the grove. Freneau's grave is marked with a monument, but the living locusts give breath to the memorial.

A row of fine catalpas planted about 1757 on the lawn of "Morven," home of the Stocktons in Princeton for seven generations, recalls Richard Stockton, signer of the Declaration of Independence. They are sometimes called "Independence Trees," because they bear pure white blossoms on the Fourth of July.

Haddonfield has two yew trees said to be the oldest of their species in America. They were brought from England on one of her three voyages in 1712 and 1713 by Elizabeth Haddon, founder of the town, whose romantic life was celebrated in Longfellow's *Tales of a Wayside Inn* and in Lydia Maria Child's story, *The Youthful Emigrant*. Elizabeth came to this country at the age of 20 to develop land purchased by her father. She married John Estaugh, a Quaker, and built a fine brick mansion for their home, setting the trees before it. When the mansion was destroyed by fire in 1842 her descendants saved the yews by spreading wet rugs over the branches. Yews are not native to this country and only rarely adapt themselves to the soil and climate. Although they have stood for two centuries, Elizabeth Haddon's yews are now in poor condition and destined to survive only a few years.

The Washington Walnut, shading the Washington Inn, 425 Ridgewood Road, Maplewood, is believed to have been planted by Timothy and Esther Ball when they built their home, now the inn, in 1743. According to the tablet on the tree, when Washington visited the home during the Revolution he tied his horse to an iron ring which the bark has since overgrown. Although many of the branches that shaded the road have been cut away, the old giant still flourishes. The trunk is about 13.6 feet in circumference.

On the property of Dr. Maurice Cohen, at Claremont Avenue and Valley Road, Montclair, where the historic Crane house once stood, is another walnut tree, surviving from the days when Washington visited there. This tree is of special interest to the children of the community because of the fantastic figures of animals and gnomes placed in its branches by Dr. Cohen.

Cedars of Lebanon are distinctly not native to this country, but in a congenial environment are known to live to a great age. One of these, imported about 1850 as a sapling from Mount Olivet in the Holy Land, stands in front of the Borough Hall in Woodlyne, Camden County. This was the site of the house where Mark Newbie established the first bank in New Jersey, if not in the country.

At Ringwood Manor in the northern part of Passaic County, recently given to the State as a historical park, are many old trees. At the Manor, during the Revolution, Robert Erskine, ironmaster and Washington's surveyor general, maintained a forge which supplied the army with part of its munitions. The Commander in Chief stopped here often while journeying between battlefields. Alongside the house and still bearing luscious fruit is a fine pear tree that was standing when Washington visited here. In front of the house is a double row of trees planted by Mrs. Martin Ryerson, wife of Erskine's successor, to commemorate the Peace of Ghent following the War of 1812.

There has been established at Washington Crossing Park an arboretum of 1,000 native trees and 1,500 small bushes with the combined purpose of keeping alive public interest in one of the great moments in the Nation's history and in the future of its forest lands.

PEOPLE

MARK NEWBIE, AMERICA'S FIRST BANKER

In 1682 Mark Newbie opened and operated the first bank in North America. In a room of his simple home near Camden, New Jersey, this Quaker ex-tallow chandler from London set up his new institution with a capital of 300 acres of land and a currency consisting of copper coins which today are valuable only to collectors.

Newbie, to escape the persecution of the Quakers under Charles II, had sold his prosperous London business in 1677 and joined a group of sympathizers who had gathered in Dublin, Ireland, while they completed plans to migrate to the colonies. They were awaiting reports from Robert Zane, one of their group, who had been sent over to join the colony of English Quakers established by John Fenwick. In 1675 Fenwick had made a treaty with the Indians for a great tract of country around Salem.

As the news of conditions in the distant colonies reached him, Newbie realized that his old trade would be of little help to him as a means of livelihood in the wilderness. He was a shrewd, farseeing man, however, and before long hit upon a scheme which he thought might prove profitable.

During the three years spent in Ireland he had taken note of the circulation of some copper coins known as Patrick's pence. These had been issued as a reminder of the terrific slaughter of Protestants by Catholics during the retaliatory religious massacres in the reign of Charles I. The coins were named for the figure of St. Patrick which

FARTHING

PATRICK'S PENCE OR MARK NEWBIE COPPERS

appeared on the reverse. The figure of Charles I in the character of King David was on the face. The original coins made of silver were used as legal tender, but copper replicas in two sizes, though not legal, were accepted by some people as halfpence and farthings at a discount. It occurred to Newbie that these coins might be useful in the settlements across the sea where civilization was loosely organized and trade was without regulation. He invested a part of his savings in all the Patrick's pence he could obtain.

In the spring of 1682 a small vessel sailed up the Dela-

HALF PENNY

vare River, entered Newton Creek and deposited Mark
Newbie together with a group of 25 men and women near
he site of what is now Collingswood, New Jersey. With
Newbie came his coin collection.

There was at this time no authorized currency in the
olony. The rate of exchange for the moneys of Spain,
France, Portugal, Holland and England was based on
he Spanish dollar. Trade was carried on by barter or with
wampum, Spanish doubloons, pistoles and dollars, French
guineas, Portuguese johanesses, Dutch ducats and stivers,
English guineas, crowns and shillings, or with whatever
currency fell into the hands of the colonists. There was
no organized system of banking. The larger local merchants with English connections usually acted as bankers
for the smaller businessmen. Thus custom prevailed until
1781, when Robert Morris formed the Bank of North
America in Philadelphia.

In May 1682 Newbie was chosen as a member of the
General Assembly meeting at Burlington. He was appointed to the Governor's council, and became one of the
commissioners for the division of land and a member of
the committee of ways and means to raise money for the
government.

Meanwhile the little hoard of Patrick's pence was jin-
gling in his pockets, and thrifty Mark Newbie decided
that the time had come to put them to work. He suggested
to the Assembly that the souvenir copper coins could be
put into circulation for use in small transactions. He agreed
to provide security by placing 300 acres of his land in the
hands of a commission so that the money could be redeemed on demand. The land was signed over to two
commissioners, and Newbie hung on the wall of a room

in his log house his charter as a banker, dated May 18 1682, reading:

> For the convenient payment of small sums, be it enacted that Mark Newbie's half-pence, from and after the Eighteenth instant, pass for half-pence current pay of the province, provided he, the said Mark Newbie, his executors and administrators shall and will exchange the said half-pence for pay equivalent on demand; and provided also that no person or persons hereby be obliged to take more than five shillings in any one payment.

This was the first legal issue of currency in the colonies and Newbie became in effect the first American banker The bank proved popular from its beginning, for the settlers found it convenient to use the coins from Ireland Although the charter specified that no more than five shillings need be accepted in one transaction, trade among the colonists was stimulated to no small extent. Gradually the use of the coins became general; some of them reached as far as Salem.

Newbie became known as a prudent administrator during the few months he lived after founding his institution He was careful that the amount of coins in circulation was kept within a reasonable figure, mindful that his charter did not grant him permission to issue or mint new money to enlarge his own credit or to keep up circulation. The coins were employed only in those business dealings that could not be conveniently handled by barter.

When Mark Newbie died suddenly in 1683 his widow Hannah, executrix of his will, ordered the bank closed The coins were called in before the estate was settled on July 4, 1684. A discrepancy of about £30 was disscovered

n the funds of the bank, probably caused by the inability
f the founder to perfect his plans. Mrs. Newbie paid the
hortage out of her husband's personal estate, and the
ommissioners released the land held as security.

Several of Mark Newbie's coins were never redeemed
nd for a time continued to circulate. Gradually they dis-
ppeared from ordinary channels and now are to be found
nly among the rare coins of collectors. Sometimes called
Mark Newbie coppers, Patrick's pence bring $2.50 for a
halfpenny piece in good condition; $5 if in excellent con-
dition. The farthing brings $2 and $3.50.

THE SWEDISH SETTLERS

Marshes and woodlands along the shores were showing the first faint coloring of spring as two small vessels came to anchor in the lower reaches of the Delaware River. From their mastheads flew proudly the royal cross of Sweden, and from their decks crews and passengers alike were anxiously scanning the shore line for a trace of Indians or ferocious beasts. Many a fabulous tale of this new world had they heard by their firesides during the cold and stormy winters along the Swedish coast— tales of the uncivilized inhabitants, of their clothes made from the skins of animals, of their strange customs, of their reverence for white men and of great wealth that might be amassed in trade with the childlike savages.

It was in the spring of 1638. Only 18 years earlier the Pilgrims had landed at Plymouth Rock. The Swedish Mayflower, the *Kalmar Nyckel* (Key of Kalmar), with her companion tender, the *Fogel Grip* (Bird Griffon), sailed up the Delaware River in charge of Peter Minuit, the famous Hollander who had governed the colony of New Netherland on the Hudson for the Dutch West India Company. Now, in the service of the Crown of Sweden, he was bringing traders and soldiers to establish a settlement.

The little company sailed into Minquas Kill, now Christina, Creek, and landed on "The Rocks" near where Wilmington, Delaware, now stands. There, under the guard-

THE FOUNDING OF NEW SWEDEN

Peter Minuit and the First Swedish Settlers Are Bid
Welcome by the Indians

(Painting in the American Swedish Historical Museum, Philadelphia, Pa.)

ing cannon of their vessels, they set up their first settlement, called it Fort Christina, in honor of the young
Queen of their home country, and surrounded it by a
palisade against any surprise visits by an Indian war party.

But the only Indians who appeared were merely curious
to discover what these strange men wanted. On March 28,
1638, five sachems appointed by the assembled tribes
sold as much "of the land on all parts and places of the
river and on both sides as Minuit requested." Minuit had
been ordered by the Swedish Crown to be fair in all his
dealings with the Indians; and so, for what they considered value received, the natives transferred all the land

extending along the creek, as far north as the Schuylkill River and stretching westward indefinitely.

When Minuit set out for the Delaware in 1637 Sweden had become one of the most powerful nations of Europe. Her rulers had forged all the Baltic countries—Sweden, Finland, Estonia and Latvia (at that time called Ingermanland, Estland, Livland and Kurland)—into one Scandinavian union. During the sixteenth century the kings of the House of Vasa had rebuilt the whole nation from its very foundations. Copper and iron mined in the rocky interior was carried to foreign lands to exchange for gold, silver, silks, spices and valuable furs, but the supplies at home grew faster than they could be carried away to be exchanged or sold. Storehouses began to bulge with reserve stocks of refined ore. Surpluses were stored in friendly foreign countries. Sweden was powerful among the nations of the world, and rich in materials, but her supply of ready cash was deplorably low.

Spain and Portugal had increased their national wealth by subjecting Mexico and the South American continent to their rule. Their galleons brought gold and silver back to the mother countries. England had explored the coast of North America and had settled Jamestown, Virginia, in 1607, and Plymouth in 1620. The Dutch had built Fort Nassau on the Delaware in 1623, near Gloucester city.

King Gustavus Adolphus was anxious that Sweden should obtain a share of the New World's riches, and between 1626 and 1632 he permitted the establishment of three trading companies for this purpose. Subscriptions of funds were slow, however, and when the King was slain at the Battle of Lützen in 1632, the plan appeared doomed. Fortunately Axel Oxenstierna, the regent for

the new ruler, six-year-old Queen Christina, was a man
of prudence and vision. One of his main efforts was to
revive the colonization plans of his royal master.

He spoke to Samuel Blommaert, a Dutch financier,
about organizing a trading expedition. Blommaert was one
of the directors of the Dutch West India Company, for
which Peter Minuit in 1625 had purchased the Island of
Manhattan from its Indian owners for the equivalent of
twenty-four dollars. After six years' service as director-
general and acting governor of New Netherland, Minuit
was suddenly recalled to Holland and summarily dismissed from the service of the company. Blommaert
himself had been one of the "patroons" of an attempted
Dutch settlement near Cape May in 1630. He had the
highest regard for Minuit's courage, self-reliance and ad-
ministrative ability, and recommended him to Oxenstierna
as the leader of the proposed expedition.

Plans for the organization of the company were completed in 1636. Funds were widely subscribed for the
New Sweden Company, and Minuit, who had been called
to Sweden in the meantime, personally supplied one-
eighth of the total capital of 24,000 guilders. Two vessels
were purchased, and on November 20, 1637, they set sail
from the new port of Gothenburg.

The dauntless Dutchman who led the Swedish pioneer
immigrants was not to live, however, to see the success
of his ventures. In June 1638 re departed from the new
colony on board the *Kalmar Nyckel* for the West Indies,
to exchange part of his cargo for tobacco. At St. Chris-
topher a Dutch merchantman, the *Flying Stag* of Rotter-
dam, was lying in the harbor, and her captain invited the
famous explorer on board. Suddenly one of the dreaded
West Indian hurricanes blew up, and the *Stag* was blown

out to sea, never to be heard from again. The *Kalmar Nyckel* had to return to Europe without her commander.

Peter Minuit's death left a vacancy hard to fill, and it was several months before the New Sweden Company could agree on a successor. Peter Holländer Ridder finally was chosen as the second governor of New Sweden and commander of Fort Christina.

Under his leadership a second group of colonists set sail on board the *Kalmar Nyckel* in September 1639. Among Ridder's company was the Reverend Reorus Torkillus, who was to act as spiritual adviser to the people of New Sweden. He was the first minister of the Lutheran faith to serve in America. In addition to the handful of passengers there were also on board the little sloop "four mares and two young horses and a number of farm implements . . . so that the colonists can make a trial with seeding in the Autumn."

This was an indication that the attitude of the crown and of the proprietors of the New Sweden Company had changed. No longer did they dream of sudden riches to be amassed by one or two lucky trading ventures. They began to understand that, if wealth was to come from America, it would come only through the gradual development of the Delaware settlements. New Sweden was to become a crown colony in fact as well as in name.

Ridder's administration was notable chiefly for expansion. The lands which he purchased from the Indians in the spring of 1641 for the first time extended the territory of New Sweden across the Delaware into New Jersey. Stretching from Raccoon Creek south along the coast to Cape May, it was by far the largest tract yet added to New Sweden. Compared with Minuit's small strips along

GOVERNOR JOHAN PRINTZ OF NEW SWEDEN

the west bank, the New Jersey purchase was the start of real Swedish dominion in America.

In 1643 Ridder was succeeded by Johan Printz, a huge man, weighing close to 400 pounds, whom the Indians humorously dubbed "Big Belly." Known as an excellent soldier in Sweden, he proceeded to rule the colony in military fashion. Almost immediately he gave orders for the erection of a new fort on the Jersey shore. His trained eye had discovered the site from which Swedish cannon might command the river. He chose a point of land that stretches into the Delaware, south of the modern cities of Newcastle and Wilmington. The site is at Elsinboro, near the present city of Salem, New Jersey, and it is said that foundation pilings may still be seen at low water. The fort was called Elfsborg after a Swedish stronghold. But to the soldiers it was known as "Fort Myggenborg," meaning "Mosquito Fort," because of the mosquitos and gnats which made life at the garrison a torment.

Another fortification, Fort Gothenburg, was raised on Tinicum Island, opposite Gibbstown in Gloucester County. Here the new governor built Printzhof, his official residence. The choice of the island for the colony's capital was particularly wise. For not merely was Tinicum centrally located, but from there Printz could also keep constant vigil on the Dutch at Fort Nassau. This old stronghold, a short distance to the north of Tinicum Island, near the mouth of Timber Creek, had been revived by the Dutch since Printz's arrival in the New World.

Under the personal supervision of the governor the primitive dugouts and sod huts that had given temporary shelter to the first group of Swedish settlers developed into substantial log cabins. These homes, reminiscent of the cabins the settlers had left behind them in the deep forests of Sweden and Finland, were the origin of the American log cabin, that structure that later was to become the distinctive mark of the frontier.

The life of the colonists was far from being as primitive as later day accounts picture pioneer existence. The deep forest of South Jersey yielded an abundance of venison, even an occasional bear. Wild ducks, geese and turkeys were plentiful. Fish, oysters and clams could be taken from the streams. In the woods was a profusion of wild fruits, berries, edible roots and herbs. The settlers grew garden vegetables, including peas, beans, squash, potatoes and turnips. The fields yielded a good grain crop.

The furniture of their tight little cabins was hand-hewn from logs. A smooth-sawed slab on four legs may have served as a table, smaller ones for chairs and stools. Beds were pallet like shelves built against the walls. A layer of straw, covered with a deer skin or bear skin, supplied a mattress, and bedclothes were more skins.

Wood also was the raw material for most household utensils. The clever hands of these early woodsmen shaped plates from smooth strips of bark; spoons and forks from the limbs of trees; cups and bowls from wooden blocks, and even the bread pans were hollowed with fire and adze out of a section of a tree trunk. An axe, a knife, a saw, several iron or copper kettles and his musket were usually the only tools for which a pioneer depended on the mother country. The rest he fashioned for himself.

Trade with the Indians continued. Although Printz had a personal aversion to the "savages," he was much too shrewd to forget the steady demands of the New Sweden Company for valuable pelts and furs. And the Indian trappers and hunters were the ones to supply that demand, at least as long as trade goods in Printz's warehouses held out.

Throughout his administration the governor had consistently sought new colonists to strengthen his lands against the threatening Dutch from New Netherland. Although Printz had gained control of the river by his strategic arrangement of forts, he could not cope with the superior force of the Dutch governor, Peter Stuyvesant. In 1651 he was forced to abandon Fort Elfsborg, which had been New Sweden's pride and protection. There followed two long years of waiting vainly for help from home, and then in 1653, disappointed and defeated, Printz returned home.

With the arrival of a new governor, Johan Rising, hopes for the strengthening of New Sweden improved. Unfortunately he antagonized the Dutch by an unnecessary conquest of their fortress opposite Fort Elfsborg, and Stuyvesant proceeded to eliminate the troublesome Swedes once and for all. In September 1655 he appeared with a formidable force in the Delaware Valley and demanded complete surrender of New Sweden. Outnumbered, Rising agreed on the condition that the Swedish settlers might be left in full possession of their lands. Stuyvesant assented, and New Sweden became a part of New Netherland.

Not long after the passing of New Sweden, the Swedes, who since 1638 had been concentrated on the Pennsylvania and Delaware shores of the Delaware River, began to migrate eastward into New Jersey. They sailed up the creeks that empty into the Delaware to find new homes and better farm lands than those on the west bank. Throughout the century following the fall of New Sweden, the migration was so steady that ultimately New

Jersey became the center of Swedish activity in North America.

By 1685 Swedes had established themselves all over present-day Camden, Gloucester and Salem Counties. They were living as far north as Pensauken Creek and as far south as Salem Creek. They founded centers such as Cinnaminson, Repaupo and Penns Neck, which were not villages in the modern sense, but central gathering spots for settlers over a wide area.

The most famous gathering spot was Raccoon, on the creek of that name. In 1702 the Kings Highway, running from Salem to Burlington, reached the small settlement and transformed it into an important town. The road was also the instrument by which the Swedes were to be joined into a closely knit social and religious community.

With travel thus made easier, the scattered Swedes began to think seriously of erecting a church of their own on the New Jersey side of the Delaware. Since their arrival in the New World steadfastness to their Swedish Lutheran faith had been one of their major characteristics, and since the fall of New Sweden it had been their sole tie with the mother country of their forefathers.

Up to the beginning of the eighteenth century, the New Jersey Swedes were obliged to cross the river to attend the Lutheran churches at Wilmington or Wicacoa (Philadelphia). It was a long journey to these churches from the outlying districts of New Jersey. It necessitated spending time that should have been applied to work on the land. The faithful had to walk and ride along trails and paths newly blazed through the woods. At the river's edge there awaited them the crude, open flatboats that would ferry them across, bucking the wild freshets of spring and fall and dangerous ice floes in wintertime.

All these hardships made the simple enterprise of going to church a dangerous adventure. Only on Christmas, Easter and Pentecost, the three high holidays of the Lutheran faith, and on the occasion of his own wedding, might a frontier farmer leave his homestead for the several days or even the week required for the toilsome journey. The occasional tours of traveling parsons supplemented the visits to church.

Discontent, ever on the increase, was finally fanned into open flames by Lars Tollstadius, an ambitious young preacher. He eventually led a secession of the New Jersey Swedish Lutherans from the Wicacoa parish and brought about the establishment of the Raccoon Church, the first and most famous of all Swedish Lutheran edifices in New Jersey. Although the ecclesiastical authorities in Sweden and America disapproved of Tollstadius, he ignored their objections and easily persuaded the New Jersey Swedes to erect their own church. Early in the fall of 1703 he preached his first sermon in a little log church which stood within a few feet of the site of the present Trinity Episcopal Church in Swedesboro, as Raccoon is now known.

Tollstadius died suddenly in 1706, either by suicide or by accident, but the religious independence of the New Jersey Swedes had been firmly established. His success led to the formation of another parish below Raccoon at Penns Neck, which was formally dedicated in 1717. Thereafter, with the exception of two years, a single pastor, sent from Sweden, officiated for both parishes.

Although the Swedes had hoped that the establishment of their own churches would help to preserve Swedish customs and language, they fought a losing battle against superior forces. Southern New Jersey was a melting pot including, besides the Swedes, English, Dutch, Scotch-Irish

and German settlers, all of whom intermarried with the Swedes. By 1750, when the great Swedish-Finnish naturalist, Peter Kalm, visited New Jersey, he found Repaupo the only settlement still Swedish in character. In dress, language and social habits the Swedes were rapidly becoming assimilated with the other nationalities, especially the dominant English. A little more than a decade later, Swedish pastors began to keep their church records in English, and it became less and less necessory for them to preach in Swedish as well as in English, for fewer and fewer people understood the language.

When the Revolutionary War broke out, the Swedes for the most part took arms against England and played an important part in southern New Jersey's military campaigns. After the war they quickly came to look upon themselves as Americans, an attitude which contributed to the final effacement of the Swedish Lutheran Church. In 1786 the tie with the mother church in Sweden had become so weak that the New Jersey Swedes finally severed it completely by joining the Episcopal Church. Only

two years before they had erected in Swedesboro a new church building which still stands.

This building was one of the centers of the New Jersey celebration in 1938 of the three hundredth anniversary of the landing of the Swedes in America. The church received a Bible from King Gustaf V of Sweden and conducted a special service attended by Prince Bertil, official representative of the Swedish government to the celebration.

THE TEA BURNERS OF GREENWICH

When the word "tea" is mentioned as a cause of the Revolutionary War most people picture howling redskins throwing cases of tea into Boston Harbor. Few know that New Jersey had its own tea party—one that was as colorful and as violent. The New Jersey patriots used fire instead of water, but the destruction was as complete. The incident occurred in the southern part of the State in the town of Greenwich, a peaceful, law-abiding community whose citizens were about equally divided in their loyalties: half Whig, half Tory. Many of the Whigs were younger persons who bitterly opposed England's treatment of the Colonies.

On that exciting night in December 1774 the inhabitants of the little town of Greenwich were awakened by a racket. People were running toward the market place, where a huge bonfire was burning. Around the high-leaping flames a band of 40 Indians, grimly silent, were opening large packages which they brought from the cellar of a house on the square. As each package was opened its contents were fed to the fire.

Many a Greenwich housewife sniffed the air regretfully as she recognized the fragrance of burning tea leaves. So this was another tea party; like the one in Boston a year ago! There were people in the group watching the destruction who deeply disapproved the rash act, while others looked on admiringly; but whatever the sentiments of the spectators, no one offered to halt the work of the young men who had disguised themselves as Indians in order to intimidate any Tories who might attempt to resist them.

This tea business was being taken seriously by the colonists. They enjoyed the comfort of a cup of tea as much as ever; but rather than submit to a tax imposed without fair representation, many refused to drink tea. All sorts of substitutes were used, raspberry and blackberry leaves, goldenrod, dittany and various other native plants and herbs. There is a story told of Hugh Drum of Somerset County who was so thoroughly in earnest that he vowed that as long as he lived he would never touch a drop of tea. Having made the vow he stuck to it even after the Revolution when the Americans were importing their own tea.

Early in December the *Greyhound*, loaded with tea for Philadelphia, had sailed up the Delaware River. At the mouth of Cohansey Creek the captain unexpectedly gave the order to come about, and the vessel headed up the stream to Greenwich. The skipper had decided that Greenwich was a safer place to unload his cargo than Philadelphia. In Greenwich he knew of a Tory named Dan Bowen who would be pretty sure to permit the storing of the tea in his cellar. Things had come to such a pass that English ships were afraid to put in at big ports, and any captain who succeeded in landing a shipload of tea on American soil felt proud of himself.

As the crew of the *Greyhound* unloaded the cargo, groups of angry citizens muttered disapproval; but the crew worked on until the last package had been carried across the square and deposited in Dan Bowen's cellar. The captain then set sail down the creek, hardly guessing that this tea would provide fuel for a blaze that would ultimately light two continents.

The skipper had figured that, once the tea was stored in Greenwich, the consignees in Philadelphia would find a means of getting it across the land and selling it. But a meeting had already been arranged at Bridgeton to discuss the problem of British imports. The townspeople of Greenwich decided to refer the tea question to this meeting. When, at the end of the first day, no action had been taken, some of the younger men decided to take matters into their own hands.

On the night of December 22 a group of young Revolutionists met at the home of the Howells in Bridgeton. From there they marched through the towns of Bridgeton, Fairfield, Shiloh and Roadstown, increasing in determination and numbers as they drew closer to Greenwich. Arrived at the square they stormed the cellar where the tea was stored and carried out package after package. Soon the crackling flames and fragrant smoke aroused the townspeople.

There was one humorous incident at the party. One of the tea burners, named Stacks, could see no harm in acquiring for himself a little of the precious cargo. As the "Indians" danced around the blaze, he snatched handfuls from the broken cases and stuffed them into his trouser legs. Before long his expanding breeches were detected. From then to the end of his days, which he spent in comparative prosperity in Dutch Neck, he was known as "Tea Stacks."

This Greenwich tea party created a great stir in the section. The Tories called it wanton destruction, and insisted that the "hoodlums," as they called them, should be pun-

TEA BURNER MONUMENT, GREENWICH

ished. There was no difficulty in finding the guilty ones, because they boasted about their work.

Encouraged by the sympathetic attitude of the Tories, the English shippers finally did start a court action. But the Whig element was so strong that it was impossible to find a jury that would bring in a verdict of guilty. Before the case could be reopened the Revolution was in full swing, and far more important things were taking place.

In 1908 the State of New Jersey built a monument in the Market Square in Greenwich to commemorate the event. The names of 23 men preserved in historical records as among the "Indians" are inscribed on the stone shaft.

NEW JERSEY'S DELEGATES TO
THE FEDERAL CONSTITUTIONAL
CONVENTION OF 1787

May 14, 1787—a convention made up of representatives from twelve of the thirteen States assembled in the State House at Philadelphia "for the sole and express purpose of revising the Articles of Confederation." Rhode Island alone did not participate in the Convention. At the end of 16 weeks of work and spirited debate—September 17, 1787—this group of 55 men had written a new law of the land: the Federal Constitution. A year and a half later the law went into effect, and today, with the addition of 21 amendments, it still functions.

The various State legislatures picked delegates with care; they sent men with experience in colonial and state government, Congressmen and lawyers. Most of the members were large landowners. This has led to the accusation that they drew up a document which would work to the benefit of the propertied classes. An opposing belief is that these men were genuine idealists, motivated entirely by interests of the general welfare. Despite the difference of opinion, one thing is certain: they were an unusual group of men possessed of high intellect and common sense.

The State of New Jersey was represented by its wartime Governor, William Livingston; a former Attorney General, William Paterson; a Chief Justice of the State Supreme Court, David Brearley; a Princeton professor,

William Churchill Houston; and a Revolutionary Army paymaster, Jonathan Dayton.

Houston became ill during the Convention and was unable to remain. Two others named as delegates were unable to serve. They were Abraham Clark of Rahway, surveyor and signer of the Declaration of Independence, and John Neilson, merchant of New Brunswick, who had commanded a regiment of New Jersey militia in the war.

William Livingston (1723-1790)

Livingston, the senior delegate, was then 64 years old and Governor of New Jersey. He had been a member of the Continental Congress, gaining the hatred of Tories and the British for his services to the Colonies. As chancellor or chief judge of the high court, an office held by the governor, he supported measures confiscating the property of those New Jersey residents who remained loyal to the King. To escape soldiers of the Crown, he had been compelled several times to flee from his home near Elizabeth to the hills of the interior.

There is a story told of one raid on Governor Livingston's house, in which the quick wit and charm of his daughter Susan averted a serious situation. The British were about to search a secretary containing important papers. Susan promised to show them where secret documents were hidden if they would leave the desk untouched, implying that it held some very private papers of hers. The redcoats agreed to the bargain and were hoodwinked into accepting a sheaf of old law briefs.

Born at Albany in 1723 of a prominent New York family, Livingston was graduated from Yale and was admitted to the bar in 1748. While practicing law in New York City he joined a group opposing the existing Church

BENNETT HOUSE AT PARSIPPANY, THE HAVEN OF GOV.
LIVINGSTON DURING THE REVOLUTION, AS IT LOOKS
TODAY

of England theocracy and British domination. He was
editor of the *Independent Reflector*, established by James
Parker at Woodbridge, New Jersey, in 1752. The printer
refused to handle the publication after 52 issues, fearing
British officials. Livingston then edited the Watch Tower
column in the *New York Mercury*, frequently writing
under such pseudonyms as Z.B.X., Z.Z. and B.X.A. At
that time, according to one authority, the Province of
New York had fewer than a score of college graduates,
among whom were Livingston and his three elder
brothers.

In 1772, asking to be delivered, as he had put it,

> From ladies, lap-dogs, courtiers, garters, stars,
> Fops, fiddlers, tyrants, emperors, and czars,

he built on his land in Elizabeth, Liberty Hall, so named
for political reasons. Several years previously he had
bought about 120 acres to devote to his hobby of fruit
growing. He had developed 65 varieties of pears, plums,
cherries, peaches and apples.

Livingston's daughters, the three "Livingston Graces,"
the best known of his 13 children, soon made the place
a resort for the very class he had shunned. In 1774 the
house was the scene of the wedding of Sally Livingston
to John Jay, already one of the prominent men of the
Colonies. Alexander Hamilton was a guest at Liberty
Hall during his student days in the academy at Elizabeth
where he was a fellow student of Aaron Burr Jr.

In Parsippany on Parsippany Road is the Bennett house,
a private home, where Governor Livingston lived while
avoiding the enemy at Elizabeth. The rear of the house,
moved across the road, now forms half of another
building.

At the end of the war the Governor returned from his
retreat at Parsippany to Liberty Hall, although complain-
ing that Elizabeth was full of "unrecommended strangers,
guilty-looking Tories, and very knavish Whigs." He had
acquired two nicknames: Rivington's *Royal Gazette* had
called him "Don Quixote of the Jerseys," while his prominent thinness and height had long ago inspired a New
York belle to dub him "The Whipping Post."

Governor Livingston was once described as a man whose
brilliance of wit exceeded the strength of his thinking.
Under his pen name "Hortensius" Livingston wrote a
humorous complaint against the sufferings of the Revolutionary soldiers during the winter cold. As a remedy, he
proposed that attention be directed to Bergen County
because "the rural ladies in that part of our State pride

themselves in an incredible number of petticoats, which, like house furniture, are displayed by way of ostentation." He urged that these undergarments be remade into clothing which would protect the soldiers from the inclemencies of the weather. To prove his suggestion wasn't unfair to the ladies, he argued that "the women in that country having, for above a century, worn the breeches it is highly reasonable that the men should now . . . make booty of the petticoats."

Jonathan Dayton (1760-1824)

Jonathan Dayton, the youngest member of the Convention, was only 27 years old when he helped to frame the Constitution. He was born in Elizabeth and joined the Continental Army immediately after his graduation from Princeton at the age of 16. Dayton served throughout the Revolution, advancing to the position of paymaster and colonel.

Jonathan's father, Brigadier General Elias Dayton, was originally named a delegate, but resigned in favor of his son. During the debates at the Convention Dayton was a prominent speaker, once pleading for the establishment of a regular standing army.

Between 1790 and 1799 Dayton was a member of Congress, serving as Speaker the last four years. In 1799 he began his single term as Senator from New Jersey. At a time when war with France was imminent, President John Adams commissioned him a brigadier general.

One commentator called him a man of "talents with ambition to exert them." Dayton held the opinion that those men in the government who had knowledge of impending changes in the Federal economy were justified in

taking advantage of their information in making specu-
lations.

He had a number of irons in the financial fire during
Hamilton's incumbency as Secretary of the Treasury. He
gambled in land and Federal currency, supporting Hamilton during the Secretary's application of his highly un-
popular policies of taxation which led to the Whiskey
Rebellion. Dayton, Ohio, the scene of one of his activities
in partnership with Aaron Burr, was named for this New
Jersey delegate.

Association with Burr resulted in Dayton's indictment
for high treason in 1807. Although he was exonerated,
the repercussions from the affair ended his political activity on a national scale.

Up to the end, Dayton retained Colonial dress and man-
ners, and was known as the "last of the cocked hats." For
his residence he bought Boxwood Hall in Elizabeth from
Elias Boudinot, president of the Continental Congress and
signer of the peace treaty with Great Britain. In 1824
Dayton entertained Lafayette at Boxwood Hall. His death
a few days later was ascribed to exhaustion following the
festivities.

Boxwood Hall, at 1073 East Jersey Street, Elizabeth,
is today a home for aged women.

David Brearley (1745-1790)

David Brearley was one of the chief spokesmen for the
small states. It was he who made the first speech proposing equal state representation. This proposal became a
part of what later was known as the New Jersey Plan.
In order to avoid the threatened domination by the
larger states, Brearley suggested, in addition, that the
existing state boundaries be erased and the country divided

DAVID BREARLY'S CAMP DESK

up into thirteen equal parts. Brearley, a conscientious member of the Convention, wrote letters to Dayton and Paterson, urging them to attend more regularly.

The Brearley family homestead, Spring Grove, still stands in the Prince Road, five miles from Trenton. When Brearley built an addition to the house, he put a lock, a memento of his service with the Revolutionary forces in Canada, on the front door.

Before his admission to the bar in 1767, Brearley had been a law student in the Newark offices of Elias and Elisha Boudinot. He became surrogate of Hunterdon County in 1771, and so outspoken was his opposition to British rule in the Colonies that he was arrested on a Tory charge of high treason four years later. Neighbors and friends rescued him, and he immediately obtained a commission as captain in the Second New Jersey Regiment of the Continental Line, later being promoted to lieutenant colonel.

Brearley served as a committee member of the Continental Congress that drafted the Articles of Confederation. He was forced to remain away from his Trenton home much of the time, because the British had put a price on his head.

In 1779 he was serving with the First New Jersey Regiment against the Indians when he was appointed Chief Justice of the New Jersey Supreme Court. While in office, his opinion that the courts had the right to decide the constitutionality of laws already passed by legislative bodies established the precedent later maintained by John Marshall, Chief Justice of the Supreme Court of the United States.

As a member appointed by Congress to the committee, Brearley helped determine and qualify the duties and powers of the President. He presided over the State Convention which ratified the Constitution.

David Brearley was Grand Master of the Masonic Order in New Jersey, and two lodges were named in his honor. He was a charter member of the Federalist Association, the Society of the Cincinnati, and was one of the organizers of the Trenton Academy.

Congress appointed him one of the commissioners to decide the land dispute between Pennsylvania and Connecticut. The ruling in favor of Pennsylvania became known as the "Trenton Decision."

In 1789, a year before his death, Brearley resigned as Chief Justice of the State and took office as the first Judge of the United States District Court for the district of New Jersey. His grave is in St. Michael's Episcopal Graveyard, at Warren and Ferry Streets, Trenton.

William Churchill Houston (*1745-1788*)

William Churchill Houston was born in North Carolina. Three years after his graduation from Princeton at the age of 22, Houston became professor of mathematics and natural philosophy. During the Revolution he was a captain of the Somerset County Militia and a member of the Continental Congress and the New Jersey Council of Safety.

Houston was admitted to the bar in 1781, became Clerk of the Supreme Court of New Jersey and receiver of Continental taxes from 1782 to 1785.

In Trenton he practiced law and was agent for the sale of some Hunterdon County lands of the Bainbridge family. Houston was a member of Congress for five terms. During his second term he became interested in John Fitch's plan to build a steamboat. It was probably because of him that the delegates to the Constitutional Convention saw a successful trial of Fitch's craft.

With David Brearley, Houston was a member of the committee that issued the famous "Trenton Decision." Although he had been very active in the preliminary proceedings, Houston attended the Convention only a short time. He fought against the proposal that a President be ineligible for a second term. Ill health, probably tuberculosis, caused him to leave the Convention before signing the Constitution. He started to travel south, but died on the way in 1788.

William Paterson (*1745-1806*)

Because of William Paterson's abilities as an orator, he is generally credited with sponsoring the New Jersey

Plan, although David Brearley first offered the proposal on which it was based.

Paterson, born in Antrim, Ireland, was brought to Delaware in 1747 when he was two years old. Profitable real estate deals in Somerville enabled his father to send him to Princeton, from which he was graduated in 1763. He read law with Richard Stockton, a New Jersey signer of the Declaration of Independence, received an M.A. from Princeton in 1766, and helped found the Well Meaning Society, revived in 1769 and still functioning at Princeton as the Cliosophic Society.

William Paterson was secretary of the Provincial Congress in 1776. On July 16 of that year the Congress ordered township committees to prepare for hostilities by collecting all the "leaden weights from windows and clocks." Through the war years Paterson served as Attorney General of New Jersey, supporting Governor Livingston in his fight to rid the State of Tories, the enemy at home.

At the Constitutional Convention Paterson emphasized that the delegates were obliged honestly to represent the citizens who had vested them with power. He expressed his political philosophy:

> Our object is not such a government as may be best in itself, but such a one as our constituents have authorized us to prepare, and as they will approve. . . .

Paterson advanced a number of proposals that were embodied in the finished document; his struggle for State rather than proportional representation led to the compromise of the establishment of two houses of Congress.

After the death of Livingston, Paterson became Governor and the leader of the Federalist Party in New

Jersey. Hamilton, the national head of the Federalists, organized the Society for Establishing Useful Manufactures in an effort to make the United States economically as well as politically independent of England. The intention of the Society was to found at the Great Falls of the Passaic a city which would be the industrial capital of the country. Paterson granted the charter, and the city was named in his honor.

In 1793 Paterson was appointed Associate Justice of the United States Supreme Court, and continued in office until his death in 1805. During his 13 years' service he democratized and facilitated court practices, and he established the policy of legal aid to the poor by free process and assignment of counsel.

He died in Albany at the home of his son-in-law and was buried there.

The New Jersey Plan

The New Jersey delegates came to the Convention of 1787, as Paterson declared, with instructions to demand equality for the Thirteen States in their votes in Congress. This principle had been recognized for more than twelve years in the Continental Congress and in the existing government under the Articles of Confederation.

New Jersey had suffered much through defects in the Confederation of States formed during the war. Each of the States, jealous of its own power and privileges, had withheld too much from Congress. There was fear in New Jersey and in other small states that a stronger national government might be controlled by the larger States, New York, Pennsylvania, Massachusetts and Virginia.

The country was still dependent on Europe for many

manufactured articles, English Colonial rule having forbidden or discouraged the establishment of factories. New Jersey had complained bitterly of duties on imports at New York and Philadelphia, the chief seaports through which goods reached her in ships. These taxes went into the State treasuries of New York and Pennsylvania and were added to the price New Jersey paid for many articles.

Freight between New Jersey and the two large ports was carried in sailboats. New York compelled New Jersey's boats to enter and clear like foreign ships, paying fees to New York. New Jersey struck back by laying a heavy tax on the Sandy Hook Light, maintained by New York for the shipping entering and leaving the harbor.

In the Convention of 1787 Paterson and Brearley assailed a plan presented by Virginia for representation in Congress entirely on the basis of the population or contribution of each State. They declared it would destroy the smaller States.

The New Jersey Plan, which won support among the smaller States, provided foremost for the equal vote in Congress of all States. It proposed increase of the powers of Congress, to permit the levying of duties on imports at any port in the country, by postage and other stamps, and the regulation of commerce between the States and with foreign countries. Congress was to elect the Federal Executive; but the question was left to the delegates to decide whether this should be a president or a committee. Punishment of offenders against the Federal laws was left to the State courts, subject to an appeal to Federal judges.

The debates that followed showed the danger of a split that would divide the States into two or more unions— "wretched fragments of empire"—as Washington wrote of it.

Paterson boldly declared that New Jersey would never join with other States on the Virginia plan. He would rather submit to a monarch, to a despot, than to see his State swallowed up.

In the end, the moderate counsel of Benjamin Franklin for a compromise was heeded. The United States Senate was formed under the New Jersey plan of equal representation for all the States, so that each, whether large or small, has two Senators and two votes. The influence of the larger States, however, prevailed in the formation of the House of Representatives, with its membership based on the population of each State.

New Jersey was the third State to ratify the new Federal Constitution, December 18, 1787.

BIRTHPLACE OF HANS BRINKER

The story of *Hans Brinker, or the Silver Skates* has delighted boys and girls in foreign lands as well as in the United States. Children of New Jersey may not know that it was written for two small boys by their own mother, Mrs. Mary Mapes Dodge, in a tiny farmhouse on the outskirts of Newark.

Mary Mapes was born in New York City in 1831. She was one of four daughters of Professor James J. Mapes, a well-known scientist and inventor. According to the custom of the day the Mapes girls were educated at home. Mary was the best student of the four sisters and spent hours poring over the great books that lined the shelves of her father's spacious library. It was from her reading of history, especially that of Holland, that she derived much of the story of the little Dutch boy, Hans Brinker. She loved to write, too, and when still but a young girl helped her father with his scientific pamphlets.

When she was 20 years old Mary Mapes became the wife of William Dodge, a New York lawyer. A few years later Mr. Dodge died accidentally, leaving Mary Mapes Dodge to care for herself and her two small boys, Harry and Jamie. She gave up her New York home, went to live with her parents, who had bought a home in the suburbs of Newark, near the present Weequahic Park, and began to write again. Almost from the beginning her stories were eagerly bought by publishers.

In her father's busy home it was difficult to find a quiet

place in which to work, but Mary Dodge was a person who always found a way out of difficulties. There was a small farm cottage adjoining the orchard on her parents' estate. With the help of her boys, she pulled down a partition here and there and arranged the old cast-off furniture, and soon had a cozy workshop away from the hubbub of the big house. There she worked while Harry and Jamie were away at the Newark Academy each day; the remainder of the day was spent at play with them after their return. It is said that the boys' birthdays were always celebrated in this little farmhouse den, with verses written by their mother honoring the event.

The children enjoyed bedtime stories, and there was no happier time in the day for the two boys than the evening hour when they sat and listened to the tales their mother told from the pictures in her own mind instead of from the pages of a book someone else had written.

It was an especially happy day, not only for them, but for countless children the world over, when she started to tell the adventures of Hans Brinker and his sister. It was in response to repeated requests from Harry and Jamie, who spent many hours skating on Drake's pond nearby, that she told the story of skaters across the seas. Each night she recited a new chapter of the story for them, and each following day she wrote it down. It was published serially in a small magazine and was most eagerly received. When eventually the story was printed in book form its popularity was overwhelming.

The story of Hans Brinker has been translated into five languages. In its first 30 years 100 editions were printed. Although Mrs. Dodge had never been in Holland, she had gained accurate knowledge of this little lowland nation from her reading and from her Dutch neighbors, with whom she discussed her work. The book was so well done that it was accepted by the Dutch people themselves as a true picture of their nation and its life.

Some years later Mrs. Dodge was traveling in Europe with one of her sons. One day she sent him into a store for a book about Holland. To her amazement he came out with a copy of Hans Brinker, quoting the Dutch dealer as saying it was positively the best book that had ever been written about his people.

Mrs. Dodge wrote many other stories and verses for children, but her outstanding service to juvenile literature was her editorship of the popular magazine, *St. Nicholas*. She was given charge of it shortly after it was founded in 1873, and credit is due her for its name. She could have thought of no name dearer to the heart of childhood than that of the good old saint. The editor of *St. Nicholas* numbered some of the leading writers of the country among her personal friends and so was able to obtain contributions from such famous people as John Greenleaf Whittier and Henry Wadsworth Longfellow.

The magazine achieved outstanding success, and it was considered a privilege to write for its pages. When Kipling, then a very young man, offered the services of his pen, Mrs. Dodge asked him if he thought he was equal to it. The story of *Little Lord Fauntleroy* by Frances Hodgson Burnett was first written for serial publication in *St. Nicholas*. It was for *St. Nicholas* that Mark Twain wrote *Tom Sawyer Abroad* and Louisa May Alcott wrote *Under the Lilacs*.

Mrs. Dodge planned the department contributed by the young readers. This section, which became one of the most popular features of the magazine, has always been known as the St. Nicholas League, and many artists and writers known far and wide entered upon their successful careers through the pages of *St. Nicholas*. Edna St. Vincent Millay first received honorable mention by the League for her verses when she was fourteen. Then she won, each in turn, silver and gold badges, and at last the longed-for cash prize.

Children of the gifted Benét family all contributed to the League. It is interesting to compare the poem called *Mystery*, written for St. Nicholas by Stephen Vincent Benét when he was only fifteen, with his long prize poem *John Brown's Body*, which has won him a high and lasting place in American literature. Faith Baldwin, Ring Lardner and Cornelia Otis Skinner are among the many other noted people who first won recognition through the department established by Mrs. Dodge.

In the Weequahic section of Newark, where the parents of Mary Mapes Dodge had their home, Mapes Avenue has been named in honor of the family. The spacious old homestead stood almost at the corner of Mapes and Elizabeth Avenues. Today a huge modern apartment house and the dug-out side of a hill mark the place where Mrs. Dodge lived with her children and where the storybook boy, Hans Brinker, was born.

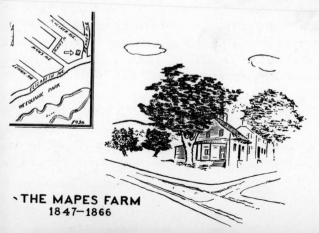

THE MAPES FARM
1847–1866

STEPHEN CRANE

Stephen Crane, who in a short life of less than 30 years won for himself a lasting place among the great American authors, was a native of New Jersey. Though in his varied career he wandered through Europe and America, New Jersey was, more than any other, the place he could call home. And it was in New Jersey soil that he was finally laid to rest among his ancestors.

On the 50th anniversary of Stephen Crane's birth the Schoolmen's Club of Newark, aided by the children of the public schools, placed in the Newark Public Library a bronze tablet bearing this inscription:

INSCRIBED TO THE MEMORY OF
STEPHEN CRANE

He attained before his untimely death, June 5th, 1900 international fame as a writer of fiction.
His novel, the Red Badge of Courage,
set a model for succeeding writers
on the emotions of men in battle.
His verse and his delightful stories of boyhood
anticipated strong later tendencies
in American Literature.
The power of his work won for him the admiration of a wide circle of readers and critics.

Stephen Crane was born on November 1, 1871, to the Reverend Jonathan and Mary Crane in the Methodis

BUST OF STEPHEN CRANE—NEWARK
PUBLIC LIBRARY

arsonage at 14 Mulberry Place, Newark. At that time
Mulberry Place was one of the city's best residential
streets. Today the house in which Stephen was born is
crowded among closely packed, tumbledown buildings.

Jonathan Crane was a man of moral and intellectual
independence. When he discovered in his student days at
Princeton that he could not honestly accept some of the
tenets of the Presbyterian Church, he had the courage to
leave it and enter the Methodist Church. Mary Crane,
like her husband, was a person of firm character and
fortitude. With such parents it was natural that Stephen
Crane should develop the hardihood to face poverty, illness and disappointment without flinching, and that his
stories were honest pictures of life as he saw it.

The Crane family had figured prominently in the affairs
of New Jersey and of the Nation for generations. Jasper

and Azariah Crane had founded the city of Montclair
which for a time was called Cranetown. Another Crane
had taken part in the Continental Congress. When his
fourteenth child was born Jonathan Crane wrote to a
friend, "we have named him Stephen because it is an old
name in the Crane family."

Young Stephen, a delicate child, was subject to severe
colds, and it was not until he was eight years old and the
family had moved to Port Jervis, New York, that he was
allowed to attend school. He had been taught to read and
write at home, and once in school seemed to have little
difficulty in keeping step with his contemporaries.

In the quiet country town Stephen lived the life of a
normal schoolboy. He liked school no more than any boy
of his age, but he did like horses and dogs. This devotion
to animals and to all helpless creatures remained with him
to the end of his life.

In 1882 the family moved to Asbury Park, where
Stephen's brother Townley was conducting a news service
for Newark and Philadelphia newspapers. Here young
Stephen achieved a small fame in baseball. He boasted
that no one could pitch a ball that he could not catch bare-
handed, and announced to one of his elder brothers that
he was going to be a professional ballplayer.

In spite of his interest in horses, dogs and baseball, he
was already beginning to show signs of his future ability.
He had a talent for unusual words, even to the point of
coining them to suit his meaning. His first step up the
ladder of literary fame was taken when he interrupted his
ball playing long enough to write an essay for a 25¢ prize.

The summer of his seventeenth year he went to work
for his brother Townley in Asbury Park. He covered
miles of hot sandy roads on a bicycle, gathering news of

the summer resorts and writing stories of clambakes and sailing parties.

In 1889-90 he had two terms at Lafayette College, followed by a year at Syracuse University. While there he was correspondent for the *New York Tribune* and contributed articles to the *Detroit Free Press* and *Syracuse Daily*.

Anxious to be independent, Stephen moved in 1891 to East 23rd Street, New York, to try to earn his living with his pen. As a newspaper reporter he was a hopeless failure. It was of more interest to him to describe accurately and vividly the color and action of a great fire than to tell where it happened or the loss involved. For a time he tried business, but the routine and restraint were unbearable.

Meanwhile he was spending his spare time exploring the odd corners of the city, sitting in saloons and standing on street corners, listening to the conversations of the people about him. He had made up his mind that he was going to write a book about the people on the Bowery; therefore he must see for himself how these people lived and talked. The book was written in the two days before Christmas of 1891. He called it *Maggie, a Girl of the Streets*. It so horrified the conventional-minded publishers of that day that, although they recognized that it was the work of an artist, they dared not undertake to print it.

All this time Crane was living in poverty and privation. What odd bits he earned came from special articles sent to the newspapers. He was too proud to ask help from his brothers, who would have been only too glad to come to his aid if they had realized his need. His brother Edmund was living in Lakeview, just outside of Paterson. It was no novelty for Stephen to walk the seven miles from the Hudson River to his brother's home for a square meal and a little rest. Perhaps it was at this time that he said, "I would give my future literary career for twenty-three dollars in cash at this minute."

In the summer of 1892 his brother Townley again gave him a job in Asbury Park writing stories for the *New York Tribune*. When Townley went away to Newark one day, he left Stephen to cover a political parade held for the Republican nominees for President and Vice President, Benjamin Harrison and Whitelaw Reid. These two men represented the narrow capitalism of that time. Crane, always sensitive to the lot of the underprivileged, was moved by the irony of laborers marching for men who opposed their interests. He forgot that Whitelaw Reid owned the *New York Tribune*; he sat down and wrote a biting article that somehow got past the copy desk and was printed in one edition of the *Tribune* (August 21, 1892). It is said that this article helped defeat the two candidates. It also cost Townley his job.

Maggie was still haunting her creator. In November Crane borrowed $1,000 from his brother William and had the book printed in a cheap paper-backed edition, to be sold at 50¢. But even this undignified approach failed to reach the American public. *Maggie* in bright yellow stacks gathered dust in the corner of his room. Some of the copies were used for fuel. (In 1930 a copy of this once despised first edition was sold to a collector for $3,700.)

Meanwhile Crane was working on the book that was to bring him lasting fame. In February 1894 he sold the serial rights of *The Red Badge of Courage* for $100 to a newspaper syndicate conducted by Irving Bacheller. This story of the Civil War called forth a shower of favorable letters. The story was printed in book form the following year. But it was not until the review of the English edition reached this country that the general public awoke. Almost overnight Crane became a person of public importance. His stories at once had a ready market; even *Maggie* was rescued from obscurity.

This belated recognition of his ability was a justification of Crane's simplicity, honesty and devotion to his art, expressed in the following extract from one of his letters:

> . . . When I was the mark for every humorist in the country I went ahead . . . for I understand that a man is born into the world with his own pair of eyes, and he is not at all responsible for his vision—he is merely responsible for his quality of personal honesty . . .

In 1896 Crane was shipwrecked off the Florida coast while on a filibustering expedition headed for Cuba from Jacksonville. Crane, the ship's captain, the cook and an oiler rowed in a dinghy for 50 hours until within swimming distance of shore. This adventure was the basis for *The Open Boat*, published in New York and London in 1898. This powerful, dramatic tale of shipwrecked men has been acclaimed as one of the greatest short stories ever written. The exposure endured in this experience was too much for Crane's delicate constitution. He was never entirely well thereafter.

His next assignment was as war correspondent for the *New York Journal* and *Westminster Gazette* in the Greco-Turkish War. In the freedom allowed a war correspondent to recount vividly the stirring episodes of war, Crane found the type of journalism he could and liked to do.

In addition to his regular work he wrote a series of letters entitled *With Greek and Turk*.

It was during his stay in Greece that Cora Taylor, a woman several years older than himself, whom he had met in Jacksonville, Florida, nursed him through a serious attack of illness. In 1898 they were married and returned to England. They went to live in Surrey, where Crane was able to indulge his love of dogs and horses. There were never fewer than three dogs that had the run of the place, and Crane spent many hours in the saddle riding through the fresh English country. This house was a rendezvous for novelists, critics and others of the literary world. Guests came in swarms and stayed for long periods, invited or not. At one time Crane had to take refuge in a London hotel in order to get some work done while his wife cleared the house of guests.

At the outbreak of the Spanish-American War Crane left England, intending to enlist in the United States Navy. He left so suddenly that many of his friends journeying down for a visit to his Surrey home were surprised to find him gone. After he had sailed the *World* cabled to obtain his services as war correspondent, but it was only after he had been turned down at the Navy recruiting office that he reported for duty at the New York office of the newspaper.

At Guantanamo Crane was caught in a surprise attack on a party of marines. His gallantry in staying to help care for the wounded under fire when he might have sought safety on a gunboat earned him mention in official dispatches.

While he was writing stories of the Battles of Santiago, San Juan, Guantanamo and the Cuban blockade, he was also working on short stories which are still among the best American efforts in that field. But his health could not withstand the climate, bad food and recurrent fevers. He left the island a very sick man.

Back in England, after Christmas of 1899 Cora and Stephen went to live in Brede Place, a crumbling baronial hall, which it was hoped would not be so accessible to his friends and where he might have quiet and peace in which to work. But Cora's famous cooking and cordiality and Crane's informal hospitality continued to attract visitors not always considerate of their hosts' pocketbook and privacy.

His health was failing rapidly, but he kept writing at a furious pace. Finally, in a vain attempt to stall off the ravages of tuberculosis, he hurried to Baden Weiler, Germany.

The Black Forest could work no magic for Stephen Crane. He died in his sleep on June 5, 1900. Cora had his body brought back to the State of his birth, and he was buried in the Crane family plot in Evergreen Cemetery, Hillside, New Jersey.

THE LAST DAYS OF WALT WHITMAN

A little gray house, once the home of a Camden workingman, is today one of the literary shrines of the world, maintained by the State of New Jersey as a memorial to the great Walt Whitman. Here "the good gray poet" spent the last eight years of his life; and here he died in the midst of the simple people he loved, whose minds and hearts he had understood and interpreted in his striking poetry.

From the far corners of the earth people have come to this quiet back street to pay homage to the man who has been ranked with the great poets of all times. Among those who have written their names in the guest book is the Japanese poet, Katsua Kawa, who has translated Whitman's poems into the language of his country, where they are as familiar to every schoolboy and schoolgirl as are the poems of Longfellow and Milton to American school children.

Whitman has been called the father of modern poetry. His subjects were the common everyday people and things about them. He found beauty in drab, sordid streets; in the harsh lines of factory buildings; in crowding chimneys and plodding ferryboats; in dull-eyed, tired working people and the problems of their daily life. The new and free style of his verse, which often disregards rhyme and adopts the rhythms of Nature rather than the pattern of earlier poetic forms, was adopted after long and patient experiment as best suited to express the things he had to say. His vigorous and colorful style reflects the abounding vitality and love of life that were his outstanding characteristics.

Whitman himself declared that his poetry would not be appreciated until 100 years after his death; but his prophecy was not borne out. Although his fame has risen slowly, he was already being acclaimed in 1873 when, at the age of 53, he came to his brother's Camden home to see his dying mother.

After his mother's death, when his brother moved to Burlington, New Jersey, Whitman chose to remain in Camden. He had spent days and nights wandering the streets and had come to love the little city and its simple, hard-working people. At first he lived in lodgings; and then, with the help of George W. Childs, a wealthy Philadelphia admirer, he bought the little two-story frame house at 330 Mickle Street. The belongings of the poet are there, his books, his work chair, some furniture that was in his childhood home in West Hills, Long Island; portraits of his father and mother, a bust of himself by Sidney Morse, a copy of his will, and a copy of the Japanese translation of his *Leaves of Grass*.

From 1884 to 1892 he worked contentedly at the parlor window of the little house until his long, last illness confined him to his bedroom. On spring and summer days the people passing his window would stop to hail him, especially the children, and he would drop his pen to greet them. Perhaps that is one reason why he was often pressed for money. His poems and articles were selling in newspapers and magazines; but Walt was more absorbed in observing life and people and in developing his art than in the practical problems of living. Admirers of his poems in England sent him $400 through the *Pall Mall Gazette*.

Friends arranged a lecture for him in Philadelphia, and he got a goodly sum for it.

Then, as he began to decline, the aging poet could enjoy life as he wished. Camden people bought him a horse and buggy, and he was the delight of the town, driving at full speed, his great white beard streaming over his shoulders. Nothing disturbed him, neither popular opinion nor physical inconvenience. He took whatever life offered, even the smell of the neighboring fertilizer plant and the shouting of a nearby congregation.

In his bedroom was an iron stove. In cold weather he kept the wood piled about its base, while in an outer circle were stacks of books and manuscripts. When he went to bed he would hang his clothes on the higher piles, dropping his shoes between the islands of books, sticking the ink bottle where it would hold. His housekeeper was a brave woman, leaving the poet to pursue his work undisturbed by any criticism of his disorderly habits. Even when he took his work to the kitchen she did not complain. His spotted dog ambled around, and the cat smoothed itself against his legs. Sometimes a rooster paraded in with his wives and pecked around contentedly.

Many famous people journeyed to the little house to meet Whitman, and he received them all with the same enthusiasm and informality that he offered the children and neighborhood friends.

In the autumn of 1891 he began planning his tomb, which can be seen in Harleigh Cemetery in Camden. The inscription, "For That of Me Which Is to Die," was written by the poet and engraved on the stone at his request.

All through the winter he lingered, confined to his bed in his cluttered bedroom, surrounded by a sea of books and manuscripts. On March 26, 1892, he closed his eyes for

WALT WHITMAN'S HOME

the last time. The tomb was waiting for his body, but his spirit has been kept alive in the little house which reflects so much of his personality and life.

CLARA BARTON, IN SCHOOL AND IN WAR

In a quiet corner of the old town of Bordentown, on a wedge-shaped lot enclosed by a picket fence, is a tiny one-story brick schoolhouse—one of the first public schools in New Jersey. The key, borrowed from the house opposite, will admit the visitor to the one-room building, not much larger than a playhouse, where a few pieces of old-fashioned school furniture are preserved.

In 1921 the school children of New Jersey contributed to a fund to restore the building and maintain it as a memorial to the little New England school teacher who opened the door to those children who were deprived of education because their parents could not afford to pay the required fee. That teacher was Clara Barton, later to become world-famous as the founder and first president of the American Red Cross.

On Christmas Day 1821 Stephen and Sarah Barton welcomed into their farmhouse in Oxford, Massachusetts, the fifth child to their family of half-grown boys and girls. The new baby was named Clarissa Marlowe, after the heroine of an early 18th century best seller by Samuel Richardson.

Her father, Captain Stephen Barton, had been a Revolutionary soldier. He liked books and saw to it that his children had access to them. Clara could not recall when she learned to read. Practically in infancy she was taught spelling, arithmetic and geography by her brothers and sisters. At four she was ready to go to school in the little one building not far away from her home. She wrote quaintly of her childhood:

I had no playmates but in effect six fathers and mothers. They were a family of school teachers. All took charge of me, all educated me, each according to personal taste. My two sisters were scholars and artistic and strove in that direction. My brothers were strong, ruddy, daring young men, full of life and business.

At eight Clara entered what was called high school, which meant boarding away from home. The timid little girl was so unhappy in the strange surroundings that it was decided to take her home, where her instruction again fell to her brothers and sisters.

Timidity was a handicap that Clara Barton had to fight all her life. Many years later, when she had faced the dangers of the battlefield and had stood before great audiences to persuade them to her ideas, she wrote: "I would rather stand behind the line of artillery at Antietam, or cross the pontoon bridge under fire at Fredericksburg than to be expected to preside at a public meeting."

Clara's sensitiveness and timidity caused her mother considerable anxiety, and, being an intelligent woman, she looked about for a way to help her youngest daughter. At this time people were taking a great interest in phrenology. This now discredited "science" claimed to read character and to estimate mental aptitude by studying the formation of the skull.

Mrs. Barton asked Mr. L. W. Fowler, author of a popular book on phrenology, what Clara ought to do in life. Mr. Fowler's answer proved that he had wisdom if not scientific accuracy. "The sensitive nature will always

remain. She will never assert herself for herself; she wil
suffer wrong first. But for others she will be perfectl
fearless. Throw responsibility upon her." He suggestee
that she become a school teacher. Both Clara and he
mother were much impressed by Mr. Fowler's recommen
dation. Years later she looked back upon Mr. Fowler'
visit as the turning point in her career.

Clara Barton was 15 at the time and barely five fee
tall, but all she needed to qualify as a teacher was to le
down her skirts and put up her hair. Her education wa
ample to meet the requirements. A position was obtainee
for her in a district school near her home.

Her success as a teacher was immediate, for she com
manded the love and respect of her pupils. Young thoug
she was, she had no trouble with discipline. In the next 1
years she was often called upon to straighten out problem
in schools where there was disciplinary trouble.

Teaching in country schools, however, did not lon
satisfy this ambitious young woman. She realized tha
these years of her youth should be spent in increasing he
own knowledge and training her own mind. Higher edu
cation for women was not taken seriously at this time, an
there were few institutions that offered Clara Barton wha
she was looking for. She finally decided on the Libera
Institute, at Clinton, New York, where she dismayed th
faculty by her eagerness to fill to the limit her progran
of study.

When she had absorbed all that the Institute had t
offer, spending her vacations there in study and reading
she accepted an invitation to visit friends, the Nortons, i
Bordentown, New Jersey. There she was offered an oppo
tunity to teach in the Bordentown school.

This was in 1852. In New England and New York fre

CLARA BARTON'S SCHOOL, BORDENTOWN

schools had been established; but in New Jersey the old fee system remained. Only those who were able to contribute to teachers' salaries and the cost of maintenance could receive an education. It was not long before the faces of the children of the poor began to haunt and worry the young teacher.

One day she approached a group of youngsters idling around the park fountain.

"Would you boys like to go to school?" she inquired brightly.

She was ready for the reply, "Lady, there is no school for us." True enough, there was no school for these urchins. But Clara Barton had quietly made up her mind that there would be a school provided—and soon.

"If there were a school opened for you, would you come?"

"We would be glad to go if there was one," was the eager reply.

That was all she wanted to know. Without delay she sought out Mr. Suydam, the chairman of the school committee, and laid the plan before him. He listened carefully to her idea for a public school and, when she had finished, proceeded in a sympathetic but superior manner to explain the impossibility of the venture. The rich would not patronize a "pauper school." The ragamuffins really belonged in a reform school; anyway how could a woman expect to control them? Since there would be no fees from the pupils there would be no pay for her.

To all his arguments Clara had a reply. She offered to work without pay for an experimental period of three months if the committee would furnish quarters. Mr. Suydam, completely vanquished, referred her to the school committee. The determined young woman overrode their objections and instilled in them, against their will, something of her own enthusiasm and confidence.

Clara Barton got her school. A little ramshackle one-room building opened its doors on the first day to six timid pupils, and Bordentown sat down to watch the results. But they had not long to wait.

The school quickly outgrew its quarters, and Clara sent word to her brother, superintendent of schools in Oxford, Massachusetts, that she had to have an assistant. He sent Miss Fannie Childs, who was put in charge of 60 pupils, quartered in a room over a tailor shop. When there was no longer any doubt of the success of the public school, the Bordentown citizens voted $4,000 for the construction of an eight-room brick schoolhouse, and proceeded to the appointment of a principal to manage it.

Today it would be natural to appoint the founder and

organizer to fill the post of principal; but the people of the middle 19th century were reluctant to place authority in the hands of a woman. It was argued that the school was too large for a woman to manage, although a woman had developed it and was managing it successfully. There was persistent demand on the part of the citizens for a male principal. The majority of the pupils would have preferred to keep Clara Barton, but in the end the appointment was given to a man.

The tireless little woman, who had given the best of her energy and talent to the building up of the public school, would not remain to occupy a second place. Whether from disappointment or overwork, she suffered a nervous collapse. Her voice completely failed her, and she was prostrated.

In 1854 she went to Washington to regain her strength, little realizing that in leaving Bordentown she was leaving the schoolroom forever. She had no more definite plan than to gain some knowledge of the Nation's Capital. Returning strength renewed her ambition. Before long she had received an appointment as clerk in the Patent Office—one of the first women to receive a government appointment.

When the Civil War broke out Clara Barton began visiting the hospitals in Washington and doing what she could to help the soldiers. She made newspaper appeals for money and supplies for the injured. She organized groups of women as nurses and took them to the battlefields to ease the sufferings of the wounded while they were waiting for transportation to hospitals.

Despite every opposition and obstacle placed in her way

by those in authority, she carried on her work. On the grounds of 16 battles she nursed the sick and wounded and comforted the dying. She was known far and wide as "the angel of the battlefield."

When the war was over and the North counted its losses, 359,528 were listed as dead. There were 315,555 graves, and of these only 172,400 were identified, leaving 143,155 graves without names. When frantic relatives flooded Washington with inquiries about their loved ones, there was the utmost confusion. President Lincoln called on Clara Barton. She established a bureau for answering the countless letters, and managed to locate over 40,000 men, dead and alive.

Once more Clara Barton had overtaxed her strength. As at the time she left Bordentown, her voice failed her and she had a nervous collapse. She was ordered to Switzerland for a three years' rest.

At Geneva a delegation from the International Committee for the Relief of the Wounded in War called upon her, urging her to do something about aligning the United States with the great cause. The war of 1870 between France and Germany was then in progress. Clara Barton was so much impressed by the efficiency of the Red Cross of the two countries that she determined to try to get her own people to join the international organization. For years she devoted herself untiringly to this great cause. From the lecture platform and in the press she issued countless appeals to her fellow countrymen.

In 1882 the American National Red Cross was formed with Clara Barton as its first president. From then on Clara Barton's life was one with the great organization she had founded. She saw it bring its priceless services to suffering people in such disasters as the Spanish-American War, the San Francisco earthquake and Mississippi floods.

She did not live to see the achievements of the Red Cross during the World War, for she died April 12, 1912, at the age of 90.

JOHN HOLLAND, SUBMARINE INVENTOR

Strangely enough the submarine, which took a terrific toll of life in the World War, was the invention of a school teacher who hoped that his invention would insure peace by making war impracticable. He foresaw the destruction of entire navies by this vessel which could steal up unseen and with one well-aimed torpedo sink a great battleship.

This peace-minded inventor was John P. Holland, born in Ireland in 1840. While teaching school as a young man of 30 in his native County Clare, he first got the idea of an undersea boat of steel. He had been much impressed by the battle of the *Monitor* and the *Merrimac* during the Civil War, but it was hardly to be expected that a generation that had laughed at the "cheese box on a raft" would take enthusiastically to his fantastic idea.

Failing to interest the British Government, Holland migrated to America in 1873, and became a teacher at St. John's Parochial School in Paterson. In 1875 he submitted plans for his undersea craft to the Navy Department, but the United States Government was no more receptive than the British Admiralty.

Holland's persistence finally won the support of an Irish brotherhood known as the Fenian Society, which enabled him to finance the construction of his first experimental craft. The little boat, only 14 feet long, could hold but one man. It was divided into three compartments. In the center was the machinery, the small engine and the

HOLLAND SUBMARINE, WEST SIDE PARK, PATERSON

apparatus for storing an air supply for the operator. This section was, of course, airtight and watertight. The two end sections were built to hold or discharge water pumped in and out by the engine, making the boat sink or rise.

On the afternoon of May 22, 1878, Holland brought his craft, which had cost $4,000, from the shops of Rafferty and Todd in Paterson and launched it in the Passaic River. The results were discouraging. The submarine had sprung a leak in transport and sank almost immediately. But a leak was only the first of a series of obstacles that were to impede the progress of Holland's invention. After the boat was raised, several further attempts were made to operate it. There was no room on board for steam boilers, so a launch was pressed into service to supply steam through a flexible rubber hose. When the hose broke, as it frequently did, Holland opened a little trap door and calmly swam to the surface.

The weight of the stem prevented floating, so the boat had to be supported by heavy casks. Disregarding these relatively minor difficulties, Holland determined to concentrate on testing the submerging possibilities. On June 6, 1878, at 6 p.m. the submarine dove beneath the surface, remained there until the same hour on the following day, and emerged with no damage to itself or the occupant. That much, at least, had been accomplished. It had been proved that the submarine was no idle dream.

Forced, for the time being, to be content with this incomplete success, the inventor abandoned the craft. It was tied up beneath the Spruce Street bridge. Forty-seven years later a group of young men, with the aid of a magnet borrowed from a nearby plant, located the almost forgotten boat. They salvaged it from the river bottom and presented it to the Paterson Museum, where it is now on display.

In 1881 Holland launched another submarine in the Hudson River. This new boat, built in the Delamater yards, was a decided improvement. Thirty-one feet long and equipped with a one-cylinder combustion engine, it could accommodate a crew of three.

By this time Holland's venture had attracted considerable notice. Cheering throngs on boats and on shore watched in amazement as the "wild Irishman" in his cigar-shaped craft ducked under the surface in the harbor off Staten Island to a depth of 100 feet, remained for an hour and rose again. The *Fenian Ram,* as the new boat was named by a newspaper reporter, caused quite a flurry in the daily news as the inventor continued to try it out. There were various conjectures as to the purpose for which it was built. There was no war in progress, nor in prospect, other than the chronic trouble between Ireland and England. This gave rise to the half-humorous suggestion that the boat was meant for the use of the Irish against the British navy; therefore the name, *Fenian Ram.*

Tug and ferryboat captains were frequently startled when the queer-looking craft rose from the bottom. Suddenly the little trap door would open and out would pop the genial smiling face of John Holland, who would hail them gaily in his thick Irish brogue. Since there was no periscope to warn the navigator of anything on the surface, there was great danger of collision. On January 3, 1881, the *Ram* was sunk when it collided with a ferryboat near the Weehawken slip. Within a week a wrecking crew had raised the boat. It rests today in West Side Park, Paterson.

It seemed that Holland's hard work was accomplishing nothing but the distinction of providing exhibits for Paterson. But the intrepid schoolmaster kept at his task, and five years later he completed another submarine. Success, however, was still far off. This third vessel was damaged in launching, and the Fenian Society, discouraged by repeated failures, withdrew its financial aid.

Holland had learned enough from his mistakes to spur him to further endeavors. Although the Navy Department still withheld recognition, the new device commanded the interest and support of those who were concerned with the improvement of war machinery, and he was able to obtain financial backing to continue his work. He worked at plans and models for seven more years and finally succeeded in getting the support of the Navy officials. In 1893, with a $150,000 contract, he started to build again. The new boat, called the *Plunger*, was launched in Baltimore, Maryland, in 1895; but Holland had been so hampered in carrying out his plans by interference from government experts that the result was a failure, and the *Plunger* was abandoned.

Holland, still under government contract, returned to New Jersey and at the Crescent Shipyards in Elizabethport started to build the *Holland* according to his own ideas, profiting by the mistakes made in the construction of the *Plunger*.

The *Holland* was successfully launched early in 1898. It was 53 feet 10 inches long, fitted with a gasoline engine for surface propulsion and an electric motor, supplied by storage batteries, for traveling under water. It carried one pneumatic dynamite gun, a torpedo tube and several torpedoes.

In February of that year, before the submarine had been accepted by the government, it became the center of a serio-comic incident. The United States was on the brink of war with Spain, and, as a protest against the presence of the *Maine* in Havana harbor, the Spanish warship *Viscaya* had been sent to New York and was anchored in the harbor.

One of those baseless rumors to which nervous government officials are susceptible in troublous times reached the ear of the Navy Department. The tale was that the *Holland* was planning to try its guns on the *Viscaya*. Admiral Bunce, in command of the New York Navy Yard, was ordered to watch the strange vessel and seize it if necessary.

The *Holland*, as yet privately owned, had set out from Elizabethport for Perth Amboy for final preparation before being tested. Just before leaving she had taken on board several dummy wooden projectiles made to fit the 8-inch dynamite gun mounted in the bow. From a distance these dummies looked very real; so real that when a Navy tug came to look for the submarine, some workmen at the shipyard told the tugboat captain that they had seen the *Holland* load up with projectiles and set off down the river. At full speed the tug went in pursuit. An all-day search of New York Harbor and the port of Perth Amboy evealed no sign of the suspect; but the *Viscaya* was still intact, so the tug returned to report the disappearance of the submarine and no harm done. Several days later, quite innocent of the commotion it had aroused, the little *Holland* was discovered tied up in the Perth Amboy docks.

At that time Holland had not yet tested the submerging ability of his latest model. The first test took place on March 17, St. Patrick's Day. It was not, however, until April 1900, after several grueling tests off Sandy Hook and Long Island, that the Government authorized the purchase of the *Holland*.

On one of these tests, in June 1899, Clara Barton, the founder of the American Red Cross, was on board as a guest. As they ran for two miles under 15 feet of water, Holland explained the mechanical devices and described the probable effect of the torpedo. If he expected any approbation from his guest he was sadly disappointed, for Clara Barton in no uncertain terms expressed her dismay that a civilized American should be guilty of inventing such a deadly instrument. Holland hastened to explain that he was confident that if all nations were equipped with submarines war would no longer be possible.

In December 1899 the *Holland* was taken to Washington, D. C., for exhibition runs up the Potomac River. Because of rough weather it was decided to take the inside passage from Perth Amboy through the Delaware and Raritan Canal to Bordentown, down the Delaware to Delaware City and through the Chesapeake Canal to Chesapeake Bay and on to Washington.

All along the route people turned out in crowds to see this new wonder. At Bordentown, where the submarine came through the locks of the canal and entered the Delaware River, public school children were dismissed and many of the stores were closed.

A few months after the successful demonstration at Washington, the Government ordered six more submarines. The following year Great Britain, Russia and Japan placed their orders.

John Holland made an unquestionable success of his invention, but he utterly failed to promote peace. Realization of this final failure was spared him by his death on August 12, 1914, at the opening of the World War. If they both had lived, Clara Barton might have reminded him of her words on that June day in 1899.

WORKING AND LIVING TOGETHER

NORTH AMERICAN PHALANX

The panic of 1837 and the long period of suffering afterward focused wide attention on plans for establishing a social order with a more abundant and secure life for all the people. Many of the social thinkers of a century ago felt the need of testing their theories to prove their worth. To do this it was necessary to organize communities where people would live and work under a plan that differed sharply from the ordinary community life in towns and villages.

As a result, hundreds of experimental projects sprang up throughout the country. Some lasted only a few months, others for several years. One of the most successful was the North American Phalanx, about five miles west of Red Bank in Monmouth County, New Jersey. Today, resting quietly in a grove of trees, a large, rambling house occupied by descendants of the original founders is all that remains of the once busy community where for 12 years men and women worked, played and educated their children with one common object—the greatest good for the greatest number.

The socially minded thinkers of the period believed that most unhappiness arose from competition in an economic order that made it necessary for each individual to work for as much profit as possible, regardless of the rights of others. This resulted in the setting up of two classes—the rich, with leisure for recreation and study, and the poor, with time for little except work.

Courtesy Red Bank Register

North American Phalanx from an Old Oil Paintin

Most of the proposed plans fell into two categories
based on the ideas of Robert Owen of England or o
Charles Fourier of France. Owen had put his socialisti
ideas into practice at his textile mill in New Lanark, Scot
land. Visitors reported that the workers appeared remark
ably happy, especially when compared with those in othe
towns where the Industrial Revolution had brought onl
exploitation and misery. Owen came to America and le
tured to huge crowds. He tried to establish a socialisti
community at New Harmony, Indiana, in 1825, bu
failed.

Fourier differed from Owen in one important way
Owen believed that mankind would never be happy s
long as the rich and the poor remained as separate classes
and that the only solution was to give every man th
means of enjoying an abundant life. On the other hand
Fourier argued that the rich man should be allowed t
keep his wealth and bequeath it to his children, eve

though it was more than was needed for a comfortable existence. He felt that the rich and poor could reach an understanding through living together in an experimental community.

Under Fourier's plan, every member of the communal enterprise would get income from three sources: interest on his investment, a share of the profits and wages for his labor. Fourier believed that a man would have to work only 10 years, from three to five hours a day, to be assured of an income for the rest of his life. His followers established many communities in France, but his plan failed to work.

Although the theories of Fourier and Owen had borne no practical results, many people maintained that they had planted the seeds of a new and happier society which needed only careful planning to bring it to flower. It was during this period that Ralph Waldo Emerson wrote to Thomas Carlyle: "Any one you meet on the street may at any time produce a new community project from his waistcoat pocket." Among the many who became infected was Albert Brisbane, father of the late newspaper editor, Arthur Brisbane. In 1840, on his return from France, the elder Brisbane published a book, *Social Destiny of Man*, inspired by the ideas of Fourier. Three years later he published a paper, *The Phalanx*, in which he detailed the Fourier plan of social reorganization.

According to this plan people would live in groups of from 800 to 4,000, away from the big cities. These groups, known as Phalanxes (taken from the Greek military formation), would be self-supporting, growing their own food and making their own clothes, furniture and other articles. People were to be housed in huge, hotellike structures called phalansteries, eliminating the duplication of housework. Three or four phalanxes would form a union and three or four unions would become a district. Several districts, in turn, would become a province. Between the phalanxes scattered over the land there would be an exchange of surplus goods. There would be no drones, no parasites, no extremes of poverty and wealth. Rich and poor would work together and learn to understand each other through equal education and opportunity for all. By successive combinations, a world unity would emerge. There would be a republican form of government with annual elections. Universal harmony would do away with soldiers, policemen and criminals.

With the idea of reaching a wider public, Brisbane purchased from Horace Greeley the use of a daily column in the *New York Tribune* in which, day after day, he expounded the theory of Fourierism. Although Greeley was to become one of the staunchest supporters of the Phalanx movement, he took care to assume no responsibility for Brisbane's articles. The column carried a statement which read, "This column has been purchased by the advocates of Association in order to lay their principles before the public."

Brisbane's teachings fell on fertile soil. A few years later one investigator listed 69 associative communities, excluding religious ones, 15 of which were called phalanxes. They comprised about 9,000 people and owned about 140,000 acres of land.

One of the most famous experiments of the time was Brook Farm, a few miles out of Boston, founded in 1842 as an endeavor in communal living based upon the social political democracy advocated by George Bancroft, the historian. George Ripley, the founder, was a Unitarian minister whose plan was

. . . to insure a more natural union between intellectual and manual labor . . . to combine the thinker and the worker as far as possible in the same individual . . . to guarantee the highest mental freedom by providing all with labor adapted to their tastes and talents and to secure for them the fruits of their industry.

Many of the most distinguished scholars and literary men of the day—Nathaniel Hawthorne, Ralph Waldo Emerson, Charles Dana, later editor of the *New York Sun;* the Reverend Theodore Parker and a host of others —were active in, or for a time associated with, the Brook Farm colony. When Brisbane's articles appeared, Brook Farm aligned itself with the Phalanx plan and for a time was known as the Brook Farm Phalanx. *The Harbinger,* the organ of Fourierism in this country, was printed at Brook Farm from June 1845 to June 1847.

Although the Brook Farm experiment has, because of its association with many names famous in literature, received more attention from writers and historians, it was not nearly so successful as the New Jersey colony known as the North American Phalanx. One reason given for this is that the Phalanx members happened to be practical, rather than literary or esthetic. Of the scores of colonies set up along the lines of Fourierism, the majority lasted not more than a year. Brook Farm lasted about six years, but the North American Phalanx flourished for 12 years.

In 1843 a small group of ten progressive families from the vicinity of Albany, with an aggregate subscription of $8,000, purchased the old Van Mater farm in Monmouth County for $14,000 and set up the North American Phalanx. There were 673 acres of well-watered arable land, woodland and meadow, plus extensive beds of marl, used as fertilizer. In addition to those who took up residence, there were some who had sufficient faith in the experiment to back it with purchases of stock. Among these was Horace Greeley, who, from first to last, was an enthusiastic supporter of the association. He had dedicated his *New Yorker* to an "advocacy of the great social revolution . . . rendering all useful Labor at once instructive and honorable, and banishing Want . . . from the globe."

In September some of the families took possession of the two farmhouses on the property. In most instances the men preceded their families in order to prepare suitable quarters for the women and children who followed in the spring.

The first two years were extremely difficult for the settlers. Nathan French later said that the first winter they lived on buckwheat cakes and sorghum, and the second winter on buckwheat cakes without sorghum. The farm was impoverished, and none of the colonists knew much about farming. There were only two farm buildings and a pre-Revolutionary barn. But the settlers were not easily discouraged. They had pledged themselves "not to rest nor turn back until the whole people were convinced of the practicability of associative living."

By 1847 the population was about 90, including about 40 children under 16. The colonists represented a cross section of people from all walks of life: scientists, writers, doctors, lawyers, artisans, farmers. New quarters had to be provided for all these people, and a multifamily house was erected on the plans of Fourier. This phalanstery was 40 by 80 feet, three stories high and was flanked on each side by the two old farm buildings. The top floor was reserved for bachelors, the middle floor for the families. Each family had two bedrooms and a sitting room. The first floor or "grand salon" was used as a dining room. When there were dances or lectures the tables were pushed aside. Here the colonists staged their amateur plays and charades. Music was often provided by a famous Negro fiddler, Caesar Johnson, who lived near the Phalanx.

Each person bore his or her share of the work of the entire community. A woman who had spent the morning in the dairy, or in canning fruits or vegetables, might in the afternoon teach French or music to a group of children. After a day's digging in the potato field, teachers, writers and farmers would congregate in the evening to discuss the political or social questions of the day. One settler declared that "our days were spent in labor and our nights in legislation for the first five years."

There was some criticism of the unconventional behavior of the colonists. Women of the surrounding communities were shocked at seeing the Phalanx women wearing a sort of Turkish trouser over which was worn a skirt reaching a little below the knees. These loose trousers, known as bloomers, were named after Mrs. Amelia Jenks Bloomer of New York, who had introduced them in 1848. The Phalanx women found the trousers more comfortable for work in the fields. So much excitement did the bloomers cause in the streets of Red Bank (a tiny settlement itself at that time) that the colonist women usually put on long skirts when they went shopping.

The Phalanx people were far beyond their time in many things. They believed in and practiced religious toleration, the 30-hour week and profit sharing. All forms of work were considered equally honorable, with no differences in pay according to age or sex. In addition to reserves for old age and accidents, a fund was to be maintained for the education of children, which was an important factor in the systems of both Fourier and Owen.

Education at Phalanx was similar to what is, even today, called progressive. The students, for instance, drew from real models instead of from an art book and studied living plants instead of a textbook on botany. They frequently spent the entire day at school, keeping busy with a multitude of tasks and incidentally leaving their mothers free for their own work. The teachers attempted to give the pupils a true insight into the business of life by presenting to them the problems of production, distribution and administration. In addition, the association maintained a day nursery and an evening school for workers. Members had the benefits of lectures, concerts, readings, plays, daily papers and a library. Every distinguished lecturer who appeared in New York was likely to be brought there.

The people ate in the main dining room and could order what they pleased from the menu, as if they were in a restaurant. Families could either sit at the long tables or enjoy the privacy of a small table. Coffee sold for ½¢ a cup, bread for 1¢ a plate, meat 2¢, pie 2¢, and everything else in proportion. "Table, laundry and room rent amounted to $2 a week and sometimes less."

The work was divided into series: the agricultural series, the domestic series, the manufacturing series, etc., and these were subdivided into groups. Each series was headed by a chief. The leaders, or series chiefs, as they were called, comprised the industrial council. Each evening the council met and planned the work for the following day

"Every able-bodied person had his or her appointed task. Because of careful planning and supervision there was no confusion, loss of time or idleness."

The rate of pay was from 6¢ to 10¢ an hour, with the series heads receiving 10¢ a day extra. The least agreeable and most exhausting work paid the highest rate. Everything was furnished at wholesale price. Food was raised in the garden and on the farm. Clothing was made on the premises. There was little need for money and less need for saving. The Phalanx contract provided for old age pensions and insurance to cover any emergency.

Soon farmers and mechanics joined the colony, machine shops and mills were constructed, and after a few years' hard work the colony was producing wheat, rye, buckwheat flour, corn meal and hominy. By 1852 the North American Phalanx farm was one of the most productive and profitable in the State. Its original value of $14,000 had increased to $80,000 and its population to 112. Philosophers, sociologists and curiosity seekers came from far and wide. Charles A. Dana, the Reverend George Ripley and other members of the Brook Farm Colony were visitors. All went away impressed with the apparent success and happiness of the members.

Soon there was enough surplus to sell to outsiders. The association purchased an interest in a steamboat plying between Red Bank and New York and another between Keyport and New York. All fruits, vegetables, flour and other products sent to market were stamped N.A.P. This trademark was recognized as representing high quality. The first packaged and trademarked cereals ever sold in this country came from the Phalanx mills.

It is probable that the success of the Phalanx was due to the wise administration of the three men at the head of the organization. Charles Sears, a businessman, was president for a time and always took a leading part in its affairs; John Bucklin, his brother-in-law, was head of the agricultural group, and Nathan French had charge of the manufacturing group.

In spite of the flourishing condition of affairs and the apparent satisfaction of the members, there was an undercurrent of disagreement. Little by little the desire for gain began to undermine the smooth surface of the colony. As news of returning prosperity came from the outside world, a teacher who was paid 9¢ an hour began to wonder if it would not be better to go where he would receive $5 for two hours' work. There was some question as to whether higher pay and independence were not preferable to the communal life. Then, following a visit by a missionary, religious sectarianism began to cause some dissension in contrast to the previous mutual tolerance.

In 1854 there was a fire that destroyed the flour mill, sawmill, smithy and machinery. The loss involved was about $9,000—not enough to ruin the association. At a conference after the fire, no decision could be reached as to the best site on which to rebuild the mills. There were some who advocated that they be built nearer to shipping points. A number of these withdrew their capital and some of them formed at Perth Amboy a new association headed by George B. Arnold, which they called the Raritan Bay Union. They thought they could make more money there. They did not.

A vote was then held on the desirability of continuing, and the majority voted in favor of dissolution. The fire, therefore, was more the excuse than the reason for abandoning the experiment.

In April 1855 the Phalanx property was broken up into

parcels and sold at auction. The nonresident stockholders
got 100% of their investment back. The resident stockholders received about 60%. The Phalanx was dead, but
the members were almost unanimous in regarding this
period as the happiest of their lives. A number of them
remained in Monmouth County, where they became substantial and respected residents.

John Bucklin purchased the phalanstery with the purpose of continuing the canning industry. Down through
the years the Bucklin family has occupied the huge building, moving into closer quarters as decrepit sections were
torn down. The Bucklin factory in the village of Phalanx,
where tomatoes and other vegetables are canned, is on the
site of the association's property.

In 1887 Alexander Woolcott, grandson of John Bucklin, was born at Phalanx. In *While Rome Burns* he writes:

> The place [Phalanx] is thronged with ghosts.
> Ghosts of the Van Mater slaves who, back in the
> early part of the 18th century, forged the nails and
> hewed the beams of the barn that went up in flames
> in 1919, and whose burial ground still stands between
> two fields, the wooden crosses long since moldered
> away. . . . Certainly the redcoats, retreating before
> Washington, to the waiting ships at the Highlands,
> ran across our fields. Once the potato diggers came
> upon a British officer's sword. Then there is the ghost
> of Mr. Greeley, who used to take his nap in a chair
> on the veranda, the red bandana, which would be
> thrown across his face, belling rhythmically with his
> snores, and all the young fry compelled to go about
> on tiptoes because the great editor was disposed to
> doze . . .

Only one of the original buildings still stands. The grand ballroom was razed in 1935. The schoolhouse is a memory. Here "with the drab old caravansary bleak as a skull in winter," the descendants of John Bucklin live among ghosts and memories.

FEMININE WEAR AT PHALANX

Henry George

FREE ACRES, A SINGLE-TAX COMMUNITY

Free Acres, a section of New Providence Township in Union County, New Jersey, is one of several experimental colonies founded about the turn of the 20th century to demonstrate the single-tax theory. This was the fourth of such colonies in this country. The first, Fairhope, was established in 1895 on Mobile Bay in Alabama. Five years later followed Arden, in Delaware. One man alone, Fiske Warren, a wealthy paper manufacturer, was so anxious to spread the single-tax doctrine that he founded 13 colonies with a total land area of 971 square miles and a population of more than 9,000 persons. Of these, Tahanto, in Massachusetts, and Halidon, in Maine, are among the best-known.

The single-tax movement is credited to Henry George whose book, *Progress and Poverty*, caused a sensation when it appeared in 1880. According to Henry George Jr., "it out-sold most of the popular novels of the day In America and England it ran serially in the columns of the newspapers and by 1905 more than 2,000,000 copies had been printed." Single tax was debated in clubs and forums and discussed in editorial columns. To many it seemed that it was a scientific solution of the numerous difficulties of a complex economic and social structure Others looked on it as just another scheme that had no possibility of success.

Nearly every celebrity of Henry George's time had something to say upon the subject of single tax—either for or against the plan. Tolstoy, the Russian novelist, contended that "no one could possibly disagree with *Progress and Poverty*." George Bernard Shaw, John Dewey and Lincoln Steffens were admirers of Henry George and his philosophy. Tom L. Johnson, onetime mayor of Cleveland, Ohio, happened to buy George's book on a railroad train; as a result he sold out his monopolies. Later he was elected to Congress on a reformist program.

Many socialists, on the other hand, argued against single tax because it was based upon the value of land not labor.

George Fallon, economist, asserted that land tax under George's scheme would benefit neither agriculture, industry nor business; would increase the cost of living, and would destroy "billions of dollars of wealth of a large number of our citizens." Another opponent, Alvin Saunders Johnson, said in the *Atlantic Monthly* in 1914 that the single tax was a "device for the spoliation of the middle class." He called attention to the fact that pioneer

ho crossed the plains, enduring great hardship, did so
ecause the land was sure to rise in value.

Lately there has been a revival in popularity of single-
ax doctrines. In 1932 Oscar H. Geiger founded the
Ienry George School of Social Science with 84 pupils.
n August 1938 the school purchased for $50,000 a build-
ig in Manhattan which will be used as a headquarters
id academy. John Dewey, the American philosopher, is
onorary president of the Henry George School. Accord-
ig to Frank Chodorov, the director of the school, the
mplicity of the doctrine is the principal reason for its
surgence in popular thought.

At present in the United States there are 21,000 stu-
ent followers of George's philosophy, and the number is
pidly growing. New teachers cannot be trained quickly
nough to supply the demand for instructors. Single-tax
lasses are conducted in about 200 cities in this country
nd seven foreign countries. Approximately 5,000 men
nd women are students by correspondence.

The advocates of single tax contend that the funda-
iental cause of economic difficulties is the taxation of
idustry, of profit and of income. Land, they say, alone
iould be taxed, never the improvements on it. This,
iey believe, would make it unprofitable for speculators
) hold land unused. Under the single-tax plan the land
elongs to the community, not to the individuals who
ccupy it. Individuals pay a tax rent the amount of which
 regulated by the cost of improvements and of providing
rvices. As community costs rise the tax rent rises, regard-
ss of whether any particular parcel of land has been
nproved or not.

Under our present system, of course, speculators may
uy land in undeveloped communities, hold it unused

while community improvements are made—meanwhile
paying a comparatively small tax—and sell their unde
veloped land at a profit when space in the community
grows valuable. Those who believe in a single tax argue
that everyone would eventually become a landholder
subject to taxation; there would be plenty of land for all
because it would be unprofitable for anyone to attemp
to speculate in land or land values. The taxes paid on the
land would furnish revenue for policing, fire protection
national defense, schooling and all the other services pro
vided by the government.

Free Acres cannot ever fully express Henry George'
theory as long as it is part of a state and country governed
by economic principles at variance with the single-tax idea
But within the limits of Free Acres a certain amount o
single-tax demonstration has been in force since the com
munity's beginning in 1910.

The land, about 60 acres originally owned by Mr
Bolton Hall, belongs to the Free Acres Association
Mr. Hall, a strong advocate of single tax, was one of the
founders of the colony, incorporated under the Coopera

ive Act of New Jersey, which prohibits selling for profit. The land is leased to residents on a perpetual lease. For occupying their home sites the people of Free Acres pay a yearly tax, or rent, to the association. The association, in turn, pays taxes to the Township of New Providence, to bear its share of the expense of public education, police and fire protection and general improvements. As improvements have been made, the tax rent paid by the landholders to the Free Acres Association has risen from about $16 an acre to about $70 or $80. The rules of the association require that no one can lease, or rent, less than one-half acre for a home site.

The governing body of Free Acres is the entire membership of the association, and it is known as the Free Acres Folk. Open meetings are held monthly where all the business of the association is discussed. Trustees and committees for all public activities are elected annually from the membership.

The children attend grammar school in Berkeley Heights, and high school at the new Regional High School at Springfield. They are gathered up each school day by busses at the entrance to Free Acres.

Free Acres was originally begun as a summer colony. The settlers put up simple shingle cottages, many without cellars, and cleared only enough woodland to make room for their homes and for roads and paths. As transportation facilities improved many of the residents found the community life so pleasant and the woodland surroundings so congenial that they remained throughout the year, commuting to their work. Many people widely known in art and literature have been members of the Free Acres community. Some of these have given up their residence; others have remained and have contributed to the interest

of the community life. The hand of an artist is evident i
the attractive signposts and bulletin boards, the rust
benches and the general landscaping of the tract.

Just inside the entrance on Wood Road is the Henr
George Common, a clearing in the woodland. Here is
rustic bulletin board on which town notices are poste
At one side is an old farmhouse, shaded by a giant syc
more tree said to be about 200 years old. This spot is th
community center; here are the libraries, one for adul
and one for children, where meetings, lectures, teas, flowe
shows and other affairs are held. The old building
familiarly called "The Inn."

In front of the building a large outdoor pavilion h
been built around a huge walnut tree that rises throug
the center of the floor and spreads its shadow over th
entire platform. Here dances and outdoor meetings a
held in the summertime. From this platform many me
and women prominent in public life have lectured. O
the end of the platform is a bell which is rung to ca
people to town gatherings.

A gradually sloping lawn leads from the platform to
baseball field, an archery court, a tennis court and a pla
ground with swings, rings and bars for the children. Nea
the center of the colony is a swimming pool surrounde
by benches in the shade of towering old trees. Across th
road from the swimming pool is an open-air theat
framed in a setting of white birch and cedar trees. Durin
the summer months plays are produced by the resident
many of whom have been professionals.

Trees are among the outstanding features and are pr
tected by a local forestry committee which supervises the
care. Most of the members prefer to keep the natur
setting of trees, bushes and wild flowers, with steppin

stone or gravel paths for their yards. Free Acres has an active Garden Guild which encourages members to plant only those flowers that will fit into this natural setting.

The winding gravel or dirt roads through the colony are cared for by the association. There are no sidewalks and no street illumination. At night each foot traveler carries his own light. Though the surroundings are simple, almost primitive, there are more than 100 persons who find Free Acres a congenial year-round residence. In summer the population is about doubled. Although many of the old cabins and bungalows put up by the original settlers still remain, modern improvements such as electric refrigeration and oil heating systems have been installed. There is delivery service from all the leading metropolitan stores.

After 27 years, there are still many of those associated with the beginnings of Free Acres and other similarly organized communities who feel that the single-tax idea must be kept alive, because it is based on Henry George's simple and forceful expression, "liberty is justice and justice is the natural law."

CO-OP

The two green pine trees in a circle and the word "Co-Op" are new to the New Jersey scene, newer than the George Washington Bridge or modernistic architecture —much newer than radio. Yet they represent a century old idea. This sign over a store front or displayed on canned goods, clothing, oil cans, or any one of a number of commodities indicates that a group of people are applying to their everyday living the great principle of coopera- tion. It means that they have taken the initiative of going directly to the source of supply for the things they need so that they may get the best value for their money.

It was the depression that gave impetus to the coopera- tive movement in America, though it had been growing steadily in Europe for generations. In 1934 the word "co-op" was almost unknown. Today it is displayed over sixteen stores in New Jersey; and there is an increasing number of groups buying goods under the cooperative plan. Throughout the United States the "Co-op" sign may be seen on clothing stores or apartment houses, bakeries or gasoline stations, restaurants or coal trucks.

Since its birth 100 years ago the cooperative movement has appealed to people who are looking for a practical solution of their everyday problem of securing food, cloth- ing and shelter. It was a group of weavers in the little town of Rochdale, England, who, faced with the problem of chronic poverty, worked out a plan so practical that today it affects the lives of 120,000,000 families in every country of the world.

The Rochdale weavers decided that if they would, as a group, buy food, clothing and other necessities directly from the farmer, manufacturer or wholesale dealer in large quantities, and then distribute the goods among themselves in their own little shop, they would save expenses. In this way each member would obtain goods at cost. What was saved after deducting the expense of freight and handling could be divided among the members.

These weavers never had enough of the bare necessities of life. It took them a whole year to save £28, equal to about $135. With this small capital they opened a tiny store in a deserted warehouse in Toad Lane, arousing the scorn of neighbors and local tradesmen. But this was only a beginning. They called themselves the Rochdale Society of Equitable Pioneers and declared that "as soon as possible this society shall proceed to arrange the powers of production, distribution, education and government."

The Rochdale enterprise was so successful that the news spread, and other stores were opened. The society then established a wholesale department to serve the various stores. Next they built factories to make many of the articles they bought. Even that was not enough—the wholesale branch bought tea plantations in India and great wheat ranches in Canada to supply the food prepared and packed in the factories. All these properties were owned and controlled by the consumers who obtained the products through the society's stores.

The rules adopted by the Rochdale society for governing their organization were so simple and practical that they have been used in every successful consumer co-

A Co-op Store

operative group since that time with only slight changes.
These rules, called the *Rochdale Principles,* are the first
thing taught to a new cooperative member. They are based
on individual rights which we today would say are essen-
tial to a democracy, although several of them did not
become a part of democratic government until years later.

One of the most far-seeing of the Rochdale principles
is that providing for the sale of goods at prevailing prices.
Since it is impossible to decide beforehand exactly how

much it will cost to run a store, it is more likely that expenses will be covered if the prevailing price is charged. Whatever surplus results goes back to the consumer anyway. In the second place, if a cooperative should start underselling it would be the signal for a price war. Young "Co-ops" have not the financial strength to stand this type of competition.

Sweden, where more than 20% of the retail and wholesale trade is carried on through cooperatives, has supplied a notable exception to this rule. In fields where monopoly control has kept the price of goods unnecessarily high, the cooperatives have stepped in and, by producing as well as distributing, have lowered prices for all consumers.

In order to force down the artificially controlled price of electric bulbs the Swedish cooperative announced that they would build their own factory. Immediately the price dropped 10¢ a bulb; and it was announced that bulbs would be distributed for nothing if the co-ops persisted in their plan. The cooperatives replied that they would consider this a very good result of their investment. Obviously, no private interest would consider investing a million dollars in a factory just to let it stand idle. But these co-op members were also consumers. If their threat resulted in the production by a private industry of bulbs below cost, it would be to their advantage. No monopoly can continue to sell below cost indefinitely. It is merely a strategy to force small competitors out of the market. The Swedish cooperative was strong enough to stand this type of competition, since its members were getting the benefit of a reduced price on a commodity. The great Luma factory is now distributing bulbs to co-ops in all the Scandinavian countries.

Today half of the families in England are members of

consumer cooperatives, and the movement is growing steadily. They employ in all their branches 450,000 workers. In most countries the cooperative provides not only consumers' goods but also banking, insurance, housing, medical care and even burial services.

The various local groups in the United States are building up a strong consumer cooperative movement. These groups have united to form regional organizations which, in turn, form a national body. This national body is divided into several groups to coordinate the business of the smaller groups. National Cooperatives is a national wholesale organization. They have copyrighted the term "co-op," which can be used only by member groups organized on Rochdale principles. In addition to the central business organization, there is a national organization, the Cooperative League of the United States, whose concern it is to provide an educational program. Their insignia is two green pine trees in a circle, the use of which is allowed only to member groups. In other words, in order to use the term co-op and the pine tree insignia, a cooperative group must meet the requirements of both national organizations.

Established groups are laying out educational programs embracing everything from art to economics, as well as the history and principles of consumer cooperation. Those groups that can afford it employ full-time educational directors to take charge of the education of their youth as well as their adult members, management and employees.

Buying on specification is an important part of the co-op plan. For example, the Wholesale purchases co-op soaps made according to a formula drawn up by chemist members, the best it is possible to make. Goods bearing the co-op label are made to meet the demands of the consumer for quality at a reasonable price. There is no incentive to cheapen materials in order to make more money. As one of the leading farm cooperators say of their fertilizer factory, "We have never made a pound of fertilizer to sell; it has all been produced to use."

Before the depression cooperation was concentrated in farming areas and in foreign groups in the urban population. New Jersey has several long-established foreign groups and stores in the rural sections. Outstanding among these is the *Germania Fruit Growers Union and Cooperative*. Started in 1888 by a group of farmers to fill a pressing community need, the store has prospered consistently. Today it occupies a modern three-story structure and supplies, at nearly wholesale prices, fertilizer, coal, farm implements, meat, groceries and many other commodities to a widespread community in Atlantic County.

The New Jersey Consumers Cooperative, Inc., is one of the most successful of the new eastern suburban cooperatives. In 1935 small groups of white collar and professional workers in Madison and Summit, who had been providing themselves with coal, organized a co-op and opened a grocery store. An affiliated store was opened in Caldwell, and the first year the business amounted to $52,000. The second year business doubled. The organization now operates stores in Fair Lawn, Caldwell, East Orange and Madison.

In 1936 President Roosevelt sent a commission abroad to make a study of the cooperatives in Europe. The committee's report supplies an estimate of the long-run effect on other businesses. From Denmark—"Their total effect is so much to improve the situation of a community that it could reasonably be said that there is more business and

more work to be done as a result of cooperative enterprise
than there would have been without it . . . Business in
general is better and industrial production steadier as a
result of cooperative enterprise . . ."

EGG AUCTION

Chicken farmers, in addition to the natural hazards of drought, storms and plant and animal disease, have had to face further difficulties in the marketing of their produce. Small producers in particular have been forced to sell their goods at prices set more or less arbitrarily by dealers who rode up and down the country bargaining independently with each farmer.

In 1930 a group of nine men from Flemington decided that the poultry farmer should be enabled to deal directly with the retailer and thus get a fair price for eggs. They formed an organization called the Flemington Auction Market Cooperative Association, Inc. The idea appealed so strongly to the citizens of Flemington that the Chamber of Commerce offered the free use of a cellar for the first meetings, and a local printer offered to print the necessary announcements without charge. The organizers of the auction were prepared to invest $500 to launch the new scheme; but from the first it met with such great success that not one cent was called for. At first the auctions were confined entirely to eggs, but in the second year poultry was added, and in 1935 livestock was offered for sale.

Farmers who live in New Jersey and produce their goods here are invited to bring their eggs to the auction, held twice a week, where they are graded for color, size and quality by an inspector from the New Jersey Department of Agriculture. Retail dealers bid for the eggs as they are put up by the auctioneer. The farmer receives about 95% of the proceeds immediately; the rest is retained to meet the expenses of the auction. At the end of the year, after all expenses are deducted and a certain amount set aside for improvements, profits are divided among the farmers in proportion to the amount of goods they have brought for sale.

The first year's business left a profit of $1,818.02 for the members of the association. So rapidly have the profits grown that at the end of two years the auction felt justified in investing in land and a building.

Today it has exchanged its small cellar quarters for a large, two-story brick building close to the Flemington Railroad station, with lofts, salesrooms, offices and shipping platform. It takes an office force of from 30 to 35 to conduct the business of the auction and keep the accounts of the members. There is a membership of more than 1,000.

The business of the auction is in the hands of a manager. He keeps in close touch with the farmers so that they will be thoroughly informed on everything done by the board of directors and the business staff, and will feel free to take an active part in the affairs of the association. There is an annual meeting of all members to discuss general business and to elect the board of directors. Details of finance and administration are handled by the nine board members.

The auction itself is very interesting to watch. It is held in a large room equipped with folding wooden seats, much like classroom chairs. The auctioneer stands on a platform in front of a large double blackboard. Behind him a clerk, writing as fast as he can—and he has to write fast to keep up with the speed of the auctioneer—posts a list of the particular lot of goods that is being offered. The auctioneer talks so fast that, until one becomes accustomed to the sound, it is impossible to understand what he is saying.

The dealers sitting in the chairs facing him, to all appearances, are quite indifferent to the proceedings on the platform. But as one looks around, a finger will be seen lifted here and there to indicate that the bid has been raised. When the auctioneer is satisfied that he has received a fair price for the goods, he signifies the closing of the bid by clapping his hands together.

Meanwhile, another clerk is keeping a close watch on the audience to see which dealer gets the goods. When a dealer has completed his purchase he steps to the front of the room, receives a slip indicating the lot numbers of the eggs he has bought, walks to a window and pays cash, and then goes downstairs to receive the lot and take it away at his own expense. The whole proceeding is carried on with businesslike efficiency and speed.

Before the establishment of this method of selling, the farmer sold his goods mostly through wholesale dealers, who in turn sold them to stores or route salesmen. The farmer received as little as 86% of the wholesale selling price. Retailers then added anywhere from 8¢ to 10¢ a dozen to the wholesale price; and the farmer had to be content with the difference. Now the auctioneer can hold the price up to meet the market price in the large cities, and all the farmer has to pay for the service is the actual expense of running the auction. In addition, he gets a return from the yearly profits of the auction.

So successful has the cooperative idea proved that today about 70% of the eggs sold in New Jersey find their way to the market through this plan. There are now auctions at Mount Holly, Vineland, Paterson and Hightstown set up on the Flemington plan. The Flemington auction, however, the largest of its kind in the world, does about 15% of the total business.

THE SEEING EYE

Coeducation is a term that is commonly applied to the education of men and women in the same institution and under the same terms. There is, however, in the village of Whippany near Morristown, New Jersey, another kind of coeducational institution—a college for people and dogs. This is The Seeing Eye, where dogs are trained to act as guides for the blind; where men and women are trained to discard canes and the shuffling, hesitating gait and to rely on the intelligence and devotion of their dumb guides.

The dogs are not merely trained; they are actually educated. They learn to obey commands, but only when it is safe for their masters that they do so. To develop this high standard requires as much as three months of painstaking education. Only those dogs especially adapted to the purpose are selected. Most are of the German shepherd breed; females are preferred because they are more docile than the male, more tractable and less likely to be drawn into a battle. One of the hardest lessons Seeing Eye dogs must learn is not to fight. No matter how deeply aroused is their canine sense of justice, they must control their inherent instinct to have it out with the enemy. To a Seeing Eye dog alumnus her master's safety is all important.

Every dog must pass a rigid health and intelligence test before being accepted for training. For example, small torpedoes are exploded to see if the dog continues to be

Courtesy L. Bamberger & Co.

THE SEEING EYE

frightened at the sound. This test reveals whether the animal will become scared by sudden sharp sounds such as backfiring automobiles.

The peak of the course is reached when the dog learns to guide her master away from impediments, such as awnings and low branches. A bit of string is stretched before the dog, too low to permit her to pass under. She invariably walks around it. Little by little the string barrier is raised until she can pass under it, although the master is stopped. Having passed under the obstacle the dog then turns to see what is preventing her master from following. Again and again this lesson has to be repeated until the dog learns to circle the obstacle. Finally she is able to judge whether any obstruction is high enough for the master to pass under safely.

Obedience is the mark of any well-trained dog. But the Seeing Eye dogs must learn also to disobey when the master gives a command that might lead to disaster.

They learn to obey the commands, "forward, left, right," only as long as it is safe for the blind person. For instance, the man may order the dog to cross a street. But she sees a car speeding toward her. Regardless of the order, she stands still. When the car has passed she looks in both directions and, when sure that the way is clear, ventures across.

The dog wears a harness with a rigid U-shaped rubber handle placed conveniently for the blind man. This intimate contact enables each to be instantly aware of the slightest movement of the other.

The blind person must also be educated. His education may be even more difficult than that of the dog, since it is first necessary to erase former habits of uncertainty and fear. When he arrives at the institution he is first allowed

o become familiar with his own room. Then he is taken
out on the grounds and whirled around, time after time,
until he is able to reorient himself.

After he has learned confidence he is assigned a dog
guide. When they have become acquainted the two pupils
are taken out into the streets of Morristown, to gain experience in stopping at curbs, passing broken sections of
sidewalk and other obstructions, and crossing traffic-
covered streets. When both have passed this final test they
are sent out into the world as one individual, fit to earn
their living in a competitive society. As in every good education, both have been subjected to a rigid discipline, with
approving words and caresses as a reward for the dog
when she acts properly.

The Seeing Eye project was the idea of Mrs. Harrison
Eustis. On her travels through Europe she saw the German shepherd dog performing remarkable tasks. The
German and Swiss police in particular made special use
of the breed. What was more important, animals of this
type showed touching faithfulness in leading men blinded
in the World War.

Mrs. Eustis was so impressed that she determined to
see if more of the dogs might not be trained to lead the
blind. At Fortunate Fields, a pleasant retreat in Switzerland, she experimented for some years with these dogs.
Mrs. Eustis was assisted in her work by Elliott S. Hum-
phries, who had had a great deal of experience in training
animals for circus work.

Then in 1928 a blind young Southerner, Morris S.
Franks, learned of their experiments through an article in
an American magazine, and wrote to offer his assistance.
Mrs. Eustis urged him to visit Fortunate Fields. He did
so, and when he felt confident in the judgment of his dog

he returned to America. The dog behaved exactly as she
had been trained. Delighted with the results, Franks wrote
to Mrs. Eustis, asking that she carry on her work in
America. The result was the establishment of The Seeing
Eye. Today Franks directs the institution and tours the
country with his dog. His first dog died in June 1938 at
the age of 11.

So, in a spacious and pleasant residence in the rolling
countryside near Morristown, Mrs. Eustis maintains her
school for men and dogs. The men come looking eagerly
for their "eyes." The dogs are procured either by purchase or donations. Many people give their female shepherd pups to the institution. Churches and schools help
the work along. All donations are accepted; although only
a nominal charge is made for training of dog and man,
many of the blind are unable to pay at once. Time is
allowed for payment in small installments while the
graduates are getting started on the important business
of earning a living.

The Seeing Eye is intended to be neither a charitable
institution nor a subject for sentimental writers. The directors are interested only in the solution of a difficult
problem.

JERSEY HOMESTEADS

In exchange for a crowded tenement, a pleasant house and garden; for a cluttered city street, sunny fields and cool green woods; for an ill-lighted, stuffy workroom, a modern glass and concrete factory set in the open country —these and the opportunity to share in the profits of their own labor are the advantages enjoyed by the group of families that has joined the Jersey Homesteads, a cooperative colony near Hightstown.

The colony occupies 1,275 acres of beautiful rolling farm land and forest five miles southeast of Hightstown in Monmouth County. A factory is the center from which spread out, fanlike, the homes of the workers, the stores and the school. A wide belt of farm land and forest belonging to the colony encircles the community. This insures freedom from the encroachment of industrial or commercial activities.

The colony was started by the Department of the Interior of the Federal Government, at the suggestion and under the sponsorship of a group of prominent men interested in social betterment. It was designed as an experiment in the decentralization of industry, to enable workers to live in pleasant homes, near their work, with enough land on which to raise some of their own food, and so supplement their incomes. The colonists have organized all the work of the community and the administration of its affairs on a cooperative basis.

Like Brook Farm, the North American Phalanx and

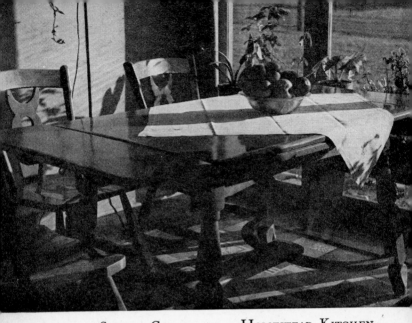

SUNLIT CORNER OF A HOMESTEAD KITCHEN

other experiments in communal living, Jersey Homesteads
is designed to find a simple and happy solution for the
complexities of modern industrial life.

Construction was started in May 1933 under the Reset-
tlement Administration. In August of the next year the
first families moved in. In planning the colony it was
decided that 200 families or about 1,000 people would
provide all the workers necessary to run the factory, farm,
school, store, post office, etc.

The greatest care was used in selecting the colonists.
First of all they had to be of good character, and each
worker had to be expert in his particular field, whether
he be farmer or hat trimmer. Second, everyone had to
pass a rigid health examination. Finally, each family had
to be able to contribute $500 toward financing the venture.

The colony is run on the same democratic principles as

WINDOWS REACH FROM FLOOR TO CEILING

club, each member having only one vote. To date only
wo families have dropped their membership.

At present the garment factory is the center of the
olony. It is designed to furnish jobs for 160 garment
orkers making men's, women's and children's clothing.
he workers are all members of the International Ladies
;arment Workers Union or the Amalgamated Clothing
Vorkers of America and are paid according to the union
age scale.

The factory is a one-story structure of glass, steel and
oncrete, sleek as an airplane. This air-conditioned build-
1g, one of the most modern garment factories in the
Jnited States, cost $95,000. It is planned to provide the
1ost efficient operation consistent with the safety and
ealth of the workers. There follow in successive steps
round the building the receiving platform and room, the

stockroom, the cutting room where 75 to 150 garment are cut at one time, the underpressing, the finishing, th final pressing, the finished stock room, and so back to th shipping room, which is shared with the receiving room The factory has a capacity of 1,500 coats and suits an 1,000 dresses a week.

One corner is devoted to hat making, with a capacit of 200 to 300 dozen hats a week. There are also a sho meeting room, a directors' room and retail department The association maintains a showroom and designers i New York.

During the first year, 1936-37, the factory disposed o its output through the New York market. The followin year they distributed through consumer cooperatives i Utah, Wisconsin, Illinois, Kansas, Ohio, Pennsylvani New Jersey, New York and New England. This exper ment proved successful enough to warrant setting up a organization, composed of representatives of the regiona cooperative groups and one representative from the worl ers, which has taken over the management of the factor as well as the distribution of its output. In this way th consumer, through his regional board, is taking his pai in controlling the production of the garment he buys an is sharing proportionately in any saving that is effectec The factory turns over to the regional bodies any mone that remains after the expenses of manufacturing hav been met. This money is turned over by each regiona group to the local consumer cooperatives, after deductin the cost of distribution. The consumer, in turn, receiv a rebate from his local group, in proportion to the amour of his purchases.

The workers' homes are good, sturdy examples of moc ern architecture, for the most part one-story and fla

Concrete Walls—Fireproof and Durable

roofed, designed for efficient, comfortable and gracious living. Windows reach from floor to ceiling. Each house has a living room, dining room, kitchen and three or four bedrooms. All are equipped with hardwood floors, gas and electricity, electric refrigerators, oil burners, and are air-conditioned. There is an attached garage and a work-room for garden and carpenter tools. A plot of ground no smaller than 100 by 300 feet surrounds each house, enough space to allow each occupant to grow whatever flowers or vegetables he desires. The homes will be paid for over a period not exceeding 30 years at a cost of $18 to $24 a month.

A space of about 500 feet between the backs of the houses is ploughed, sown and cultivated by community-owned machinery. The families have decided on the vege-tables which they all want. These are grown and cared for by the community, but the produce belongs exclusively to the family on whose land it is raised.

The cooperative farm of about 500 acres gives work to six members. It has been so successful that wages of $2 a week have been paid the year round and a considerable amount returned to the credit of the whole colony. The produce has either been sold to other members or disposed of through a farmers' cooperative auction market in Hightstown. The quality of the vegetables has been praised, particularly the Irish potatoes, which in 1936 were judged second best of all raised in Monmouth, Mercer or Middlesex Counties. The first year's crop showed a profit of $17,000 after repaying a Government loan of $26,000. During the planting and harvesting seasons the women help in the fields. When work is slack in the factory the coat makers and milliners join the farm workers.

A cooperative poultry project has been started with 3,000 chickens. This gives work to two members of the colony. The colony has also acquired a dairy which is run cooperatively like all the other community projects.

A consumer cooperative store owned by all the members as consumers is run on the same principles which govern other such ventures the world over. The savings were 8¢ on the dollar after the first four months of business. The young people of the colony opened in the spring of 1938 a small cooperative tearoom which was needed to serve the many visitors to the colony.

The two utilities which serve the community cooperatively and which eventually will be owned by them— water supply and sewage disposal—are models for their size and have attracted the attention of engineers from all over the country.

A fine school building with a capacity of 500 opened in the fall of 1937; in addition to the usual subjects the school offers training for future workers in the colony. A nursery school is conducted in one of the old farmhouses that stood on the property. A community center has been established in a farmhouse, and the factory is used for movies and dances on Saturday evenings.

At first the surrounding Monmouth County residents looked askance at this community of pioneers. But little by little they are coming to accept them. Neighboring farmers have been impressed with the methods of the city-bred newcomers; and the Hightstown people are coming out to buy clothes from the factory.

Jersey Homesteads, now incorporated as a borough with its own mayor and council, welcomes visitors interested in studying this new adventure in social and industrial planning.

SERVICE FOR THE PUBLIC

SAFEGUARDS OF OUR COAST

New Jersey, except for a small strip along the northern border, is surrounded by water, nearly 300 miles of which is navigable. The gentle coast line is bordered by many miles of broad beaches where children romp safely in the breakers; it is indented by coves and inlets that offer safe harbors for gay yachts and fishing boats. But beyond the level shore are treacherous shoals and sand bars that have been the dread of mariners from the days of Henry Hudson and the Dutch, Swedish and English settlers who followed him. The newcomers to these shores in the early days, without a signal to warn them, took their chances on being grounded on a sand bar and battered to pieces by the waves.

The first American lighthouse, built to protect the shipping of Boston, was hailed as an epoch-making event when it was lighted September 17, 1716. Sixteen oil lamps placed in groups of four furnished the illumination. The cost of maintaining the light and the salary of the keeper were paid from a tax imposed on all vessels putting into the harbor. In the next 40 years two more beacon towers were built along the rocky New England coast.

As late as 1761 there was no warning signal or other aid to navigation in New York Harbor. The merchants of the city organized a lottery to raise funds for the construction of a lighthouse and bought four acres of land on Sandy Hook. So apathetic was the public that a second lottery was necessary to produce enough money to complete the project.

On June 11, 1764, the Sandy Hook light first shone out over the dark ocean. The nine-story, octagonal masonry tower, rising to a height of 85 feet, was a notable skyscraper at the time. The light of 48 oil blazes set in glass sided lanterns made it the most powerful on the continent. Of all the early Colonial lights the sturdy Sandy Hook tower with its brick-lined walls, seven feet thick at the base, is the only one remaining intact and in service today. At the time of its construction it stood about 500 feet from the northern extremity of the Hook. The tides of almost 175 years have piled the sand around it so that today the shore line extends a quarter of a mile beyond the tower.

When the British fleet gathered off New York Harbor in 1776, a party of adventurous Americans dismantled the light so as to confuse the enemy. A British landing party was forthwith dispatched to restore it. Shortly afterward the Americans tried again to destroy the light by using a small field gun mounted on an open boat. They succeeded in damaging the tower somewhat before they were driven off.

One of the first agencies established by the Congress of the United States in 1789 was the Lighthouse Service. At that time there were twelve lighthouses in operation. The Sandy Hook tower was one; nine were in New England waters; one was at Cape Henlopen, Delaware, and one at Charleston, South Carolina.

In 1903 lighthouse work was placed under the Department of Commerce, and in 1910 the present Bureau of Lighthouses was created under the same department to direct the establishment, construction, maintenance and

SANDY HOOK LIGHTHOUSE

operation of all lighthouses, lightships, buoys, marker
and other navigation aids on the 40,000 miles of seacoast
the Great Lakes and navigable rivers of the country
Supervision is divided among 17 districts with a personne
of 5,050 employees, 42 of whom are employed in th
bureau at Washington. The seacoast of New Jersey lie
in the Third District, which includes the waters of Rhod
Island (excepting Narragansett Bay), Connecticut, New
York and New Jersey, with headquarters at Staten Island
The Delaware Bay and River waters are under the Fourth
District, with headquarters in Philadelphia.

The efficiency of the lighting devices is an importan
factor in lighthouse equipment. The older lighthouses had
to depend on simple whale or coal oil lanterns set in front
of reflectors to direct the beam. In 1822 a French engineer
Augustin Fresnel, developed a lens consisting of a serie
of prisms to collect and concentrate the light. This was an
important step in lengthening the beam. Not until the
beginning of the century did electricity come into use for
lighting, although there are still lighthouses operating
with vapor oil lamps. Electricity is also used to revolve
the lens to produce a flashing light. In the past the
lens was revolved by a clockwork device controlled by
weights which the lighthouse keeper wound every few
hours.

Lighthouses placed on exposed points of land or shift
ing shoals are at the mercy of the very dangers they are
set to guard. There have been many lighthouses literally
washed into the sea as their foundations crumbled under
the pounding waves or collapsed beneath crushing ice
jams. The towers have to be constructed to withstand the
force of the wind that batters at them from all directions.
Though they are designed for utility rather than beauty,

1any lighthouses are notable for the graceful lines of the
tpering towers; others are famous for skillful design and
1genious construction.

The color of the light and the length and frequency of
1e flash are significant features that help the mariner to
ifferentiate between the beacons and thus confirm his
)cation. For the same reason the lighthouses are painted
1 varying colors and designs. Special coloring also helps
) make the structures stand out more clearly from their
ackgrounds.

The most powerful light in the country is at Navesink
.ighthouse on Beacon Hill, Highlands, New Jersey. It
as a 9,000,000-candlepower beam. Two lights were estab-
shed here in 1828, and the first Fresnel lens used in
merica was installed in 1841. The present stone structure
'ith two towers, looking much like an old fortress, was
uilt in 1862. The electric lamp in the south tower, which
; the only one in use today, is set in a lens weighing over
even tons that revolves in ten seconds and gives a flash
very five seconds. Its light can be seen 22 miles at sea,
eyond which it is obscured by the curvature of the earth.
t has been reported, however, that its beam has been seen
1 the sky 70 miles from shore. Since its establishment
Javesink has been considered the principal light for New
"ork Harbor, although it has lost much of its importance
'ith the improvement and increase in the number of
oating aids—lighted buoys, fog signals, sounding buoys
nd lightships.

The Absecon light in Alantic City was abandoned in
933 and three years later deeded to the city, which
1aintains it as a landmark. When it was built in 1854 it
'as placed at what was thought to be a safe distance from
1e shore, 1,300 feet, but the sea kept tearing at the shore

until the waves were breaking within 75 feet of the towe
In 1876 the United States Government built stone jetti
to protect it. Then the tides brought in tons and tons
sand until there was $10,000,000 worth of new buildir
property around old Absecon. Now, instead of bein
lapped by the ocean, the lighthouse is safely tucked awa
among summer houses and is no longer useful.

The 167-foot tower, painted in three alternating banc
of black and white, is set on a foundation of piling 30 fe
thick. The light may be seen for more than 20 miles
sea. On the lighthouse grounds are a Coast Guard and
Weather Bureau Station.

At Barnegat Inlet, where the sea pours past the sout
ern tip of Long Beach Island into Barnegat Bay, is th
now abandoned Barnegat Lighthouse, one of the mo
famous beacons along the Atlantic Coast. The first tow
built at this point in 1834 was brought down by the se
The present structure was built in 1858 under the dire
tion of the father of F. Hopkinson Smith, the famo
author and playwright. In fact, F. Hopkinson Smith hir
self was an engineer who at first did all his writing in h
spare time. It was while working on the lighthouse
Barnegat City that he started his well-known book, *T*
Tides of Barnegat.

When the lighthouse was first built it was about a mi
back from the shore, but today the bay and ocean me
at its very feet in Barnegat Inlet. Its foundations hav
been weakened by so many storms that in 1930 the Fe
eral Government finally decided to abandon it.

The State of New Jersey bought the lighthouse fro
the Federal Government for $1 and raised funds to fi
in around the base of the tower and so preserve the famo
old landmark. This work is being carried on by the Sta

BARNEGAT LIGHTHOUSE

Bureau of Commerce and Navigation. An automatic light still remains burning as a warning to sea travelers. Visitors are welcome.

The Cape May Lighthouse, built in 1823 to guard the entrance to Delaware Bay, was the second in the State. Its site has long since vanished in the sea. A second tower, built in 1847, was also swallowed by the ocean. When the present lighthouse was built in 1859, it was placed 1,000 feet inland. Near the tower are the buildings of the U. S. Coast Guard Life Saving Station. The 145-foot white tower with its red lantern stands out boldly against the sky. Its light, flashing every 30 seconds, can be seen 18 miles out to sea.

The Brandywine Shoal Lighthouse, erected in 191. eight miles from the entrance of Delaware Bay, mark a dangerous shoal where two lighthouses have succumbed to the pounding of the waves and the grinding of the ice For years the spot was marked by a lightship. The aban doned lighthouse is still standing close to the new one. A 225-ton reinforced concrete pier forms the foundation fo the circular concrete structure. The beacon itself stand at the center of a group of nine iron legs. Surrounding th entire structure are 30 heavy iron piles driven into th sea bed.

Fourteen Foot Bank Lighthouse, lying just a little abov Brandywine Shoal about in the middle of Delaware Bay is one of the greatest achievements of lighthouse engi neers. The lighthouse is named for the 14 feet of wate covering these dangerous shoals. At this point, in 1887 was built the first lighthouse in the United States on submarine foundation. A timber working chamber built on shore was encased in an iron cylinder and sunk 20 fee into the bed of the river. Through the center of th cylinder rose an air shaft through which the workmen entered the working chamber where they dug out th sand, which was blown out by air pressure. Eight men working in four-hour shifts sank the caisson 35 feet int the bed of the shoal at the rate of about one and one-hal feet a day. As the caisson sank into the river bed, the wall of the cylinder were built higher to keep them above th level of the water. The completed cylinder was then filled with concrete and upon it was built the keeper's dwelling topped by the light tower.

Opposite Cohansey River in the middle of Delawar

Ship John Shoal Light

Bay, east of the main ship channel, is Ship John Lighthouse, one of the oldest lighthouses on the Delaware, built in 1877. The lighthouse is named for the ship *John*, which grounded on the shoal in the early winter of 1797. By spring it had been cut through by heavy ice and storms and gradually it settled into the sand. Drift accumulating around the sunken hulk has increased the area of the shoal, which is marked by a 65-foot tower surmounted by a light visible for 13 miles. The tower is surrounded by 3,700 tons of stone for protection from ice and the sea. One of the souvenirs at the lighthouse is the wooden figurehead of the ship *John*, which, along with much of the assorted cargo, was salvaged from the wreck. In the Museum of the Cape May Historical and Genealogical Society at Cape May Court House is the bronze frame of the ship's rudder, which was caught in an oyster dredge and brought to the surface by Captain Zadok Sharp, who presented the relic to the museum in 1930.

Lightships

The first lightship in the country was moored sever
miles off Sandy Hook in 1823 at the entrance of New
York Harbor. It was known as the Sandy Hook Light
ship until 1908, when its name was changed to Ambrose
to identify it with the Ambrose Channel which it now
marks. Though this ship is not within New Jersey waters
it is one of the links in the chain of navigation aids for
New York Harbor.

Three lightships are anchored in New Jersey waters.
Scotland Lightship, three miles off Sandy Hook, was
placed in 1868 to mark the wreck of the steamer *Scotland*
The encumbrance has long since been removed, but the
Scotland Lightship has been kept in service as an additional safeguard. Barnegat Lightship, the most recent of
the New Jersey lightships, took over the functions of the
abandoned Barnegat Lighthouse in 1930. Five Fathom
Bank Lightship, 16 miles southeast of Cape May Point
was established in 1839. In a hurricane that raged for
two days, August 23 and 24, 1893, the lightship stationed
at this point foundered. Four of the crew were lost.

Unless relieved, a lightship is not allowed to leave her
station on any pretext. The more serious the weather conditions, the more important it is that her light and fog
signals be kept in operation. There are many accounts of
terrific hardships suffered by the crews of these lonely
guardians during ferocious storms or dense fogs.

Lightships are placed in exposed positions at the mercy
of gales and cross-currents. To keep them at their station
they are equipped with mushroom anchors weighing up to
7,000 pounds with iron or steel chains in some cases as
long as 900 feet. A modern lightship has the advantage

Courtesy Bu. Lighthouses, Wash.

Scotland Light, Sandy Hook

f engines to relieve the strain on the mooring during a
ard storm and radio to communicate with shore stations
nd ships at sea in case a storm drives it from its position.

Great advances have been made in the design and
quipment of lightships since the first small boats were
owed out and anchored at harbor entrances or dangerous
oints and left at their stations without a crew. Someone
ad to go out each day to see that the light was kept
urning.

The modern, snub-nosed, sturdy ship, designed to ride
ut every kind of weather and withstand every strain,
s a more comforting than beautiful sight. The dark hulk
obbing serenely on the waves or dimly glimpsed through
he thick curtain of fog, its name painted in large letters
n its side, assures the navigator of his position. From the
all masts, which in the larger ships raise the light 57 feet
bove the water, the flashing signal can be seen 14 to
o miles at sea.

In addition to fog signals, all lightships are equipped
with a radio beacon, which sends out an assigned dot and
dash signal which can be picked up 100 miles or more a
sea by any vessel equipped with the proper radio receiving
apparatus. By this device an approaching vessel, even
though far below the horizon and out of sight and sound
of the lightship's other signals, can keep a check on it
course.

Depending on the size of the ship and the importance
of the station, the crew varies from 6 to 15 men. Except
in the stormy season, when no one is allowed to leave th
ship, the work is arranged so that the men have ampl
shore leave to compensate them for the monotony and
loneliness of their life. The crews of the lightships hav
the most liberal vacation allowance of any men in th
service. Time on duty and ashore is arranged in rotation
so that each man has a maximum of 90 days' annual leav
without interfering with the operation of the ship.

At regular intervals each ship must make a trip to th
nearest depot to be overhauled. Meanwhile a relief shi
takes its place, sending out the same signals. Not for
moment is the station allowed to go unguarded.

Lighthouse tenders, the messenger boys of the service
carry supplies and equipment to all lightships and light
houses in addition to inspecting and placing the variou
buoys, markers and other aids. In the stormy season specia
care is taken that the lightships have a full supply of foo
and equipment, in case they are cut off from the shor
by a protracted spell of bad weather.

Before the coast was amply provided with lightship
and lighthouses, the shoals off New Jersey were a grave
yard for ships, shipwrecked sailors and passengers. Amon
the many shipwrecks with dreadful loss of life were thos

of the passenger ships *Powhatan* and *New Era* in the 1860's. In the former 311 lives were lost, and 260 in the latter.

The duties of the men in the lighthouse service do not include lifesaving. This work is delegated to the Coast Guard service, which has 39 stations along the coast equipped with devices for saving the lives of bathers from the shore and of shipwrecked travelers. Nevertheless, because of the exposed and isolated positions of light-houses and lightships, there have been many instances of rescues undertaken voluntarily and at great risk. Employ-ees receive no remuneration for such hardships endured or dangers faced. Commendation by the Department of Commerce, or, in rare instances, the award of a medal are the only rewards for deeds of notable heroism per-formed as a matter of course in the line of duty.

Captain C. W. Atkins of the tender *Iris* in June 1930 received commendation from the Department of Com-merce for rescuing eight persons from a burning yacht in the Delaware River. When the *Iris* reached the yacht the people were in such great peril that they had jumped overboard and were clinging to the sides of a small swamped boat. Two men, two women and four children were saved.

FOREST FIRE FIGHTERS

For many years New Jersey's 2,000,000 acres of woods and forests were left to the mercy of fires that destroyed vast acres of valuable timber, left the land barren and desolate, and robbed the birds and wild animals of refuge. This area, 120 miles long and averaging 30 miles in width, only recently has been placed under the protection of the State. The first attempt at organization of fire prevention was in 1903, when local firewardens were appointed under township ordinance. This haphazard system worked pretty well, but there was still an average loss of 51 acres per fire each year.

In 1923 there was a reorganization of the system. The work was placed in charge of a State Fire Warden with headquarters in Trenton. Under this system, the State is divided into three divisions: Division A extends from the New York border to the Raritan River; Division B from that point to the Mullica River; and Division C covers the remainder of the State. These divisions are subdivided into 40 fire sections, each in charge of a State-paid section fire warden. The sections are split into districts under district wardens, making 372 districts. To each district warden is assigned a crew of from 10 to 25 helpers who are paid only when fighting fires. Altogether there are 9,000 men available for fire duty. Seventeen towers overlook the State's forest areas. These and the 13 district offices are connected to headquarters at Trenton by short-wave radio. In addition, the State Fire Warden has at his disposal an airplane manned by a pilot and an observer. Thus the headquarters office is in constant communication with every portion of the field.

Although through education of the public the State Forest Fire Service has done much to diminish the number of fires, its greatest accomplishment has been in reducing the loss in acres per fire. With the entire State under constant observation from lookout towers and the well-organized crew of trained helpers that can be marshaled quickly and efficiently, there is now less likelihood of a fire getting out of control and destroying great areas. As an example, instead of losing 51 acres per fire, as was the case before 1923, the recent average has been 17 acres.

Each division is equipped with three fire trucks which may seem primitive when compared to the elaborate fire-fighting apparatus used in cities, but they are most efficient for the rough work they have to do. The trucks are stripped of fenders to give them better clearance through narrow lanes between trees. Their equipment includes a portable gasoline-driven water pump, 2,000 feet of 2½-inch hose, and a bristling load of long-handled shovels and brooms of a special type—the most efficient of all forest fire-fighting appliances—as well as axes, brush hooks, buckets, steel drums, lanterns, hoes, mattocks, sprayers and torches.

Combatting forest fires depends on eternal watchfulness and speed in getting out to fight the flames. All that a forest fire-fighting service can do in the way of preventing fires is to have laws passed that discourage fire hazards, to post the woods with warnings and educate the public in the dangers of carelessness. The causes of forest fires are far too numerous and varied and the area to be protected is far too extensive to permit more than the most general preventive measures.

A forest fire may start in any number of ways—from a spark thrown by a passing locomotive or a lighted cigarette tossed into dry grass. Picnickers or hunters may have lighted a campfire in restricted areas. Glowing ashes knocked from a pipe into a bed of dried leaves or grass can start a blaze that will burn over miles of country and keep crews of men fighting for hours to control it.

Fire Warden Fales reported in the winter of 1937 that hunters were responsible for setting 42 blazes in the fall of that year, several of which were of major proportions. One of these larger forest fires was in Sussex County and was started by sportsmen who set fire to a hollow tree to rout out a squirrel. The hunters did their best to put out the fire, but it got beyond them.

The increasing number of devastating forest fires led to the enactment of many laws pertaining to the care of the forests and the duties of the fire wardens. A person starting a fire in the woods without obtaining permission from the local fire warden may be fined as much as $400.

When engaged in fighting a fire the warden in charge may summon any male person between the ages of 18 and 50 within his jurisdiction to assist in extinguishing the blaze. No physically fit person can refuse. Such recruits are paid the same rate as the warden's regular staff of helpers. The fire warden also has the right to use personal property and material if they are needed to beat back the fire.

The men of the forest fire service do more than merely wait for fires. There is much preparatory work to be done to make the actual work of fire fighting more effective. During the off season, December 20 to March 1, each

Men Against the Flames

district warden and his crew go through the woods removing dry branches, digging up patches that threaten to produce dry grass and cutting away underbrush and trees of less than three inches in diameter. Sand piles are deposited to be ready to scatter on the flames.

At certain points, strips or "lanes" are cut through the woods. These are cleared of all vegetation and are cut wide enough to allow the fighters to get through to start a "backfire." In case a forest fire gets a serious start, a "backfire" is set toward the onrushing flames so that when the two meet neither can proceed for lack of fuel on the already burned area.

The dangerous and expensive practice of backfiring may be eliminated, however, with a new pumping unit developed by the department. The outfit, which can reach about 30% of the fires in a district, is capable of pumping 11

gallons of water a minute at the end of a 10,000-foot hose
The unit is equipped with tanks to wet down the road
bordering the burning area, a two-way radio, hand spray
ers, axes and other fire-fighting equipment. Water can
be pumped into the apparatus from a 22-foot well, and
the intake hose needs only three inches of water in which
to operate. The department is planning to have one of
these in each of the three divisions.

The average forest fire is not spectacular unless it breaks
into tree tops where it roars or crackles from tree to tree
sending flames sky high, making an awe-inspiring scene
Man power is what counts in the struggle, for the fire has
to be beaten down with shovels, brooms and other imple
ments before it has the chance to spread upward into the
dry foliage of the trees.

Of the three sections into which the forest areas have
been mapped, Division B and parts of C in the central and
southern sections of the State are the danger spots, for
here are dense forests of evergreens filled with resin and
volatile oils. Many of the sections in this division are
covered with scrub pine and underbrush tangled into a
jungle so thick that even hunters refuse to penetrate it
Once these pines catch fire they burn so quickly and cast
off so much heat that men cannot come near enough to
fight the flames. This section of the State, abused and
neglected by man in earlier times, is one of the greatest
fire hazards in the United States.

When the railroads were built through this region to
carry people to the Atlantic coast resorts there was a great
increase in forest fires. Little attempt was made to extin
guish the blazes. They were allowed to burn until arrested
by some natural barrier—a swamp, stream or road. Not
only have the trees been weakened and destroyed by fire

quent burnings, but the soil, robbed of its richness through the destruction of humus and ground litter, has been so impoverished that it will take 100 years to restore it to productivity.

The procedure of reporting a forest fire has become an exact science. High in one of the observation towers sits the lookout, a licensed radio operator. Smoke from chimneys in the villages and hamlets that lie in his district do not interest him. But let smoke appear where it should not, or let the chimney smoke appear suspiciously heavy, and immediately he is all attention.

Around swings his range finder and the smoke is located on the map—plot 62. He watches to see if the smoke is increasing. If it does, he calls the section warden, giving his tower location and the number of the burning plot. The warden calls another tower and gets a location from the lookout there. From this tower it looks as though plot 51 is afire. A glance at the map shows where the two bearings cross, and the fire is located. The section warden then calls the district warden, who drops whatever work he is doing and races for the garage, stopping only long enough to notify his men. Then down the street and across the fields, sometimes as much as eight miles, the truck jounces with its load of men and equipment. On the way more men are picked up. In the woods, the smoke leads the crew to the fire.

Just as the causes of forest fires vary, so do the methods of fighting them. These depend on what headway the fire has made, on the nature of the vegetation on which it is feeding, on the terrain—whether the ground is level, uphill or downhill—and whether or not there is a high wind. As a rule, the easiest fires to handle are those near farms or wherever else it may be handy to set up the

water pump, drop its suction hose down a well or a cister
and let the water spray. Hillside fires are next most easil
disposed of, because the draught created by the flame
is deflected by the slope of the hill instead of fanning th
fire. The most difficult fires to handle are those on a leve
among the evergreens in Divisions B and C, because o
the heat and speed of the flames. In cases like these th
fire lanes that have been cut and prepared are a godsenc
If the blaze occurs where no fire lanes have been cut th
fire fighters are rushed ahead of the fire to cut lanes fo
backfiring.

Backfiring, however, is not undertaken except whe
necessary, and only under favorable conditions. In a hig
wind there is danger of spreading flames in the wron
direction unless, of course, the lanes are very wide. Th
safest backfires are started on the downhill side of slope
where the flames progress far more slowly than uphill
Except where backfiring is used all forest fires are attacke
from in front and beaten out with shovels.

In these days of fire-fighting efficiency the attack i
more interesting than spectacular. The choking, acri
fumes of blinding smoke that rise from the charred are
over which the fire has traveled on occasion are hot enoug
to scorch shoes. But the army of shovelmen piles throug
this, choking and coughing, whether the fire front be
half-mile or a mile in length. Each tries to beat a gap i
the line of flames, thus putting a stop to further advanc
at that point, and then along the line of fire so as to out
flank it.

Relatively small fires are quickly disposed of, especiall
in the northern end of the State where trees of the pin
family are scarcer and where the chief fuel for the flame
is little more than dried grass, dry underbrush and leave

But fighting a real forest fire is a he-man's job. The smoke is so thick that the men are discernible only as shadows. The heat, the ash dust and the smoke parch their throats, blacken their faces and send streams of tears out of reddened eyes.

There is no such thing as time out for a breathing spell or food or even drink; and throughout, without a moment's cessation, the shovels are pounding, sometimes for hours and hours while even the strongest lungs, joints and muscles weary. On one occasion, in Division C, the fight continued eight hours. Then, reeling, the men came back from the front, black and sooty, red-eyed, swollen-lipped for want of a drink and so absolutely exhausted that many were obliged to sit or lie down before proceeding home. For this work the "extras" are paid $1 for the first and 40¢ for each succeeding hour of work. But it is not the money, it is pride in belonging to a splendid service, that commands the loyalty of every man.

STATE POLICE

In 1921, when mounting automobile casualties and the increase of crime in rural communites were beyond control of local facilities, the New Jersey State Legislature authorized the creation of the State Police with a force of 140 men. In 17 years its duties have been expanded to include a variety of services, from conducting safety education classes to tattooing poultry as a protection against thieves. Even though the personnel has been doubled Col. Mark O. Kimberling, Superintendent, feels that the present force cannot adequately cope with the growing population and the increasing traffic on the State's 8,20 miles of roadway.

An applicant must be more than 5 feet 6 inches tall weigh at least 135 pounds and be between the ages of 24 and 40. Very few over 32 apply because of the rigid physical test. Applicants who pass a thorough character investigation are invited to take the periodic mental and physical examinations. On these tests they must attain an average of 65% to be put on the eligible list. When vacancies occur, those highest on the list are called to the training station at Wilburtha, near Trenton.

For three months the training classes of 50 to 75 recruits are not permitted to leave Wilburtha except in cases of serious illness at home. On Sundays they may go to church with an officer and receive visitors in the afternoon. The student is carefully watched to determine whether or not he is temperamentally fit for police work

Many are eliminated for this reason alone. Life in the training school under the rigorous schedule is a test of stamina, mental and physical alertness and adaptability:

5:45 a.m.   Rise.

6:00 a.m.   Roll call, calisthenics and foot drill.

7:00 a.m.   Breakfast.

8:00 a.m.   Road run. A quarter of a mile the first day, and this distance is increased until the daily limit of five miles is reached. This is followed by a shower, more calisthenics, jiujitsu, boxing, wrestling, broadswords and horsemanship, motorcycle riding or automobile driving, until noon.

12:00 noon   Dinner.

1:00 p.m.   Lecture. These include talks on the legal phase of a policeman's work, first aid and a practical knowledge of medicine. The lecturers are doctors, lawyers, judges and police officials.

2:00 p.m.   Study of the police manual. This includes the State, criminal, game, forestry and motor vehicle laws; Federal statutes, State geography, court procedure, courtesy and consideration toward prisoners and complainants, scientific crime detection, including the study of fingerprinting, toxology and making of moulage casts.

4:30 p.m.   Marksmanship, livesaving and resuscitation. Colt pistols are used on the rifle range. A candidate must be able to shoot with both hands and attain an average of 85% in marksmanship. The use of gas

hand grenades to quell disturbances is also
part of the study.

5:30 p.m.   Supper.
7:00 p.m.   Classroom.
8:00 p.m.   Recreation.
9:30 p.m.   Lights out.

Those selected for service sign up for two years, but they
may resign at any time. The $100 monthly salary which
begins in training continues for a six-month probationary
period served under the supervision of a veteran trooper.
At the end of nine months a trooper's pay is $1,600 a year.
This is increased annually until at the end of six years he
reaches $2,200—the limit for trooper's grade. At the age
of 50, after 20 years of continuous service, State police
men are pensioned at half of salary and maintenance.
Troopers disabled in line of duty receive between one
quarter and three-quarters of their pay, depending on the
degree of disability. Widows or dependents of men killed
in the service receive an amount not in excess of one-half
of salary and allowance.

Following the six months' probation the rookie becomes
a full-fledged State policeman. "Duty, Honor, Fidelity,"
the motto of the State police, are the first three words in
his lexicon, and the rolling road becomes his home for 1
or 13 hours each day, 6 days a week.

A State trooper is subject to call 24 hours a day. To
keep criminals from knowing the exact whereabouts of
troopers at certain hours, there are no set "beats" or
mileage limits. Nor does a trooper know from day to
day to which of the three trooper headquarters or the
25 substations he will be assigned. Transfers are made
"for the good of the service" and are never questioned.

Troopers are seldom removed from stations except for good cause.

State headquarters are maintained at Trenton, where Superintendent Kimberling, former Army officer and warden of the State Prison, directs the activities of the department. The three troop headquarters are at Hammonton, Morristown and Wilburtha.

A captain, or troop commander, is in charge of each troop headquarters and eight substations. He is responsible to the Superintendent for the men and for police conditions in the area. Substations are commanded by a sergeant or corporal who in turn is accountable to the troop commander.

Although crime prevention is an important part of the work, the particular responsibility of the State police has been patrolling the roads that carry the commercial and pleasure traffic to and from the great cities of New York and Philadelphia. Despite the efforts of the police to educate drivers, there is still an appalling number of injuries and deaths from automobile accidents each year. State policemen are trained to treat the motorist, as well as the law, with respect. Minor offenders may receive only a warning; but the deliberately reckless driver can expect the full penalty of the law. To this particular public nuisance the State police have dedicated a parody on *Trees:*

> I think that I shall never see,
> Along the road an unscratched tree,
> With bark intact and painted white,
> That no car ever hit at night.
> God gave them eyes so they could see,
> Yet any fool can hit a tree.

TRAINING IN HORSEMANSHIP

Colonel Kimberling has devised an accident-control system that has cut down mishaps considerably. Every reported accident is recorded by a pin placed on a huge map of the State; in addition, a detailed description of the accident is filed. When the pins become massed in any spot on the map, that spot is marked off as an accident center and is subject to special policing.

In the last few years the airplane has proved very effective in untangling traffic snarls, especially on holidays. Observers fly over the highways and by radio inform headquarters of the extent of traffic jams. The news is teletyped to station WOR, which broadcasts warnings of possible delay and suggested detours. Meanwhile, extra details of troopers are rushed to untangle the traffic knots. Eight white patrol cars and 55 motorcycles are used for this work.

RUNNING; PART OF THE TRAINING
EVERY TROOPER WHILE IN TRAINING MUST RUN FIVE
MILES DAILY

School Safety Patrols

The Safety Education Bureau was started in 1929 when angry Camden County parents protested against the mounting number of automobile accidents in rural districts. Since then the bureau has carried on a broad program of instruction for children and adults. Police especially trained for this work are assigned to certain territories to supervise and instruct the safety patrols of school children. In country schools in 1937 there were 405 active safety patrols under the supervision of the State police.

There is a keen rivalry among these young traffic directors, whose motto is "Safety, Service, Citizenship." Good work means promotion to the rank of lieutenant or captain. Advancement is decided upon by a board in each school consisting of the principal, a teacher and the trooper in charge.

Organization and supervision of the school safety patrols is only part of the work of these trooper-teachers. Twice each month they visit the schools in their territory to direct safety training from kindergarten to high school classes. The course is planned to follow the seasons from October until spring. Instruction in November and December is devoted to methods of preventing Christmas accidents, while in March the hazards of roller skating, bicycling and kite flying are discussed. During May and June the troopers tell of summer dangers, with emphasis on July Fourth mishaps.

The State police have proved good teachers, enlivening the talks with stories and moving pictures. The confidence placed in the troopers by their young charges is illustrated by a recent incident. A little girl about seven called the telephone operator and asked for the State police. The operator relayed the call to the nearest barracks, and the trooper on duty heard a small voice ask that a State policeman be sent to her home to keep her company.

"Why?" asked the desk man.

"Because my mama's gone to the city and I'm alone and afraid. A policeman teaches me in school and I'm never afraid when he's around," the youngster explained. The trooper on the nearest beat was told to drop in and see how the child was faring.

Adults, too, may receive instruction through lectures before civic groups, luncheon and social clubs, church groups and parent-teacher associations. The police urge the importance of broadening the educational program, because a preponderance of accidents occurs as a result of violation of simple safety rules.

Crime Prevention

The clocklike precision with which the troopers spring into action in an emergency has often resulted in the apprehension of a criminal, the uncovering of telltale evidence or the saving of a life. As soon as an emergency call is received, the telephone operator plugs in the nearest substation. The troopers make regular calls into their stations so that the officer in charge has a constant check on the movement of every man in his detail. In case of a sudden call for help, the substation orders a light placed in the window of a home, store or garage along the trooper's beat. The trooper, recognizing the signal, calls up the station for orders, and off he goes to the scene of the accident or crime.

An idea of the speed with which the State police function can be gained from a recent attempted burglary near Stanhope. An aged woman, left alone in the house, heard someone prowling donwstairs at midnight. Locking her bedroom door, she opened the window and screamed for help. Neighbors telephoned the barracks at Stanhope, five miles away, and seven minutes later a State policeman was at the scene. The would-be thief had fled when he heard the woman's cries, but by noon the next day he had been arrested, tried and sentenced to a year in jail.

In 1930 the legislature authorized the installation of a State-wide police teletype alarm system to be connected with similar systems in New York, Pennsylvania, Massachusetts, Connecticut, Rhode Island, Delaware and Ohio. This method of communication has been responsible for apprehending many criminals.

In the crime laboratory at Wilburtha are kept the rogues' gallery and fingerprint records of thousands of

ONE OF THE TROOP HEADQUARTERS SHOWING NEWEST
TYPE CARS

lawbreakers. In addition, the laboratory is equipped with almost every known scientific device for checking evidence: microscopes, cameras, violet-ray and X-ray machines, equipment for making ballistics examinations and chemical analyses, machines for making photomicrographs (pictures made through a microscope), for enlarging photographs and making photostats. Fingerprint files, to a great extent, have taken the place of the rogues' gallery as a means of identifying criminals. Experts estimate that the chance of two fingerprint impressions being identical is one in 64 billion. When no fingerprints are left at the scene of a crime, the investigators must rely on other devices. A cast of a footprint or the chemical analysis of a single hair may lead to the solution of a crime.

The uniformed force of the State police is augmented by the detective bureau of 25 men. These plain-clothes men, selected because of special aptitude for the work, cooperate with the troopers and local police. In 1937 the

letective force investigated about 1,300 criminal cases, of
vhich 566 have been completed and 728 are still under
nvestigation or awaiting trial.

Rendering first aid, policing disasters and quelling riots
are vital parts of the troopers' work. One of the best examples of their efficiency in this line of duty was the
Hindenburg tragedy. At 7:23 on the night of May 6,
1937, the giant dirigible from Germany exploded and
took fire as it neared the mooring mast of the Naval Air
Station at Lakehurst. A few minutes later, troopers on
duty at the station were connected with the Trenton headquarters. Messages were sent out over the teletype, speeding ambulances, doctors and nurses to the scene. At 7:33
every available State policeman was on his way to Lakehurst. Their heroic work that night brought praise from
passengers, naval officers and government officials.

Many other demands are made of the State police from
time to time. The cooperation with the Fire Warden in
fighting forest fires has been a factor in keeping the damage at a minimum, and poultry thefts have been greatly
reduced by the State police system of tattooing a number,
registered like automobile license numbers, on the fleshy
part of the birds' wings.

The efficiency and courage of the State police have
earned the respect of the public. Many troopers have left
to accept positions as chiefs of local police departments or
for police work in private industry. Most of them, however, remain in the service, well satisfied with the healthy
outdoor life and the secure economic future.

RESTORING LOST FORESTS IN THE MULLICA WATERSHED

The Mullica River and its branches, once important arteries of commerce for the industries of southern New Jersey, drain nearly 450 square miles of silent woodland and barren waste in the heart of the pine belt. Here in five State forests, scientists are conducting experiments that look to the rebuilding of the 3,200 square miles of New Jersey forest area so that the soil of the southern pine lands, which produced the valuable forest of Colonial days, will again grow timber, hold the rainfall and give service to man.

Early settlers in this region found the land covered with giant pine, cedar and oak trees, an abundance of wild life and many streams, well stocked with fish. They set up furnaces, smelting iron from the bog ore found along the banks of the streams, and built glass works that drew upon the rich deposit of glass sand underlying the area. In the vast forests they ruthlessly cut down the trees to supply charcoal for the furnaces and timber for ships that plied the clear, swift-flowing Mullica, carrying cargoes to New York, Philadelphia and other cities.

Today only crumbling ruins of furnaces and mill wheels are left as reminders of this former activity. Shipyards along the banks of the Mullica closed long ago. Here and there ghost towns are decaying. The few people remaining in the vicinity earn a living in the cranberry bogs and by exploiting the remnants of the forest.

Much of the timber left standing by earlier inhabitants was destroyed by fires which again and again ravaged the area. Even the leafy covering of the soil was burned away in spots, and wind and rain eroded the thin mold, laying bare the unfertile subsoil of sand and gravel. Trees forced by the heat of fires sprouted too often, ever weaker, until they became dwarfed, crooked and feeble.

It is through these denuded forests that the Mullica River flows southeastward across New Jersey for 35 miles, starting at a point near Berlin, Camden County, and emptying into Great Bay, an arm of the Atlantic Ocean about 15 miles north of Atlantic City. Its many branches reach into three other counties—Burlington, Ocean and Atlantic. Along the lower stretches of the river the meadows covered with reeds and grasses are feeding grounds

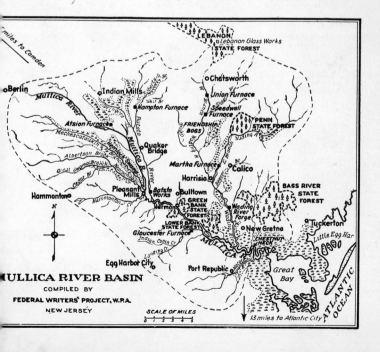

MULLICA RIVER BASIN
COMPILED BY
FEDERAL WRITERS' PROJECT, W.P.A.
NEW JERSEY

SCALE OF MILES
0 1 2 3 4 5

for countless birds. Large vessels can still navigate th
Mullica for several miles above its mouth, and smal
ships can travel 20 miles upstream, as far as Pleasant
Mills, but today there are no large towns to attract com
merce. For 20 miles above Pleasant Mills, where the
stream is joined by four others, it is sometimes called
Atsion River.

The State forest reservations along the Mullica and it
tributaries, centers of large-scale forest planting, compris
35,000 acres, or more than two-thirds of all the Stat
forest reserve. Fine groups of trees that somehow escape
the woodman's axe in the two centuries preceding th
Civil War still stand in scattered spots. Tall fire-tower
give silent evidence of the value the State places on
these forests.

The Mullica, once called Little Egg Harbor River, ha
two State forests on its shores, Green Bank and Lowe
Bank. Trees cast their shadows on the smooth surface of
the broad stream. Here are picnic grounds and camping
places which are increasing in popularity each year.

The rising quest of outdoor life that has come with the
automobile and motorboat has brought new activity into
the Mullica River region. Many residents of Philadelphia
and Atlantic City have found its forests and streams ideal
for a summer vacation land. Small cottages have been
built in recent years around the Colonial village of Sweet
water or Pleasant Mills. The summer visitors spend much
time in fishing, hiking and horseback riding along the
woodland paths that lead to berry patches and ghosts of
towns. Hunting also is a favorite sport.

Canoeists, attracted by the beauty of the clear-flowing
river and its tree-shaded banks, make their way up as fa
as old Atsion, once an iron center. The tides flood th

treams as far as old Batsto, where there is a dam. Boys'
nd girls' camps may be seen on the shores near cabins of
unters, fishermen and summer residents invited by the
ilent woods. The balmy scent of pine fills the air. Out-
ide of the many bogs the soil is dry and porous.

The Bass River branch of the Mullica River reaches the
3ass River State Forest, while the Wading River branch
ises from the springs and brooks of Lebanon State Forest
nd Penn State Forest, named for William Penn. Pictur-
sque Oswego Lake, made by damming the Oswego River
ranch of Wading River, is at the southern border of
'enn State Forest.

In the Bass River reserve the forest supervisor recently
ound an old dam mysteriously repaired and flooding
even acres. He discovered that the work had been done
y beavers, most of which had vanished from this section,
aaving been killed for their valuable skins in Colonial
lays. The founders of the new beaver colony are believed
o be descendants of those deported from northern New
'ersey about two years ago at the request of human
aeighbors.

On the experimental area in Bass State Forest are lob-
olly pine trees planted in 1913 that have grown 50 feet
aigh and 10 to 16 inches in diameter. Here also are white
aines which in the same period have reached a height of
10 feet. These are the largest of the experimental plant-
ngs, though the foresters also have set out jack, red,
Scotch and Austrian pines, Norway spruce, Douglas fir
ind European larch trees.

The foresters have been and still are thinning out the
white swamp cedar trees to relieve crowding and to permit the best trees to develop. Where the soil is shallow,
he oak scrub is cut away to permit the growth of yellow

pines, which thrive better than oak in this locality. In thes
forests and the land around them the deer, protected b
law, have been increasing for the last 20 years. At on
time deer were almost extinct in New Jersey, but the
have been replaced by bringing Virginia whitetail deer t
the State forests.

The State operates two nurseries for producing youn
trees, one of them close to the Mullica River near Gree
Bank Forest. In recent years the Civilian Conservatio
Corps, stationed at several camps in this region, has aide
the State Forester by planting millions of young trees. I
the entire State this corps has set out 40,000,000 trees an
collected between 7,000 and 8,000 pounds of seed.

State engineers have offered plans to save the soft wate
of the Mullica basin for the drinking supply of New Je
sey cities. This would include the building of an aqueduc
13 feet in diameter stretching 84 miles northward t
Newark. Two reservoirs of 54 square miles would be cre
ated on the Mullica and Wading Rivers by dams, eac
four miles long. Unfortunately these reservoirs woul
bury old Batsto, Pleasant Mills, Gloucester Furnace an
other historic points beneath their waters.

Another report made by the State Board of Conserva
tion and Development favors purchase of the Wharto
tract for its forest and park value. The Wharton Estate
covering 148 square miles, takes its name from Josep
Wharton of Philadelphia, who purchased large tracts o
pine land along the Mullica and its branches before th
Civil War. Wharton proposed to build a reservoir whic
would furnish a future water supply for Philadelphia
Since State legislation forbids water to be taken out o
New Jersey, these vast areas in the river basin have re
mained a part of the Wharton estate. The small cottage

now at Batsto were built for workers who protect the Wharton forest lands against timber thieves. The fine old manor house was rebuilt as it now stands by Mr. Wharton.

Little farming is possible in the Mullica Watershed, but cranberry culture has been a growing industry in the bogs that once yielded iron ore. New Jersey's crop is now the second largest in the United States. In recent years the development of the swamp blueberry has been fostered in this region as a result of successful experiments by the Federal and State Departments of Agriculture. Sphagnum moss is also gathered in the woodland in large quantities for the use of florists.

One of the early furnaces with forge attached, the Batsto Iron Works, was built on the Batsto River, about two miles north of its junction with the Mullica. Across the river from the village was the Colonial settlement of Sweetwater, now Pleasant Mills, where lived timber cutters, charcoal burners and teamsters serving Batsto. The ruins of an old cotton mill which opened in 1821 still stand. The mill was later converted to the manufacture of paper, using wood pulp made from the surrounding forest. In Batsto is the Aylesford House built by Charles Read, the ironmaster. His daughter Honoré, heroine of the novel *Kate Aylesford*, was rescued from Tory outlaws by a young Continental officer, Major Gordon, whom she later married.

The leader of the bandits was Joe Mulliner, a South Jersey Robin Hood who robbed the rich and sometimes aided the poor. He held up wagon trains carrying supplies to Batsto Furnace and sold "protection" to other teamsters. Joe's lieutenant, "Big Dan" Johnson, who had a shrill high voice, would hide himself under a blanket and call to passing drivers for a lift. When the wagon stopped,

the gang swarmed out of the bushes and looted the load
Tradition relates that Mulliner loved Honoré Read and
kidnaped her when she failed to invite him to a party a
here home. Honoré was returned that night, but the part
was a failure. The militia, stirred to action, tracked Joe t
his den in Hemlock Swamp a few miles up the Mullic
River. They dragged him to a birch tree near the Rea
manor house and hanged him. A wooden sign now
beneath the tree reads: "Joe Mulliner, Hung. 1781."

The Mullica River, so important in the State's earl
industrial history, received its name from Eric Mullica
who came to this country with other Swedish settlers i
1663. About 1697 Mullica led a party of Swedes from
their settlement on the Delaware into the wilderness an
cleared a strip of forest land along the north bank of th
river close to the present village of Lower Bank, near th
State Forest in Burlington County. Mullica remained her
until he was 80 years old, when he joined his sons at thei
home near Raccoon Creek, close to the present village o
Mullica Hill, which also took the name of this hard
pioneer who lived to the age of 87.

In the more than 240 years that have intervened sinc
Eric Mullica led his little band of pioneers into the Mu
lica region, it has been despoiled to supply the utilitie
of a rapidly expanding nation. Now that science has taugh
greater respect for the gifts of Nature, future generation
may benefit from the forward-looking program of th
Department of Conservation.

AGRICULTURE

CRANBERRIES

Early New Jersey settlers were introduced by the Indians to a small red berry with a distinctive acid flavor. Before long they discovered that the new fruit had a certain tonic value and was particularly helpful as a cure for scurvy.

This fruit, the cranberry, is a native of the bogs of the northern United States and belongs to the same botanical family as do blueberries, huckleberries and snowberries. It is closely related to the European cranberry which grows in colder bogs in Europe and Asia and between Labrador and Alaska and Michigan and British Columbia. The American variety is comparatively large, ranging in color from a light yellow to a very dark red, almost black. The fruit may be bell-, bugle- or cherry-shaped.

The first colonists were satisfied to gather the cranberries in their wild state. In 1835 the first bog in New Jersey was set out by Benjamin Thomas near Burr's Mills in Burlington County. Many bogs were established in the early fifties, but it was not until after the Civil War that production was begun on a large scale. Since then the industry has flourished, enlisting the aid of science in its fight against its natural enemies, insects and disease.

There are few States with the climate and soil necessary for cranberry cultivation. Massachusetts leads in production with New Jersey in second place. The level, sandy, well-watered soil of the southern part of the State is particularly suited for this enterprise, which is rapidly becoming the most important small fruit industry of New Jersey. Burlington, Atlantic and Ocean Counties produce about one quarter of the entire cranberry crop in the United States. There is plenty of room for expansion, for only a little more than 10 percent of land suitable for cranberries has been cultivated.

The primary requisite in cranberry cultivation is an available water supply, since periodic flooding is important. The most desirable soil is sandy with a top layer of acid muck or peat and a hardpan base that will retain the water until it is drained off. Throughout the pine barren section of New Jersey there are miles of bog land watered by small streams which can be dammed and controlled to provide water to flood the bogs.

The preparation of the land takes several years. First the soil must be cleared of all vegetation, the usual method being to burn everything after the site is cleared. The land is then ditched and covered with two to four inches of clean sand. Cuttings are next planted at six-inch intervals in rows 16 inches apart. Care is taken to weed out any cutting showing disease. Working on his knees and using an ordinary dibble, a man can plant about 10 square rods a day. In about four years the ground is completely covered by the vines, and they start to bear fruit.

The cranberry plant or vine is a trailing runner along which are distributed numerous erect branches and roots. Both the runner and the upright bear leaves, but only the upright bears fruit. During the winter all the leaves are red, but in the spring they turn green.

Fruit buds first appear in August. In the following spring the new uprights grow from the terminal bud. The vines flower in June and early July and bear fruit in September or October.

In January of each year the bogs are submerged and kept flooded until early May in order to prevent winter killing and a too early start of growth. Bogs are flooded again during late May or early June to kill insects, and the treatment is repeated after the fall harvest. Occasionally a reflow in August is necessary. These periodic reflows must be very carefully controlled. If the plants remain submerged too long the entire crop may be ruined. In most cases the flow must be put on and taken off in 24 hours.

The most troublesome disease is the false blossom, which is spread by a tiny leafhopper. Growers, working with the cooperation of experiment stations, are now able to fight this disease, but in recent years it has been the main cause for the cutting of the cranberry crop from some 200,000 barrels a year to a little over 100,000. Other diseases, such as scald, blast and rot, are caused by fungi. Insects that injure the plants include the yellow-headed fireworm, the black-headed fireworm, blossom worm, cranberry girdler and the common grasshopper.

Although flooding is the most common way of fighting these pests, new methods of control are being developed. Many growers use pyrethrum dust, sprayed by hand dusters, by traction dusters or from autogiros and airplanes.

Frosts are another worry to the grower, for the cranberry bogs are much colder than the surrounding upland on clear, still nights because of lack of air circulation. Growers watch the temperatures, and when conditions threaten frost during the growing season they flood the bogs enough to counteract the cold. The water, which is warmer than the surrounding atmosphere, raises the temperature above the danger point. It is important for the grower to know just what minimum temperature the plants can stand so that the water may be used without waste or without damage to the plants.

Another problem is that of forest fires. Since many of the bogs are in woodland, and the vines are combustible a system of fire lines or burned-off strips is employed to protect them. The ordinary methods of fighting forest fires are used when flames threaten the bogs.

Harvest begins in early September and lasts until late October. Entire families, men and women, young and old spend the season in the fields. They are housed in makeshift shelters provided by the owners. They are paid on the basis of the quantity of berries picked. As each box is filled the picker receives a ticket which represents so much money and is accepted as currency in the stores in the vicinity.

Pickers are assigned to certain places and are held responsible for that section. A group of four or five pickers may be assigned to a strip one rod wide. Eight to 12 such groups are supervised by a foreman, who walks up and down between the strips to see that the plants are picked clean and that few berries are dropped on the ground. Unless the picking is carefully supervised as much as 25 percent of the crop may be left on the vines by the workers. The pickers must work hard and fast during the brief season to make their employment profitable enough to meet their needs.

The method of keeping track of the harvest is simple. If 30,000 bushels of berries are to be picked in 40 working days it means that 750 bushels must be picked daily. With a force of 200 or 250 pickers the average is three to four bushels. As the picker presents a filled box he receives a numbered ticket. If the first ticket issued in the morning is No. 569 and the last one at night is No. 1,232 the grower knows that 663 measures have been harvested.

Recently a new method of picking, called scooping, has changed the labor problem on the bogs. A cranberry scoop has steel teeth so arranged that the operator can comb through the vines, catching the berries in a boxlike compartment. It is a heavy tool that requires handling by men. An ordinary laborer using a scoop can gather 6 to 12 bushels a day, while an expert can average 20 bushels.

The scooping method, used on more than half of the bogs in New Jersey, reduces the cost of labor and saves in housing and supervision. But there are disadvantages. More berries are dropped to the ground, and the vines are often damaged. Some growers have tried paying on an hourly basis instead of by piece rates. This slows up the work somewhat, but makes it more thorough.

Cranberries should be picked and handled only when dry and should be kept at an even temperature during storage. A temperature of 34 to 40 degrees is desirable. The berries are placed in storehouses built to allow free circulation of air. During cool nights the doors are left open, and then closed by day to retain the cool air. Some of the elaborate storehouses are fitted with cold storage walls.

Methods of cultivating and marketing the cranberry have been vastly improved since the formation of the American Cranberry Exchange, which functions as a selling agency for its members. All the important cranberry growers are members of the exchange and benefit from the information it distributes impartially. New discoveries in producing methods, disease control or handling of labor problems become common property. There was a time when an individual grower regarded any improvement he had worked out as his personal property to be used in competition. Now the growers work together to prevent glutting the market and to develop better methods of production. In addition, the exchange has developed an extensive advertising program to interest consumers in the cranberry's place in the everyday diet.

The canning of cranberries has also become a profitable industry in this State. About 20% of the crop is packed as canned cranberries, cranberry jelly or cranberry cocktail.

Some of the New Jersey bogs have odd names. One, a few miles south of Toms River, is known as Double Trouble. The story is that a minister lived at this little settlement on Cedar Creek many years ago. Whenever the muskrats burrowed through the dam it was his job to make repairs. Once the muskrats dug two tunnels at the same time. Exasperated upon finding twin leaks, the minister cried: "Here's double trouble!" The name stuck.

JERSEY TOMATOES

The long white road cuts through the fields of green plants hung thickly with bright red tomatoes. Up and down the rows men and women, young girls and boys stoop over the heavily laden bushes plucking the fruit from the stems and piling it up in baskets. All day they keep at their task in the hot sun, calling pleasantly to one another, or singing now and then to while away the long hours. A steady procession of wagons and motor trucks winds down the road, each vehicle piled high with a tottering load of baskets. All day and night the wagon train moves in a steady stream toward the canneries and the waiting city markets.

In five of the southern counties of New Jersey—Gloucester, Salem, Burlington, Cumberland and Camden—33,000 acres of tomato fields stretch mile after mile, each field sprinkled with its group of industrious pickers, its piles of overflowing baskets. In Monmouth, Mercer and Middlesex Counties, too, there are great tomato fields.

During the picking season, July to October, South Jersey looks as though it had been invaded by an army of gypsies. From Philadelphia and other nearby cities whole families move into the district and spend the summer traveling from farm to farm. They camp in temporary quarters supplied for them. The parents and all the children large enough to work spend their days in the fields.

Grandmothers of today can remember when a tomato was considered poisonous. They were called "love apples"

TOMATO PICKING IN THE FIELD

because they were used in France in courtship as a token
of love. The tomato then was a far smaller fruit than that
now grown. It is only within the last 50 years that the
large, luscious and highly nutritive product of today has
been deveolped.

The tomato was discovered in South America by the
Conquistadors, who introduced it to Europe. About 1600
the Italians discovered its value in making sauces, especially for spaghetti, and no one has been able to surpass
them in this particular use of it. The rest of the civilized
world was content to let the Italians take the risk of poi-
soning, and it was not until the middle of the 19th century that the tomato was considered seriously as a food.
People began growing a few plants in their gardens, but
no one thought of a tomato farm. The first seeds found
their way to New Jersey from Florida in 1812, when Dr

Ephraim Buck of Cumberland County began experimenting with them.

Few other foods can be enjoyed in so many different forms. Cooked, pickled or raw tomatoes are equally tasty and healthful. New Jersey, about 1931, first produced for sale the latest form of this valuable food—tomato juice. Sales of this delicious drink are mounting steadily.

Most farmers contract for their entire crop with the canning companies, of which there are 35 in New Jersey. Among the prominent canneries are the T. J. Ritter Company and E. Pritchard Inc. of Bridgeton, the Edgar F. Hurff Company of Swedesboro, the H. J. Heinz Company at Salem, and the Campbell Soup Company at Camden. The farmer and the canning company agree on the number of acres to be planted and the price that a certain grade of fruit will bring.

Tomatoes are divided into two acceptable classes according to standards set up by the United States Department of Agriculture for tomato canning and the manufacture of strained tomato products. Except for the elimination of decayed and green tomatoes, called culls, the grower is not required to grade his own crop. Ton loads of tomatoes arriving by truck, train or boat at the canneries are graded by inspectors from the New Jersey State Department of Agriculture. These men, trained in the inspection of cannery tomatoes and other farm produce, are licensed by the Department of Agriculture at Washington. Three baskets are taken at random from each truck and examined. Upon determining the percentage of culls and of grades one and two by their proportionate weights, the inspector presents certificates showing the percentage of each grade to both the canner and the grower.

If the shipment does not meet with the specifications in the contract, the canner may reject it; or if he accepts the load anyway, he pays for it according to the percentage of each grade. When there is more than 10 percent of culls in the crop, the canner usually refuses it. The inspector has nothing to do with rejecting the shipment; he merely determines its quality. Payment for his services is made to the State Department of Agriculture by the canner, or by the canner and the grower together.

Throughout the picking season the roads leading to Camden, Bridgeton, Salem and other canning centers are crowded with trucks waiting to approach the weighing platforms. Sometimes the lines stretch for seven miles. The success of a farmer's harvest is reckoned by the tons of tomatoes an acre. An average tomato field will yield four or five tons an acre, but farmers who use scientific methods of propagation and cultivation have raised this to eight and often to twelve or more tons. In 1937 the farmers of New Jersey received $2,012,000 from the canning companies for their tomato crop.

There is in New Jersey an organization, called the 10-Ton Canhouse Tomato Club, composed of growers who have cultivated at least five acres and produced 10 tons of tomatoes per acre. Sponsored by the Canners' Association, the State Horticultural Society and the State College of Agriculture, the group accepted for membership 70 qualified growers in 1936. In the following year only three growers were admitted because the crop had been damaged by rainy weather. The club publishes an annual report from which other farmers may learn the successful methods followed by those who obtain the highest yields. Individual members write accounts telling what sort of fertilizers and seed or plants they used, how and when

hey planted and cultivated their crops, and what methods
hey found most effective in fighting disease and pests.

The larger canning companies maintain farms and laboratories where they experiment with different types of
tomato plants. Through careful selection of parent seed
stock and crossbreeding, they have developed heavy, juicy
tomatoes with better color and flavor, especially desirable
for the manufacture of tomato juice. Scientists at the New
Jersey Agricultural Experiment Station have also made
valuable contributions to the development of improved
high-yielding varieties which are adapted to New Jersey's
soil and climate.

New and improved strains are constantly being developed by the process of crossbreeding. When a promising
plant has developed enough to have some small green
fruit and some buds and blossoms, the fruit is all cut off
so that the strength will go into the remaining blossoms.
Instead of allowing the plant to pollenize itself, the sta-
mens in the blossoms are removed with surgical tweezers.
The flower clusters are then tied up in little balloons of
oiled paper or fine cheesecloth and allowed to develop.
This protects them from receiving pollen borne from
other flowers or plants of unknown parentage.

When the buds are in full bloom, pollen from selected
plants is applied to the style of the pistil of each flower.
The coverings are then replaced. These experimental
plants are then staked and tied, and the fruit is allowed
to develop. A record is kept of the qualities exhibited.
Seed selections to reproduce this strain are based on the
quality of the fruit in terms of flavor, color and ability
to yield heavily.

After eight years of such scientific selection and crossbreeding, in 1934 the New Jersey Agricultural Experi-

The Best Tomatoes Have Thick Walls and Few Seeds

ment Station developed a super-tomato which they named
"Rutgers" in honor of Rutgers University, with which
the Station is affiliated. The Rutgers Tomato has advantages which make it desirable to all concerned with tomato
production. Because it ripens from the center out, it provides excellent fruit for the manufacture of a richly
colored tomato juice. Its firm body contains few seeds and
is finely flavored. It can be picked early in July, and it
grows with an abundance of foliage which protects it from
sunscald. This last factor is especially important, because
the bleaching rays of the sun cause heavy damage to un-
protected plants. Analysis of the Rutgers variety has

hown it to have a high content of mineral salts, iron, alcium and phosphorus.

Farmers buy crossbred plants from the experimental arms maintained by the canning companies and from lant nurseries. The tomato plants are certified by official nspectors to be true to type and free from disease. Two arms of the Campbell Soup Company, for example, one t Riverton and another in Georgia, supplied 50,000,000 omato plants to New Jersey farmers in 1936. Many New ersey tomato growers and most members of the 10-Ton anhouse Tomato Club use southern-grown plants in their elds. Plants are delivered to Jersey farmers 40 hours fter leaving southern soil.

When home-grown plants are used, the seed is sown uring the first weeks of March so that plants of good uality may reach the fields by the middle of May. Usu-lly, before planting, the seed is treated with a solution f mercuric chloride and then coated with red copper xide dust. Under certain conditions the soil is also steri-zed by steam or a solution of formaldehyde to prevent lantbed diseases.

After the seedbeds have been prepared for planting, the eed is sown in rows in order to permit air and sunlight reach the entire plant. The sowing is done either in ats of soil, in coldframes or in hotbeds heated by pipes. he heat in the hotbeds is controlled so that the growth f the plants may be speeded up or delayed. In the flats e seed is covered with one quarter of an inch of soil and atered through a burlap bag to prevent the seeds from eing washed away. Then the flat is covered with paper r a few days to hold in moisture and heat until the seed as begun to develop.

Temperature, moisture and ventilation are important in

the cultivation of tomatoes. Requiring a day temperatur
of from 75 to 85 degrees Fahrenheit and a night tempera
ture of 65, the plants are susceptible to disease if watere
too much or too often. A good ventilation system, regu
lating temperature and humidity, reduces and often pre
vents the spread of plantbed diseases. During cold weathe
it is often necessary to protect the seedbeds by coverin
them with waterproof tarpaulin cloth or salt hay. Th
salt hay, which is gathered in the New Jersey marshe
is more effective than the burlap bags, wooden shutters c
straw mats used by some farmers.

Tomato fields are prepared in April by thorough plov
ing and harrowing. Fertilizers containing the necessar
properly balanced plant foods are applied, and rows ar
marked off about four feet apart across the fields. In Ma
the plants are set out in the fields about four feet apar
in each row. Nearly 3,000 plants are required for eac
acre. They are "hardened-off" or acclimated to field co
ditions by removing the glass from the coldframes an
regulating irrigation.

Then the struggle begins against the natural enemie
that lie in wait. Particularly vicious is a variety of aph
which completely covers the plant and sucks out the sa
Other pests are cutworms, tomato horn and fruit worm
flea beetles and potato bugs. Many tomato growers kee
apace of the times by using sprayers and even airplanes fe
dusting the fields with poison to fight off these menaces.

After raising a fine crop of tomatoes, the farmer sti
has the problem of seeing that it is carefully picked ar
properly handled on the way to market and cannery. Fe
the canhouse he requires good, red ripe tomatoes. Whe
destined for distant markets the fruit is picked as soon
it begins to redden. For nearby markets it is permitted

ipen almost completely on the vine. Tomatoes that are not fully ripe when picked are allowed to stand in baskets for only one day. During this time they are kept under cover. This conserves the heat in the baskets and gives the fruit time to darken. The picker, like the grower, is paid according to the grade of tomatoes he gathers.

There are still farmers raising tomatoes by the hit and miss method; but the farmer who wants to produce the greatest yield per acre and market his crop with the big canning companies is the one who follows closely every scientific improvement in methods of propagation and cultivation.

BABY CHICKS BY THE MILLION

New Jersey hens lay more than 36,000,000 dozen eggs annually, or enough to provide every man, woman and child in the State with 100 eggs a year. Once the farmer used to expect 60 eggs a year from his hens; now it is not unusual to get 200. A white Leghorn holds the records with 352 eggs a year, almost one each day! This amazing improvement in laying capacity is the result of scientific breeding, which produces a "pedigreed" chicken.

Next to dairying, poultry raising is the most important agricultural business in the State. The area around Vineland, in Cumberland County, has been called the Egg Basket of New Jersey; in this one section alone 3,500 poultry farms yield products worth $1,750,000 annually.

Although many New Jersey farmers are today producing their own chicks, there are still great hatcheries that ship chicks throughout the Middle Atlantic and New England States. In the center of the Vineland area is the Wene Chick Farm, which produces almost 3,000,000 chicks a year. They are packed the day they are hatched in corrugated containers, 25 chicks into each of the four compartments, which are padded with wood wool to absorb the droppings and to protect the baby chicks against the cold. A newborn chick has absorbed enough strength from the egg to do without food for some time, so that it may safely be shipped when only a day old to considerable distances. Only the sturdiest chicks are shipped

BATTERY OF INCUBATERS

Those which are not able to stand squarely on their feet on the incubator trays are immediately destroyed.

The Kerr Chickeries, which ship by the same method, has a 240-acre farm at Frenchtown in Hunterdon County. Its battery of incubators, looking like a row of giant refrigerators, have a capacity of 1,100,000 eggs. These mechanical hens, with temperature, moisture and ventilation regulated electrically, each holds 52,000 eggs. Real motherhood has gone out of fashion in the poultry business.

Eggs are taken from the nests as soon as they are laid and placed in the incubator, where it takes three weeks to hatch them, just as long as it takes when set under a hen. Before science took a hand in chicken farming the Biddy of the barnyard, after she had laid about a dozen eggs in the spring, would set on them and, feeling that one job at a time was enough, would stop laying. Now she has no

ONE DAY OLD

excuse to take a vacation. In fact, by using electric lights
poultry farmers lengthen the days for the hens. The
longer the day, the more they eat; and the more they
eat, the more eggs they lay.

In both of these great egg baskets of the State the
methods of poultry raising are the same. The business has
developed from the haphazard to the scientific. In the old
days the farmer kept chickens merely as a side line, feeding them with anything handy, letting them drink when
they pleased, and lay where and when they pleased. If the
flock increased beyond the needs of his family he sold eggs
and chickens wherever he could.

The layout of the Kerr plant is typical of the large
up-to-date poultry farm. Of the 240 acres about 80 are
planted with wheat and corn for feeding. The rest is used
for free range, brooding, and housing the breeders.

Many smaller farms which raise chickens for their own use or for selling in the neighborhood use the same methods on a smaller scale.)

During the busy season, January to July, a force of 60 men is required to carry on the various operations connected with the business. One of the most important steps is the blood testing of each bird so as to base selection of the parent stock on standards of health and vigor. These tests are taken by trained experts within a five-month period before the hatching season. Each hen is tagged with a numbered metal leg band; a sample of its blood is taken from beneath the wing, collected in a test tube bearing the same number and sent to the laboratory for testing. If traces of Pullorum disease are found in any of the samples, the bird, identified by its number, is removed from the flock and disposed of. This is called "culling out the reactors."

Pullorum disease is incurable; but, because it is inheritable, it can be controlled by destroying carriers of the germ. If the disease is not checked a whole flock may be wiped out. Any survivors will carry the germ and endanger the next generation. Diseased chickens are likely to be low egg producers.

Although Kerr Chickeries is the only hatchery in the state maintaining its own laboratory, there are many smaller chicken farms making use of the same scientific methods of breeding. These send samples for blood testing to the laboratory of the Bureau of Animal Industry of the Department of Agriculture.

Another important phase of chicken farming is the breeding of hens for high egg production. This is developed by a process called "trap nesting." When the hen goes on the nest to lay an egg a door springs into place and holds her until she is identified by her number and a record made of her laying. Those who produce more than the average number of eggs are separated from the rest of the flock so that their eggs can be used for breeding purposes. Trap nesting birds requires expensive equipment and extra help to keep watch over the nests and make the records. But it has enabled poultry farmers to improve their stock.

There are many varieties of domestic chickens. Among the more common breeds classed as white-shelled egg producers are the Leghorns and Minorcas. The Leghorns originated in Leghorn, Italy. This breed is used on large scale commercial egg farms throughout the country. The white-shelled eggs they produce bring a top price in many markets. The Minorcas are probably the second most popular breed of the white egg type. There are also large flocks of Rhode Island Reds, New Hampshire Reds and Barred Plymouth Rocks maintained for both egg and meat production. These are known as dual-purpose breeds.

Although 90% of the poultry raising in New Jersey is concerned with egg production, some poultry farms specialize in raising chickens for meat. The Plymouth Rock, Rhode Island Red and Wyandotte are all highly desirable meat breeds. The Jersey Giant, which originated in New Jersey, is developed largely from Asiatic stock. It is similar to the Plymouth Rock in type, but is longer, deeper and broader. This particular breed, confined mostly to farms in the central section of the State, is in great demand for roasters and capons.

New Jersey poultrymen, by their progressive methods of production, aided by the experimental work being done at Rutgers University and by the marketing program of the State Department of Agriculture, have brought the State to first rank in the value of poultry per acre.

DAIRY FARMING IN NEW JERSEY

The cows of Sussex are the most important element in the county. Not only are there more dairy cattle than people, but there is ample evidence that the people regard them with great respect. Housed in modern buildings, their fodder, care and comfort sedulously watched, these animals accept calmly the devotion they receive. Sussex County farmers have proved that the care they lavish on their cattle is well worth while; for these cows are among the most productive in the Nation, with an average annual yield per animal of about 3,010 quarts.

There are several factors which have contributed to New Jersey's rank in this important branch of agriculture. The great metropolitan areas of New York and Philadelphia within easy distance over fine roads are ready markets for the products of New Jersey farmers.

It takes more than a generous supply, however, to satisfy milk consumers. The public has been educated to demand that milk fulfill certain requirements: that it have sufficient food content, and be fresh and clean. Pure, fresh milk comes from healthy, carefully handled and well-fed cows. Therefore, from pasture land to milk wagon or grocery store, every step of milk production is checked by State authorities, local health boards and conscientious producers. Indeed, the growth of the industry in this and other States may generally be attributed to the confidence with which people can use milk and milk products.

Other States with dairy farms at a greater distance

A Sussex County Dairy Farm

from market convert much of their milk into butter, cheese and evaporated canned milk, but New Jersey's dairy farmers take advantage of the short haul to market in glass or stainless steel-lined trucks and deliver practically all of their milk in fluid form within a few hours of milking.

New Jersey farmers have been greatly aided by the New Jersey State Agricultural Experiment Station organized in 1880, which, through research and experiment, has raised the standard of the State's agricultural products.

On the experimental farms at New Brunswick and at Beemerville, in Sussex County, the State maintains large herds of cattle for testing methods of breeding and feeding. It is to the intelligent supervision of State authorities as well as to their own energy and care that New Jersey's dairy farmers of today can attribute their success.

Although Sussex County leads the State in milk production and in cow population, dairy farming is conducted generally throughout New Jersey. In the northern section, where much of the ground is rolling and unsuited for cultivated crops, many farms are devoted exclusively to dairying; but in the southern sections, where the farms yield tomatoes, potatoes, beans and other garden produce, dairying accounts for only part of the income.

The flood of 408,000,000 quarts of milk produced by New Jersey's 136,000 cows in 1937 reached the New York and Philadelphia metropolitan areas from two great milksheds: that from the northern section of the State supplying the New York area and from the southern section supplying Philadelphia and New Jersey suburbs.

Coastal cities receive a considerable supply from the dairy farms in the "Cream Ridge Area" in counties bordering the shore. In the summertime, when their population increases substantially, large quantities of milk are diverted from both the Philadelphia and New York milksheds to the shore.

The metropolitan areas of New York and Philadelphia and the smaller cities surrounding them have imposed strict regulations governing their milk supply. This was not always so. The time was when the typical dairy was housed in a stable next door to a distillery or brewery, from where the dairyman obtained waste grain to feed his cattle. Rising land values and more stringent sanitary regulations both operated to drive the industry into the country, increasing the average distance from cow to customer from ten miles a generation ago to 50 miles today. Improved methods of transportation, refrigeration and preservation also facilitated this trend.

Important in this respect was the work of Louis Pasteur, the French scientist who in 1871 startled the world by announcing the discovery of a method for destroying the organisms in milk which caused it to turn sour or depreciate rapidly in quality. Progressive New Jersey dairymen were quick to sense the value of this discovery, and pasteurization became common practice in this State before the close of the 19th century.

Prior to this time inadequate use of milk, and in some cases use of impure milk, had been factors in infant mortality. About 1900 Nathan Straus, the philanthropist, began a crusade to provide milk for the needy. He established free milk stations in New York City to distribute milk processed by the Pasteur method. The resulting decline in the infant death rate convinced the public of the food value of milk and the desirability of using milk treated in this way. Today milk must be pasteurized before it is admitted into any well-regulated area, unless it has met the still more rigid requirements of certified milk.

Pasteurization consists in heating milk to a temperature of 142 to 145 degrees Fahrenheit, keeping it at that heat for half an hour, and reducing it rapidly to a temperature of 50 degrees. By this process the milk is freed of any harmful bacteria while little if any of its nutritive value is eliminated. There is evidence that pasteurization does destroy some of the scant vitamin C in milk, but orange juice has the same vitamin in abundance, and the loss can therefore be compensated.

Certified milk does not require pasteurization, because it is produced under such rigid supervision that any danger of infection is reduced to a minimum. In 1909, five years after it had pioneered in America by introducing certified milk, New Jersey enacted a law governing its production.

Certified milk is expensive to produce and therefore has a limited market. At present there are only five or six farms in the State producing this grade of milk. Each of these farms is under the direct supervision of a board of five physicians known as the Medical Milk Commission. They superintend the activities of a chemist, a veterinarian, a physician, a bacteriologist and a sanitary inspector, who check every step in the production. The chemist sees that the milk contains at least 4% of butterfat; the veterinarian tests the cattle for disease and rejects from the herd any cow which is not in perfect health or which produces less than three quarts of milk a day; the bacteriologist superintends blood tests and bacteria counts; the physician examines the men who handle the milk at least once every six months and visits the plant at least once a week to guard against communicable disease; and the sanitary inspector sees that the barn equipment and the surroundings comply with the specifications of the law as to light, air and cleanliness.

Uniforms worn by the men are examined, utensils are carefully checked for contamination and rust, and the corners and crannies of the barns are investigated. After such control, one can be quite sure that milk from certified farms is pure. In addition, certified milk must be delivered to the consumer no later than 36 hours after production.

More extensively distributed are the New Jersey Official Grade A Pasteurized and Grade A Raw, standards for which were set on August 31, 1931, by the State Department of Agriculture. If a dealer wants the approval of the State and the right to cap his bottles with the official cover, bearing an outline map of the State and the legend, *"New Jersey Official Grade A Pasteurized"* or *"New Jersey Official Grade A Raw,"* he must comply with the regulations specified by the Department of Agriculture.

New Jersey Grade A milk must contain no less than 3½% butterfat and no less than 12% in solids. It must be cooled to 50 degrees not later than 60 minutes after production. Delivery to the consumer must be made within 48 hours, in mechanically filled and capped bottles or single service containers. All herds are subject to the cooperative supervision of the State and Federal Departments of Agriculture, and all cows must be tuberculin tested periodically. The dairy employees are examined twice a year.

These premier grades of milk, however, constitute only about 30% of the milk sold in New Jersey. Grade B, most commonly used, is subject to standards set by the communities in which it is sold. The milk companies that gather the product from widely scattered farms are responsible to the health authorities of the communities in which they distribute milk. For their own protection, therefore, they must keep the farms which supply them under close supervision. They impose regulations as to housing, fodder, health and handling of the cows. The farmer who hopes to sell his product through a first class dealer dare not become careless or allow any contamination to creep into his herd.

In general, dairy farmers fall into two classes: the producer and the produce-dealer. The first has only to cool the milk immediately to 60 degrees Fahrenheit or below and deliver it to the distributor's creamery. There it is tested, weighed, and piped into an insulated truck where it will be kept cold until it reaches the pasteurization plant. A producer-dealer must cool his milk, pasteurize it if it is not to be sold as raw, bottle it, and then make deliveries. There are about 800 of these producer-dealers in New Jersey.

After the milk has been cooled a small amount may go to a machine called the separator for the extraction of cream. The milk is whirled around in a metal container. Centrifugal force drives the milk, which is heavier than cream, to the outer edge where it is drawn off, while the cream finds an exit near the center. The skim milk is used for cultured milks, cheese or animal feeding.

The large dealers, who obtain their supply from many producers, organize their plants so that the milk passes from one process to another without exposure to the air or human touch, and with amazing speed. Drawn from the trucks, it goes directly by way of pipes into the pasteurization tanks. From there it passes through a series of artificially cooled pipes and is immediately bottled by a high-speed automatic process which fills and caps 120 bottles a minute.

The last word in high speed production of milk is the Walker-Gordon farm at Plainsboro, near Princeton. At this highly organized "milk factory" every step of the process, literally from the ground up, is studied to effect the production of the best quality milk with maximum efficiency. Here the cattle are housed in clean barns, in a setting of sunny pasture land. The soil of the fields where fodder is grown is fed with the minerals necessary to supply nutritious crops so that, although confined to the barn, the cows are assured a balanced diet. When the fodder is cut it is dehydrated mechanically. This method eliminates the moisture quickly and preserves more of the elements that make for better milk than is possible by sun drying. The fodder is then stored away in silos as tall as five-story buildings until the time of use. At that time a train of small carts carries it from the silos to the clean, white barns where it is fed in accurate quantities to the cows. The cows, clipped, clean and manicured, eat their fill and

THE ROTOLACTOR

then are led to a unique device in mechanical production of milk—the rotolactor.

This giant electric contrivance, capable of milking 250 cows an hour, is comparable to the assembly line in an automobile plant. Three times a day the cows are driven from the barns or pastures through a covered runway and are literally "taken for a ride;" for the rotolactor is a revolving platform, a merry-go-round for cows. As the platform turns, the cow steps on, her head is secured in a stanchion, and she is given a mechanical shower bath. As she continues her circular trip she is dried by an attendant in a white uniform; then she passes an attendant who takes a sample of her milk and examines it. Should it appear abnormal in any way, the cow is not milked in the rotolactor. If the cow passes muster, the milking device is applied. This is a rubber nipple which draws the milk

rom the cow mechanically and pumps it into a large
terilized jar attached to the side of her stall. The milking
ontinues as the platform revolves.

Meanwhile, one by one, more cows step into place on
he platform and go through the routine. When a cow
as completed the revolution she is released, a record of
er milk is taken, and the milk is discharged through a
anitary sluice direct to the coolers. The rotolactor is in
he center of an air-conditioned room with tiled walls and
loor. Above the "merry-go-round" is a glass-enclosed
oom from which visitors may observe every step of the
rocess.

But care, cleanliness and food are not the only fac-
ors to be considered by the dairy farmer. Since he is in
he milk business, he must see that he is operating effi-
iently. This means a study not only of the process and
he equipment, but also of the materials which go to make
is product. And it is, after all, the cows which make the
iilk. The amount of milk yielded by a cow varies with
he breed and the physical condition of the animal. In
New Jersey, Holsteins and Guernseys predominate, but
here are also many important Jersey, Ayrshire and
rown Swiss herds. There are 24 cow-testing associations
nder State supervision recording production of milk and
onsumption of feed and planning continual improve-
ents in methods of breeding and feeding. It is gener-
lly felt that an animal possessing a wide barrel, which
s the part of the body between the shoulder and the
ips, a wide muzzle and mouth, velvety skin, and coming
rom a family long established as a plentiful producer of
iilk, will turn out to be a good investment. A first class
ow will give an average of 10 to 15 quarts a day.

The question of what is a reasonable profit for farmer

and dealer and a fair price for the consumer has resulted in considerable conflict. In some States there have been violent disturbances and destruction of property by farmers, who complained that they were not receiving enough for their milk to pay them to produce it. Because New Jersey's dairy investment in land, buildings and equipment approaches $100,000,000, one-third of the agricultural investment of the State, and the annual yield comes close to $25,000,000, it was thought necessary in 1933 to create a Milk Control Board to regulate the price of milk from farm to table. The board, composed of five persons appointed by the Governor, has fixed the prices of milk in the various areas of New Jersey. It regulates the price the processer must pay to the farmer, the price he can collect from the subdealer or storekeeper, and the final price the consumer must pay when he goes to the store or orders from his milkman.

The progressive farmer bases his calculation on the average yearly production of every animal in his herd. He checks his fodder, pasturage and equipment carefully. He knows about how much milk to expect from each cow in a year, and he knows that this must represent substantially more than the cost of feeding a cow. At his disposal he has the facilities and the experiments of the State agricultural agencies in feeding and caring for cattle.

In addition to the problems of milk production, the scientists are conducting constant research to introduce new elements into milk, or alter it to meet special needs. The vitamin content of milk can now be increased by artificial means. The addition of colonies of certain bacteria produces cultured milk, particularly suited to certain types of digestive disorders.

So that the New Jersey of the future shall not lack its

quota of capable farmers, the 4-H Clubs, organized under the Agricultural Extension Service, are doing valuable work in educating boys and girls in the best methods of agriculture. The clubs are divided according to the various branches of agriculture. The 4-H Dairy clubs are composed of young people from the ages of 10 to 21 who meet regularly to receive training and discuss the various phases of cattle raising. A member must own at least one purebred dairy animal no younger than four months or older than five years. This calf is raised according to the most progressive methods, fed the best available forage, and, if a good milk producer, is entered in one of the local, county or State 4-H contests. The highest reported record of milk from a cow bred by a 4-H member was 6,616 quarts, more than twice the State average of 3,000 quarts.

For those children who cannot borrow the money for a calf from their parents the New Jersey Junior Pure Breeders' Fund was established in 1921 by former Senator J. S. Frelinghuysen and Julius Forstmann. This fund, originally of $30,000, has enabled 1,318 young people to take up dairying. The amount loaned does not exceed $100, and the interest is 6%. By taking advantage of this fund, and by buying an animal under the supervision of the county club agent, the youngster is fairly certain of a profitable venture. Many of the members of 4-H have gone on to the colleges of agriculture and to the ownership of large and thriving farms, applying to excellent purpose the first lessons learned under the banner of Head, Hands, Heart, and Health.

JERSEY PEACHES

The reputation of a peach depends not only on its beauty but on its flavor. For the last 32 years the job of making peaches taste better has been carried on most effectively in New Jersey, but the history of the improvement of peaches extends far back to ancient China, where some of the rarest specimens can still be obtained. New Jersey has been building toward better-tasting and better-looking peaches to increase the income of the peach growers in the State.

One of the oldest fruits known to man, the peach was once reserved only for the tables of emperors and nobles. During the Crusades they were brought from China, India and Persia by caravan, and later they were grown in Spain and England. By extensive culture they became more common, spread throughout Europe and were brought to America by early colonists. It is certain from early letters and writings that the peach flourished throughout New Jersey in the 18th century.

The peach growers in the Colonies from Delaware to Connecticut were more successful than the Europeans. Though at first the crop was limited and probably of little commercial value, the industry developed by experimentation. In 1806 the catalogue issued by Daniel Smith of Burlington, one of the first fruit tree nurserymen of record in America, listed 67 varieties of peaches. It was not until 1823, however, that Nation-wide attention was directed to a New Jersey peach. In that year a Mr. Gill—

then residing on Broad Street in Newark—developed the Grosse Mignonne peach, which originated in France. Michael Floy, a Hunterdon County farmer, obtained several of Gill's peach buds, grafted them to his own stock and renamed his fruit the George IV, in honor of the King of England, patron of peach breeding and honorary president of the London Horticultural Society. In 1824 he sent a sample of this peach to the Society, where it was recognized as a valuable new variety.

New Jersey grew in importance as a peach-growing State with the development of such varieties as the Early and Late Crawford, named for a peach grower of Middletown. In the middle of the 19th century most of the orchards were in Hunterdon and Warren Counties, but during the next 50 years the industry shifted to the southern part of the State.

By the turn of the 20th century the industry had almost gone. Attacked by fruit pests known as the San Jose scale, peach yellow and peach borer, peach trees were dying by the thousands. Returns had dwindled to such an extent that growers were neglecting their orchards, and it seemed that New Jersey farmers would soon lose this once important source of revenue.

This was the situation in 1906 when Maurice A. Blake, a young professor of horticulture in the New Jersey Agricultural College at New Brunswick, began to investigate the cause of the decline.

After making a preliminary investigation, he established a research and demonstration orchard at High Bridge. In 1908 another peach orchard was set up on the grounds of the Training School at Vineland, and a third was later established at the College Farm at New Brunswick. In these orchards large scale experiments were carried on, while Blake kept an eye on the crops of other peach-producing States and the prices their products brought in the market. He decided that the only hope for New Jersey peach growers was to develop new varieties that were particularly suited to New Jersey climate and soil.

No one realized better than Professor Blake that this was a task that would take years of patient work. At the Vineland Training School, in 1914, peach trees were imported from many foreign lands and from other States for crossbreeding. The new seedlings that developed from the crossbreeding were numbered, examined and tested not only in the experimental orchards but on private farms in various sections of the State. Not until Professor Blake was positive of the results and possibilities of any one seedling was a peach given a name.

Today, at New Brunswick, Blake has control of the largest peach-breeding grounds in the world. On 20 acres of land he has planted and propagated the most widely diversified collection of the fruit in existence. A total of 350 named peach varieties have been tested, and no fewer than 20,000 peach trees have borne fruit in these orchards. There are nearly 4,000 peach seedlings under preliminary observation, and experimentation still goes on.

Most famous, most delicious, and the highest-priced of Blake's crossbreedings is the Golden Jubilee peach. It received its name from the fact that the "Mother Jubilee" tree first bore fruit about August 17, 1925, on the 50th anniversary of the formation of the New Jersey Horticultural Society. Eighteen years is a ripe old age for a peach tree (the average life is from 12 to 14 years), but in 1938 the "Mother Jubilee" tree still yielded her fruit. No one knows the extent of her family, but in this State alone it constitutes about one-fourth of the industry.

MOTHER JUBILEE TREE

Among some of the important species and varieties developed at the College Farm under Professor Blake's direction are several of rather curious shape. One of these, the Peen-to or Saucer peach, of China, is broad, shaped somewhat like a flat tomato. Another curious peach introduced from China is called the Eagle's Beak because of its long, curved tip. The flesh is very sweet, much like the so-called Honey peaches, also from China. A third is the result of the crossbreeding of the Chinese Blood (an immense peach with blood-red flesh, but rather acid flavor) with the Sargent's Chinese, a variety which is white, almost free of red color, and exceedingly sweet.

The New Jersey Station is now experimenting with crossbreeding the J. H. Hale, a large, well-known variety, and Prunus Kansuensis, a bush peach obtained from the mountains of Tibet by plant explorers of the United States Department of Agriculture. This wild peach can withstand the cold when in blossom better than the domestic varieties. If the hardiness of the bush peach from the Orient can be combined with the size and flavor of the home peach, the season in New Jersey will be lengthened.

The latest sensational product of Professor Blake's developments is the improvement of the nectarine. This is a peach without fuzz, often seen on the fruit stands. It has a delicious flavor, but it tends to be smaller than the peach.

Five counties in the southern part of the State supply the majority of the industry's output: Burlington, Cumberland, Camden, Atlantic and Gloucester. Many tourists visit this section in the spring to see the flowering trees that stretch for miles. The peaches are sold in various centers of these peach-growing counties (Glassboro, Hammonton, etc.) at peach auctions and then shipped to the nearby markets in Philadelphia and New York.

One step which helped the growth of the industry was the formation, in 1929, of the New Jersey Peach Council, an organization of leading peach growers who distributed 226,000 peach trees (mostly to Jerseymen) for testing under commercial conditions. Results from experiments with new varieties have encouraged growers to increase their plantings.

Today New Jersey, the fourth smallest State, is the fourth largest peach producer with an annual output of about 15,000,000 bushels. That is enough to supply a peach pie to every school child in America, every day for a month. "Jersey Peaches" are once more market favorites.

INDUSTRY

THE VANISHED BOG-IRON INDUSTRY

The "Pine Barrens" of New Jersey, a fan-shaped section spreading over parts of Ocean, Monmouth, Burlington, Atlantic and Cape May Counties, is a region of silent woods and bogland, of lazy streams and sluggish rivers. With cranberries, blueberries, and a few other crops the inhabitants manage to wrest a bare living from the swampy lands.

Once these woods resounded with the blows of axes, the shouts of workmen and the ring of anvils, as flames from charcoal burners, forges and furnaces lighted the sky. The streams, now trickling over the flat land, rushed vigorously enough to supply water power for the wheels of gristmills, sawmills, forges and furnaces. The rivers, shallow now and deserted, carried tall ships with heavy cargoes on their way to New York, Philadelphia and other large centers.

This was the home of the bog-iron industry, which in the early history of the country gave New Jersey high rank in iron production. The metal dug from the banks of the streams and the beds of watercourses in southern New Jersey, while softer than the iron from the northern hills, had the advantage of being more easily mined and could be shipped quickly and cheaply to the outside markets. Land transportation, depending on horse- or mule-drawn wagons, was slower and very expensive. Twenty miles of road transportation cost 30 shillings a ton, whereas shipping the same distance cost only five shillings.

A successful bog-iron furnace required at least 20,000 acres of timberland for a constant supply of charcoal. The densely forested tracts, where the iron works were situated, were usually divided into sections of 1,000 acres each, one of which would furnish a year's supply of charcoal for a furnace. By the time the last section had been used up, trees on the first section had grown large enough to be cut.

Bog iron is found in the lowlands and meadows of many parts of the State where water tinged with vegetable matter percolates through beds of marl or strata containing iron deposits. The iron material is picked up by the water and held in solution in the form of iron oxide. As the water emerges from the ground and becomes exposed to the air the solids are precipitated and leave the reddish, muddy iron deposit along the banks of streams or in the beds of swamps and wet meadows. The process goes on continuously. An exhausted bed will renew itself in from 20 to 40 years.

As soon as the early settlers discovered the presence of iron deposits, they set about establishing forges and furnaces. By 1750 England was allowing the importation of American iron free of duty, and the iron could be shipped as ballast at a slight cost. But as early as 1719 English iron manufacturers had agitated to curtail the manufacture of iron goods in America. Nevertheless, iron works sprang up at various points throughout the colony, and during the Revolutionary War they were taxed to their capacity turning out much-needed cannon and other munitions for the Continental Army.

Compared to the vast production of today, the yield of iron before the 19th century seems insignificant. In 1783, according to a report written by Samuel Gustaf Hermelin, a Swedish engineer who had come here to investigate the iron industry, the entire annual pig-iron output of New Jersey, including that of the hard-iron furnaces in the north and the bog-iron furnaces in the south, amounted to only 3,500 tons. Today one New Jersey furnace alone produces more than 300,000 tons annually.

The bog-iron communities were set up much like the feudal estates of medieval Europe. Sometimes as many as 500 people would be living in one of these communities close to the furnace or forge in the heart of the woods. The center of communal life was the master's (manager's) home, called the "big house," usually an elaborate establishment with a vegetable patch and flower garden. Here the workmen brought their problems and grievances, and the stranger could always find supper and a night's lodging. Schools, stores, churches, sawmills and gristmills were built for the workers and their families. These were exempt from taxation only as long as they produced just enough for the needs of the community.

Skilled workers from the iron-producing countries of Europe were offered every inducement to immigrate, and yet their rate of pay seems ridiculously low today. Wages varied between $20 and $25 a month, paid mostly in goods. In some cases the price of goods such as flour and pork was marked up 25% over the wholesale cost, while such things as tea, coffee, cloth, sugar and rum, which were imported, were marked up 50%. Many preferred to work for lower wages in cash.

Much of the work was done by slaves and indentured servants, who were brought overseas under contract to pay off the cost of their passage in three years' time. During this period they were given food and lodging but no money. The ironmaster was obliged to supply them with a suit of new clothes when the three years were up.

Smelting and Forging

The ore was transported by wagons or floated downstream in barges to the nearest furnace for conversion into pig iron. The furnace, a four-sided stack of stone or brick, 20 feet or more in height, tapered from a 24-foot base to about a 16-foot peak. Where possible, the furnace was built against a rise in the land to permit the construction of an incline, or ramp, from the top of which the tons of charcoal, ore and lime could be passed into the structure to form alternate layers.

The fire was started, and "tub bellows," operated by water power from a nearby dammed stream, supplied a forced draft. As the ore heated, the vegetable matter was burned away, and the lime reacted on the hot iron salts to form molten iron.

The impurities rose to the surface as slag and flowed off through a tap hole at the top metal line. The molten metal, drawn off at the bottom of the furnace, was led through runners to the "sows" and "pigs," molds cut in the sandy floor. The sows, as the name implies, were larger than the pigs.

Near the furnace was the forge, where the pigs were heated and hammered into bar iron by a giant 400- to 600-pound hammer, which beat out the impurities. One end of the hammer was attached to a beam that was alternately lifted and dropped by a cam on the water wheel. The blacksmith who operated the heavy hammer was required to produce one ton of bar iron from 2,800 pounds of pig. For anything in excess of that amount he received extra pay; for any less he had to make up the deficit.

From the bar iron, by the same primitive, slow methods, were hammered out the pots, pans, kettles, fire irons and nails for the homes of the settlers, spikes for their ships and, later, cannon and munitions for the Continental Army. Early in the 19th century stoves, lampposts, water pipes and other iron articles were being manufactured. Day and night the glare from the fire glowed in the sky above the dark treetops. From about the middle of April, when the furnace was put in blast, there was no let-up in the work until January, when ice formed in the stream and stopped the water wheel. Then the furnace was blown out, and there was a celebration.

Some Early Furnaces

Charles Read, an enterprising politician, gave the South Jersey iron industry its greatest impetus. Collector of the Port of Burlington, a member of the Provincial Assembly, a Judge of the Supreme Court and an outstanding leader in public affairs, Read determined to become the greatest ironmaster of the Province. About 1750, having recognized the possibilities of the bog-iron resources, he set about developing the industry on some large tracts of land which he owned. Shortly, however, he was forced by poor health to dispose of much of his property and to leave his affairs in the hands of trustees, keeping only a part interest in some of the iron plants he had started. But the industry he had set in motion was to continue for 80 years and to attract to the unbroken forests thousands of people.

Four of the most important bog-iron works grew from Read's dream: Taunton, Aetna, Atsion and Batsto.

Taunton Furnace, about 11 miles southwest of Mount Holly, on what is now called Haines Creek, opened in 1766. Four years later Read offered it for sale, calling

INGOT AND DIGGER FROM TAUNTON FURNACE

attention to the fact that it had an advantage over many
other works farther back in the woods because transporta
tion to Philadelphia cost only 10 shillings a ton. The fur
nace, according to Read, had a capacity of 80 tons of pig
iron a month. The plant continued in operation until abou
1847, when the mill pond and the adjacent property wer
converted into a cranberry bog.

The second of Read's iron works, Aetna Furnace, whic
was in full operation by 1768, was about 10 miles from
Taunton, on the southwest branch of Rancocas Creek. I
is not certain just when this furnace closed, but by 179
the water power was being used to operate a gristmill an
sawmill, the foundations of which are still visible. Th
old dam has been rebuilt and the mill pond is now calle
Aetna Lake.

Atsion Forge, on Atsion River about 20 miles south
east of Medford, was an important one with a capacity c
150 or 200 tons of bar iron annually. During its earl
days many Indians from the Edge Pillock reservatio
three miles away, were employed there. After the Revo
lution the forge turned out pots and kettles of variou

OLD MILL AND POND AT BATSTO

sizes, as well as stoves. Two of these old stoves, made probably about 1815, are in the old First Presbyterian Church in Bridgeton. The products of the forge were carried to merchants in New York, Albany and Poughkeepsie on the *Atsion*, a schooner which ran regularly between the Mullica River and Albany. Unlike most of the south Jersey forges, the Atsion Furnace converted "mountain ores" from north Jersey as well as the bog ores, and in 1828 was getting $100 a ton for bar iron, as compared to the present price of about $20 a ton.

Batsto Furnace, established in 1766, figured conspicuously in an episode of the Revolutionary War commemorated by a monument near Chestnut Neck, an important Revolutionary shipping point on Mullica River. In October 1778 the British had made a surprise attack on the Chestnut Neck colony and destroyed the storehouse. Captain Ferguson set out with 800 British troops to dismantle Batsto Furnace, about 10 miles farther up the river, which was working at fever heat to make munitions for Washington's army. One of the patriots at Chestnut Neck, suspecting the plan, warned the commander of the militia. As the British pitched camp in the woods a few miles from the furnace, a general alarm was sounded by messengers riding furiously through the darkening countryside. By midnight a force of 90 woodsmen, iron-workers and farmers had gathered for an ambush. Almost every bullet found its man as the British advanced at dawn, and the invaders retired in confusion. Batsto and its stores were saved.

After the Revolution a glass works was built at Batsto, and a host of workmen were kept busy. An advertisement in a Philadelphia paper gives an idea of the variety of articles produced.

Manufactured at Batsto Furnace in West Jersey, and to be sold, either at the works or by the sub-scriber in Philadelphia: A great variety of iron pots, kettles, Dutch ovens, oval fish kettles, either with or without covers, skillets of different sizes, being much lighter, neater and superior in quality to any imported from Great Britain—potash, and other large kettles from 30 to 125 gallons; sugar mill-gudgeons neatly rounded and polished at the ends; grating bars of different lengths, grist-mill rounds; weights of all sizes from 7 to 56; Fuller's plates, open and closed stoves of different sizes, rag-wheel irons for saw-mills; pestles and mortars; sash-weights and forge hammers of the best quality. Also Batsto Pig-iron as usual, the quality of which is too well known to need any recommendation.

At Batsto also were made the iron pipes that replaced many miles of wooden water conduits in Philadelphia and

Camden in the early 19th century. The Batsto works continued in operation until 1848, when, like the other New Jersey forges and furnaces, it was forced out of business by the development of the Pennsylvania iron fields.

Relics and Remains

Batsto today is a ghost of the thriving settlement of a century ago. Beside the macadam road that runs through the lonely pine woods is an old mill where lumber is still sawed, and there are scattered frame houses, unpainted and weather-beaten, inhabited by families who barely manage to earn a living from odd jobs and small gardens. The old company store, a plain stucco building, is closed; the great stucco mansion with a tower, now owned by the Lippincott family of Philadelphia, is silent except for occasional week-end parties. The sound of water pouring through a gate beneath the bridge is all that disturbs the quiet.

Not even this much marks a site on Landing Creek, a branch of the Mullica River, opposite the present village of Lower Bank, where John Richards in 1813 established Gloucester Furnace, which employed about 125 workers. His uncle was Colonel William Richards, then owner of the Batsto and Atsion Furnaces. Once important as a stop on the stage route from Camden to Leed's Point on the seacoast, the village is slowly sinking into the dust. No one is left.

Only a few iron relics in the soil, the half-obliterated outlines of the furnace foundation and two long piles of slag among scraps of castings evidence the work that once went on here. The old sawmill is now a pile of decaying sawdust; a portion of a sluiceway and a rusted water wheel are the remaining parts of the gristmill; and the once broad Mullica River has narrowed into shallows.

In Ocean County, about seven miles south of Barnegat near the present village of Staffordsville, Stafford Forge Cranberry Bog now covers the site of old Stafford Forge. The forge was built on West Creek in 1797 by John Lippincott, who did a large business here for 10 years.

The bog-iron industry has been dead for more than 80 years. What has become of the furnaces, the villages, the communal life, the schools, the taverns? Where did the people go?

Today piles of slag, an occasional dam, a chimney, the foundations of a house, old cannonballs, crumbling remnants of forges and rotted splinters of the homes of the men who worked the bog-iron mines are all that remain of these once busy woodland villages. The forests echo only the sounds of birds, or the roar of motor cars on their way to and from the Jersey coast. The lonely rivers flow through miles of empty country, inhabited sparsely by people called "Pineys."

The section is traversed by highways, wide and hard surfaced, with signposts, gas stations—everything to provide comfort and safety for both car and driver. But off the road is the barren, fire-swept, decaying land of the "Pineys." Few tourists come here. There are no gas or electricity, no service stations, no billboards in the woods. The few road signs are dilapidated, and, more often than not, misspelled. It is a different world—this pine belt where once the bog-iron industry flourished. Apathy has settled on the land as on its inhabitants. They live close to modern progress, yet remote from it.

TWO CENTURIES OF GLASSMAKING

The early settlers on the American continent needed window glass badly. They were building log cabins and leaving rectangular openings in the walls which served well enough to let in the air and sunshine in the summer. But in the winter, when they needed all the sunshine they could get and less of the cold breezes, they had a problem on their hands. Some used oiled paper which let in a little light but, because it was very thin, also kept the cabin cold. Others tacked skins over the windows and endured the gloom all through the winter. Only the wealthiest traders and proprietors could afford glass for their windows, for it had to be imported, and the loss from breakage on the rough voyages made the cost prohibitive.

The glass industry was founded in New Jersey in 1738 by Caspar Wistar, an enterprising German button manufacturer from Philadelphia. There had been previous unsuccessful attempts to make glass in America in Jamestown, Virginia, New York State, Vermont and New Hampshire. Wistar came to New Jersey because it was ideally equipped for the manufacture of glass. It had a limitless supply of white sand to furnish the chief ingredient, silica, and acres of pine forest to provide charcoal for fuel.

When Wistar decided that opportunity was awaiting him across the Delaware in South Jersey, he lost no time in acquiring a parcel of land. A native of the glassmaking section of Germany, Wistar realized that if his new ven-

OLD WISTAR GLASS

ture was to be a success he would need expert workmen. He bargained with a sea captain, James Marshall, to bring from Europe workmen who would teach him and his assistants the secrets of their craft. In return for the formulas and their help he agreed to pay for their voyage, furnish them homes, food, servants, and give them a third of the profits of the enterprise. About three miles southeast of the present town of Alloway he built a glass furnace, workers' homes, a general store and a mansion house. The little settlement around the glass works soon came to be known as Wistarburgh.

At first Caspar Wistar and his artisans made only window glass, in five sizes; many kinds of bottles, lamp chimneys and drinking glasses. But, as their skill increased, they made ornaments in a great variety of shapes and colors. They developed a technique of decorating their colored glass objects with whorls of white or contrasting colors. The delicate tints of blue and green found in Wistarburgh glass have, according to many authorities,

never been reproduced, nor have other makers successfully copied the intricate designs that characterize this
antique glass, now a collectors' prize. The Wistarburgh
works also produced a great deal of glass in deep tones,
amber, brown and very dark green and blue. To Wistar
is given the credit for having been the first to produce
flint glass, a particularly clear glass made from powdered
flint. This term is now applied to any colorless glass made
with lead oxide, such as that used for windows.

So wide was the renown of this first glass plant that a
highway was constructed from Philadelphia to the doors
of the glass house. Stages brought the fashionable people
to watch the intricate process and to carry away as me-
mentos some of the novel ornaments produced. The tiny
scent bottles, favorites of the ladies of the day, were said
to be so small and delicately formed that they could be
slipped into a glove without being noticeable.

Caspar Wistar died in 1752, leaving the works to be
managed by his son, Richard. Richard seems, however, to
have preferred the city. He moved to Philadelphia and
left a manager in charge of the glass house. In his absence
the Wistarburgh works gradually declined. The depression that followed the Revolution finally forced it to close
its doors. Some of the secrets of the process that made
Wistar glass distinctive died with Richard Wistar in
1781.

But the Wistarburgh glass works had started an industry that spread rapidly throughout southern New Jersey.
Glassmakers, having learned the art, would set up in business for themselves or be lured away to other glass works
by promises of higher pay or better working conditions.
A glass plant was started at what was to become Glassboro, in the Township of Clayton, then a collection of

perhaps a dozen log cabins, by a German widow, Catherine Stanger, and her seven sons. They had learned their trade under the master craftsmen employed by Wistar. The Stangers founded their plant in 1775, and became famous for flasks, bottles and vials which were much in demand by distillers in Philadelphia and New York. The brothers proved capable glassmakers but poor business men. Only nine years after their plant was opened, it was purchased at a sheriff's sale by Thomas Heston and Thomas Carpenter. From them it passed to the Whitney Brothers and later to the Owens Bottle Works, subsidiary of the Owens-Illinois Glass Company, present operators of large plants in Bridgeton.

Despite the failure of New Jersey's two best-known glass manufacturers, the industry developed rapidly throughout the first part of the 19th century. The delicacy and artistry of the Wistar and Stanger products were replaced by more commonplace workmanship on a sounder business basis. Glassmakers pushed east into Cumberland County and concentrated their work at Bridgeton and Millville, which continue today to be the center of glass production in the State. The Whitall-Tatum Company of Millville bases its claim to the title of "the oldest glass plant in the United States" on its descent from a company founded there in 1806.

Attracted by the sand, fuel and water resources, glassmakers soon spread over the wide section. By 1837 they had moved into Atlantic County at Estelville and Hammonton. At about the same time important plants were in operation at Winslow and Clementon in Camden County and at Malaga in the eastern part of Gloucester County. In many cases bog-iron manufacturers set up glass houses near their furnaces.

About 1850 a syndicate of glass and iron interests was responsible for the construction of the Camden and Atlantic, South Jersey's first east-west railroad of any importance. At first it ran only as far east as Winslow, but in 1854 the road was extended to Absecon, which later became Atlantic City.

At the close of 1868 the number of glass factories in the State had risen to 13, with 10 furnaces producing about $1,000,000 worth of window glass, and 20 other furnaces capable of a yield of $1,500,000 worth of hollow-ware goods, plates, saucers, bowls and similar items.

In the boom days following the Civil War, a number of speculators came into South Jersey and set up glass works on little capital and less experience. Towns grew up overnight, only to be abandoned when the great financial panic in 1873 wiped out many of these manufacturers and hurt the glass industry in general. Two memorials to such enterprise are Hermann City and Bulltown. In 1873 the former was a boom town with at least 60 or 70 houses, a store and a hotel clustered around the glass plant. Before the year was out the town was little more than a crossroads spot. It is little more today. Rotting rails for cars that were never built, ruined kilns, cold for decades after a brief, intense heat, and crumbling wharves along the Mullica River are the unpleasant reminders today of the high hopes of Hermann City. Nor is there more at Bulltown. A few pieces of brick kilns mingled with glass on the sandy road are hardly enough to recall the demijohns and jugs made here for a brief time.

In addition to speculation, other factors contributed to the decline of the glass industry in southern New Jersey. Railroads and highways were slow in linking the region with the rest of the State and Nation. Coal had taken the place of wood as fuel for the glass furnaces, and freight charges from the coal fields of western Pennsylvania to New Jersey made the location of the industries in this State an unprofitable business. Finally, a more desirable pink sand was discovered in the Ohio Valley and in Illinois, closer to the source of fuel. Once again glassmakers followed the call of superior materials and cheaper rates, and gradually Ohio and Illinois have displaced New Jersey as the leading glass states.

The glass industry in New Jersey today is centered in Cumberland and Gloucester Counties. According to the 1935 U. S. Census of Manufacturers, there were eight glass establishments in the State, employing 4,666 people, with a total value of manufactured products of $15,941,-622. The most important plants are the Owens-Illinois Glass Company, Bridgeton; Gaynor Glass Works, Salem; Kimball Glass Works, Vineland; Whitall-Tatum Company, Millville; and the Owens-Illinois branch in Glassboro. The discovery of a 100-foot bed of glass sand extending under five southern New Jersey counties may become an impetus to the industry in the State.

Along with many other great industries that are reaching out into every corner of existence, glass, because of modern methods of mechanical production, is constantly widening its field of usefulness. The millions of incandescent electric bulbs and the miles of thin glass tubing for neon lights could never have been produced by the old time hand-blown methods. Likewise, increased knowledge of tempering and grinding fine glass for lenses has made possible the powerful microscope. The tremendous 200-inch telescope at Mount Wilson Observatory in California will have a mirror with a glass base that will expand or contract less than would metal, thus providing the accuracy necessary for astronomical observations.

Until the beginning of this century the methods of making glass had changed very little from those employed by the artisans of ancient Egypt and Venice and the latter day European and American manufacturers. Modern machinery has speeded up production and reduced what was once a fine art to a mechanical trade. In an up-to-date factory, from the weighing of the ingredients to the final delivery of the finished product at the end of a carrying belt, the entire process is carried out automatically. There are still small sections, however, even in the most highly mechanized glass factories, where the old methods are used to produce ornaments and other objects requiring special care. Here one may see the glass blowers practicing their ancient art.

In the making of glass the chief ingredients are sand, lime and soda. These, with whatever other materials are required to produce the desired color, are mixed together to form the batch. In the old days the batch was mixed on the floor of the glass house, shoveled into clay pots and placed in the furnace to melt. The men worked until the pots were emptied. They then had to stand around while another batch was prepared. To avoid this delay the continuous tank furnace was developed. In it the heat plays along the surface of the pool of glass instead of underneath, so that new batches may be added at the melting end without disturbing the glass that is being melted, while melted glass can be withdrawn continuously from the "refining" end without interruption. The capacity of the modern furnace of this type varies greatly, many being able to produce 100 tons of glass a day.

The molten glass is raised to temperatures ranging

from 2,800 to 3,400 degrees Fahrenheit, the hardness of the finished product depending on the temperature and the ingredients.

In handwork, now a minor factor in the industry, the furnace has several apertures for the introduction of blow-pipes. The glass blower is equipped with a blow-iron, a tube of iron one-half to one and one-quarter inches thick and about four or five feet long. The amount of glass gathered depends on the article to be produced. A wine-glass requires but little, and one immersion of the tube in the tank is sufficient. The blower works on a low chair with two long arms, slightly inclined, along which he rolls his iron. This enables him to turn the object with one hand and shape it with the other. When necessary he works with shears to cut away portions of glass no longer of any use, with "pucella," or small tongs, for widening or reducing the open forms, and with the "battledore," or pallette, for leveling the bottom of glass receptacles.

In the assembling of a wineglass, three distinct pieces are joined: the bowl, the leg and the foot. First, sufficient glass to make a bowl is gathered on the iron and shaped along the edge of the "marver," a small steel table, to give it the initial form. Then the blower puffs the glass out into a hollow bulb similar in size to the pattern from which he is working. He then adds a piece of hot glass to the bottom of the bulb and returns the iron to the furnace so that the joints fuse; again he removes the iron and blows out the leg, retaining a button at the end of the leg for the glass which is to be the foot. Again he adds glass, and with his tongs or a burned-wood paddle he forms the foot of the container. The glass is still crude, however, with sharp edges and imperfect contour. Another trip to the furnace and reshaping with the tongs leaves the glass ready for the annealing furnace or "lehr," where it is heated and then slowly cooled.

Heavy glass objects are formed in a mold which consists of two parts, one stationary, the other capable of being lifted or dropped. The molten glass is placed in the mold and blown into shape by the worker's breath or by compressed air.

Most modern, average-priced articles, such as shallow bowls and saucers, are pressed. The method consists of placing the glass in the mold and releasing a plunger which presses the glass to shape.

The making of window glass is a good index of the general progress of the industry. In the early days, a huge mass of molten glass was held on the pipe and after great labor blown into a cylindrical bubble weighing up to 40 pounds. Then it was cut along the side, opened, and returned to the furance. When it had reached the required temperature it was withdrawn, flattened, and cut to size. The modern practice is to draw the glass out in sheets through slots in floating planks. These large sheets are sent through rollers and pressed. They are then ready for cutting and cooling.

The plate glass method is different. In this instance the glass is ladled out onto a long table, and there, after it has settled to the proper thickness, it is rolled out by a moving roller. Expert polishing with various abrasives produces a sparkling surface.

Lenses require the most conscientious attention. They are made from the purest silica and soda, and carefully checked for deficiencies in strength and clarity. It requires a great quantity of melted glass to produce an acceptable lens or mirror surface.

The first successful machine to blow bottles was made

in America in 1906. The latest type has six, ten or sixteen arms—each a complete bottle-blowing machine, requiring at least nine separate parts. A ten-arm machine will make a complete revolution, producing ten bottles, in from 10 to 60 seconds, according to the size. The "Corning" bulb machine makes bulbs for incandescent lamps at a rate of 400 to 600 a minute.

The manufacture of tubing and vials for use in chemical laboratories, formerly a hand process, has also become a machine operation. An apparatus attached to the glass tank pulls out mile after mile of tubing, uniform in diameter and thickness of walls, and cuts it into commercial lengths. Another machine turns the tubing into vials of uniform construction and capacity. The production of chemical glassware was enormously stimulated during the World War when foreign importations were cut off.

Glass is colored by the use of chemicals. For a greenish tint a small quantity of marl is added to the batch. More marl is added for a deeper shade of green. For blue glass, oxide of cobalt is used; for purple, brown or black glass various quantities of oxide of manganese are added. Oxide of iron and manganese are used for amber and claret hues. Ruby glass, the most expensive type manufactured, is colored by the addition of gold to the batch. Formerly a $20 gold piece was dissolved in acid and added to a batch of 300 pounds of molten glass to achieve the red in signal lights on railroads and highways. The unminted gold is now used. A special type of colored glass keeps out part of the heat of the sun's rays.

Research is being carried on continually to produce not only different kinds of glass but better glass. The goal is a product that will be transparent, permanent, hard, and resistant to heat and electricity, all at the same time. A glass that will withstand high temperatures and from which cooking dishes are made, under the trade name of Pyrex, is one of the fruits of this activity. It was found that by adding borax to the batch such a glass could be produced. The first product dissolved in water, however, and it was only after seven years of experiment that satisfactory heat-resistant glass dishes were made.

Also highly resistant to heat is quartz glass or fused glass, but it is much too expensive to be used for kitchenware. The proper quality of clear quartz crystals which are used in the manufacture of quartz glass can be obtained in quantity only from Brazil or Madagascar.

Because it transmits a third more ultraviolet rays than ordinary glass, quartz glass has been an important factor in broadening the use of these curative rays. Water, run through a length of quartz pipe, can be purified by ultraviolet rays which pass through the quartz. For the same reason the material is particularly desirable for windows of hospitals, schools and similar institutions. Quartz glass is also used for telescope mirrors and ultraviolet-ray lamps.

One kind of shatterproof or "safety" glass is produced by the process of case hardening. Quick cooling of the outside of a sheet of glass compresses the inside and renders it five times stronger than ordinary glass. It breaks into minute, harmless particles instead of dangerous slivers. Such glass is well suited to the needs of airplanes, automobiles and busses.

Glass bricks are also being manufactured for building purposes. Ribs on the inside of the hollow blocks scatter the light in all directions, thus preventing objects from being seen through them and yet leaving them translucent. A wall of glass brick one foot thick will insulate as well as a wall of concrete two feet thick. A windowless, air-conditioned six-story department store of glass brick was opened in Chicago in the fall of 1937.

Spun glass was produced in Venice during the Middle Ages by dipping a rod into a pool of molten glass and pulling it away rapidly. It is now produced by machines and used to insulate buildings, refrigerators and hot-water tanks. Four inches of spun glass between the walls of a house provide as much insulation as would ten feet of concrete. Research chemists of a large glass company, while working on a totally different problem, recently discovered that they could produce a fine quality of this glass in quantity.

In 1937 these chemists demonstrated the production of "Fiberglas," which can be spun into a colorful cloth that is soft and warm. The process begins with the melting of glass marbles in an electric furnace. The flux is forced out through tiny holes in the bottom. The filaments thus formed, finer than human hair, are united to form a single thread one-fortieth of an inch thick. The thread is wound on spools which can be used on ordinary textile machines. One marble, about the size of those used by children, produces 325 miles of thread, and a cubic foot of the fiber weighs only a pound. This fiber is used as filter for acids, but it has been spun into sample gloves and neckties.

Glass fibers will not stretch like wool or silk, and cloth spun from them will therefore not allow freedom of movement to the body. The chemists admit that it would be irritating to the skin, but they are now working to overcome these disadvantages, and people may eventually be wearing glass clothes.

BLOWING QUARTZ GLASS

LEATHER MAKERS OF NEWARK

A map of Newark dated 1806 shows in one of its corners the picture of a shoemaker at work at his bench. Known ever since as the "shoemaker's map," it has been reproduced in bronze by the Schoolmen's Club of Newark and dedicated to the memory of Moses Combs, the enterprising tanner who began the State's first large scale production of shoes shortly after the Revolution.

The shoemaker's map is symbolic of New Jersey's early leadership in the preparation of leathers and the manufacture of shoes. Forests of oak and hemlock, natural sources of tannic acid, first attracted tanners to New Jersey in Colonial days. When Newark became a city in 1836 almost the whole of its working population was employed in some branch of the leather industry, and leather continued to dominate Newark for the next 50 years.

Although the loss of its great forests has forced leather makers to seek tanning materials in other states and abroad, leather tanning remains an important New Jersey enterprise.

Though Newark has been vitally interested in leather working for so many years, its "leather age" is almost nothing compared to the many centuries that have elapsed since a prehistoric man first used an animal skin for protection—perhaps for a foot wound. And this became the first shoe.

In a very few days, however, this man of ancient times must have discovered that all animal matter decomposes

The piece of rawhide that seemed like such a good idea must have become something of a problem. How was he to prevent this hide from decaying?

This was the first problem facing the early leather makers. But just as important was finding a method of keeping the hide flexible. The process that solves this dual problem is called tanning. Though no date can be established for the invention of tanning, leather articles have been unearthed in Egyptian tombs that have lain undisturbed for 33 centuries. It is known, however, that people in various parts of the world developed the art independently. Centuries ago, the Arabians used a tanning process that enabled them to produce the beautifully tooled saddles for which they became famous.

The American Indians developed their own crude method. After skins were washed and scraped clean of all fat and tissue and sometimes buried until decomposition loosened the hair, they were tanned by sprinkling them with pulverized rotten wood—a forerunner of the oak bark method used in some plants even today.

The early settlers in America learned from the Indians many new uses for leather. Leather moccasins, coats, breeches, boots, canoes and shelters earned for the frontiersmen the title "Leatherstockings."

The progress of leather making in the Colonies, however, depended on European advances which were brought here by English tanners. The first of these was Experience Miller, who arrived at Plymouth on the ship *Ann* in 1623. He was followed, in 1628, by Thomas Beard and Isaac Rickman, sent over by the Plymouth Company to set up their trade in exchange for "their dyett and house room at the charge of the companie."

Continued English colonization increased the demand

for leather. The frontier was pushed steadily westward, and the development of travel and communication required an increasing supply of saddles, harnesses, saddlebags and heavy leather straps for the support of coaches. Extensive tanning operations to meet this demand began in Elizabeth and Newark.

As early as 1664 a tannery was established in Elizabeth by the family of John Ogden of Long Island, and succeeding generations of the same family carried on the work in primitive fashion. In 1680 Samuel Whitehead of Elizabeth came to Newark at the invitation of the town fathers to "come and inhabit among us, provided he will supply the Town with Shoes, though for the present we know not of any Place of Land Convenient." The first tannery was established in 1698 by Azariah Crane.

The widely scattered farms were served by traveling shoemakers, who stayed at a farmhouse for weeks while making shoes for the entire household and dispensing the gossip of the towns and other farms. The leather soles were cut to a rather loose pattern drawn to individual measure and then joined to the uppers, sometimes with brass or wooden nails, but more often by stitching. When all had been well shod, the shoemaker moved on.

As the forests gave way to cleared fields, and towns continued to grow, tanners set up shop in every village or market center where farmers brought their produce. In return for their service to the farmers, they received one half of the hides. The tannery and vats were usually established on a hillside close to a waterfall which turned the slowly moving wooden cogwheel that crushed the tanning bark on an oaken floor.

About 1724 a tanyard was established in Acquakanonk now Passaic, by Stephen Bassett, a New York tanner attracted by the low prices of skins supplied by the Indians and the abundance of tanning materials, bark, lime and salt. He closed his Manhattan tannery and became the first leather manufacturer in old Bergen County. For nearly 50 years, until his death, his business flourished.

Slowly, as stagecoach transportation developed, the larger towns became the centers of shoe, harness and saddle manufacturing. Before the Revolution had ended two Newark tradesmen were advertising for journeymen shoemakers, and in the 1790's Moses Combs opened the first large shoemaking shop in the State. With prices as low as 50¢ a pair, Combs successfully invaded the New York market. His shoes gained a reputation in other states, and the value of his shipments increased until he was completing orders worth as much as $9,000.

Apprentices came to him from the Dutch families of Essex County, and Dutch took equal rank with English as the language of the shops. Each apprentice was expected to produce an average of seven pairs of shoes a week. The employer was required to supply a home and a certain amount of schooling for the young workers. Combs used to call his boys together after work for moral and religious instruction, and for years he hired a teacher at his own expense to conduct night classes which were open to the neighborhood. This was probably the first free night school in America.

Like the other leather makers, Combs used ground oak bark, almost the only vegetable tanning agent known until the beginning of the 19th century. Then Sir Humphrey Davy, the English scientist, discovered that tannic acid could be obtained from hemlock, sumac, chestnut and mimosa. New Jersey had vast resources of all these in her forests.

FLESHING A HIDE

Research and mechanical invention went hand in hand.
In 1809 the perfection of a hide-splitting machine began
a long series of "machine age" improvements that brought
mass production to the leather industry. The splitting machine, invented by Samuel Parker of Newburyport, Massachusetts, did away with the wasteful process of "planing"
leather to a desired thickness as a carpenter shaves down

lumber. The planing process was wasteful because the leather shavings were useless. With a splitting machine a skin could be divided into several thin sheets of leather with very little waste. The resulting economy was measured in millions of feet of leather.

Seth Boyden, who at his home in Foxborough, Massachusetts, had also developed a machine for splitting the heavy cowhides, was operating a harness shop on Newark's Broad Street in 1818. One day he was attracted by the enameled leather peak of a German officer's cap. It flashed across his mind that here was a valuable harness ornament. His analysis of the coatings and varnish led him to the invention of patent leather. The glossy finished European products were brittle and of little commercial value, but Boyden's process of sun drying and baking the varnish coatings made possible the manufacture of flexible patent leather.

Although Boyden's inventive interests turned to other fields, Newark forged ahead to become one of the leather centers of the United States. By 1860 the city had 30 tanneries, which employed more than 1,000 workers. A decade later leather was again ranked as the city's leading industry. After about 1875 tanneries began to consolidate and their number decreased, although their output for 1880 doubled that of 1870. As late as 1890 leather was referred to as "Newark's chief industry."

At this time the conversion of hides into finished leathers by curing and tanning still required months of patient labor. Improved methods have speeded up the tanning, but the preparatory process remains much as it was when leather activity was at its height in Newark. To restore the porous fresh hides to their original flexibility they are immersed in rectangular soaking vats.

Proper soaking requires from one to seven days, depending upon the condition and thickness of the hides. When they are adequately softened, they are transferred to a lime solution to loosen the outer skin on which the hair grows. After three to nine days the hides are ready for the "rehairing" machine. Surplus flesh is then removed either by hand or with the aid of a "fleshing" machine. The lime is then removed, and the hide is ready for tanning.

The older and slower method of vegetable tanning is still used to produce heavy leathers for shoe soles, belting, harness, upholstery and luggage. In this process the hides, suspended on rocker frames, are first immersed in vats of a weak tanning solution for two or three weeks and moved up and down in the solution to insure even absorption. Next the hides are placed in layers, sprinkled with ground bark and submerged in a stronger tanning solution. During this treatment, which may last from two to six months, the solution is changed from four to seven times. When completely tanned, the hides are placed in a vat filled with hot water to dissolve any excess tanning liquor, and then in a scrubbing machine to remove any remaining sediment or bark.

With a view to shortening the process, a New York chemist, August Schultz, developed and patented the formula for a tanning solution of chrome salts. The leather thus treated was stiff and blue and unfit for use. In 1890, however, a young Philadelphia tanner, Robert Foerderer, by treating the chrome-tanned leather with an emulsion of soap and oil, produced a product that was pliable and could be dyed any color. Foerderer gave Schultz $60,000 for his patent rights and called his new product "vici kid" —"vici" from the Latin, meaning "I have conquered."

Chrome tanning has made possible the production of fine leathers in a great variety of colors, multiplied the uses of leather and cut the tanning process to a matter of hours. Cured skins that are to be chrome tanned are placed in a drum containing the chrome chemicals, where they are tumbled about for five or six hours. When the skins emerge they have become leather. To give life and flexibility to the leather, natural oils and greases that have been dried out in the curing and tanning must be restored. Again the leather is placed in huge revolving drums where it is tumbled about in an emulsion of soap and oils known as fat liquors. Then dye solutions, if the leather is to be colored, are introduced.

Dried in darkened lofts, the leather is stretched and smoothed and made ready for the final operation, known as finishing, or glazing. For dull finishes a revolving brush is used, while high lustre is produced by friction with a glass cylinder.

Patent leather is put through a special grease-removing process and stretched on frames where paints and colors are applied by hand in several coats, each time being baked and rubbed down with pumice. Sun baking, for which no substitute has been found, gives it a hard, bright finish.

New Jersey is outstanding for the variety of its leather products. Newark has the only sharkskin tannery in the United States, two of the largest reptile tanneries and one of the three kangaroo tanneries. Sharkskin is tanned like other leathers except that the outer scaly skin, harder than steel, is first removed by special treatment. Of the more than 100 varieties of shark, only about 10 are used commercially. Many varieties of reptiles are used: alligators and iguanas from the United States, Mexico and Central America; boa constrictors, anacondas, lizards and chameleons from South America; Java ring lizards and Karung water snakes from the Dutch East Indies; pythons from India and Indo-China.

Besides these, the hides of calf, sheep, goat, pig, deer, ostrich, kangaroo, seal, walrus, horse and buffalo are in constant demand by leather buyers and constitute a vast international trade.

Goatskin, which has furnished leather since ancient times, is now used mainly for fine shoes, gloves and high grade bookbinding. Camden has one plant where 30,000 goatskins are tanned daily to produce ladies' shoe uppers, handbags and other articles.

A Newark firm which has been in continuous operation since the Civil War supplied virtually all the leather used in the lounges, halls and Rainbow Room of Radio City. This leather was the first of its kind to pass the underwriters' test for fireproofing of finished leather. Newark, at one time considered the center for the production of leather, still has a dozen or more tanning plants which supply leathers for shoes, furniture and luggage.

THE GOLD BEATERS

The art of hammering gold by hand into thin leaves for use in ornamentation is one of the rarest and most ancient of industries. The gilding found on old relics, books and art objects was prepared for the artist in the Middle Ages in much the same manner as it is for the picture frames, signs and furniture of today. In the whole country not more than a thousand people are engaged in this highly specialized work, and these are found in only 13 of the states.

In Red Bank, New Jersey, there is a colony of these gold workers distributed in three shops that owe their existence to William Haddon, a gold leaf manufacturer of New York who, after his retirement, practiced his craft in a small shop in his home at Red Bank. He taught the craft to others, who have carried on the business for more than 60 years.

The manufacture of gold leaf begins with the purchase of pure (24-carat) gold from the United States Government. One ounce of gold will produce 2,500 sheets, $3\frac{3}{8}$ inches square, hammered to a thinness of $1/200,000$ of an inch. A book of gold leaf which sells for about 75¢ contains 25 sheets packed between protecting layers of paper.

It is difficult to conceive of anything as thin as these gold wafers being visible to the naked eye. One way of estimating their thinness is to realize that it would take about 400 sheets laid on top of each other to equal the thickness of this single sheet of paper.

The process by which mined gold is reduced to such extraordinary thinness is one requiring time, patience and unusual skill. First, the gold is colored to any one of the 10 acceptable shades by the addition of alloys, such as copper and silver. In the deeper, or reddish shades, there is a preponderance of copper; while a larger proportion of silver produces the paler shades. As alloys are added the metal becomes less malleable, therefore it is not adulterated below a 23-carat grade. The gold, with the added alloy, is then melted in a clay crucible which may not be used a second time for fear of breaking. Once is too often to spill a pot of gold in the ashes. The molten metal is poured into a mold one inch wide and several inches long, and it forms a bar about ¼ of an inch thick.

This bar is then pressed between steel rollers again and again to extend its length. During this ironing process the operator guides the bar so that the width does not increase. When the gold bar has attained a length of about 10 yards and a thickness of 1/800 of an inch it is cut into squares, and each one is placed between sheets of vellum, made from calf or lamb gut, imported from France. These vellum sheets are three inches square. The inch squares of gold are bound closely in the larger vellum squares by parchment bands. This pile, called the "cutch," is now ready for the first beating.

The "cutch" is placed on a padded granite block 18 inches square which is supported by a wooden block embedded in ashes, to assure the necessary resilience as the 18-pound hammer descends. It requires more skill than strength to guide the strokes of the hammer so that the little squares in the packet will be evenly beaten.

When the gold has reached the edge of the 3-inch vellum wrapper, the squares are removed with long wooden pincers and are folded and cut in quarters by a steel knife. Six or seven hundred of these are placed between pieces of goldbeater's skin, four inches square, bound and packed as for the first beating. This packet is called the "shoder."

Goldbeater's skin is prepared by a secret process from the intestines of cattle. In all the world there are only a few companies, and these are in England and Germany, that undertake its intricate preparation. So carefully is the secret guarded that it is said that once, when an employee of a certain firm seemed to have learned too much of the process, it was arranged that he marry the daughter of his employer to insure his loyalty. The intestines of 500 cattle are required to make a single packet containing about 850 leaves. Alum, isinglass and white of egg are used in the toughening treatment, and the process is long, complicated and somewhat revolting.

A "mold" of 1,000 skins sells for about $10 and lasts not more than two to three years under the punishment it receives from the hammer on the granite block.

Now the gold leaves lying between the 4-inch squares of goldbeater's skin are beaten once more, this time by a 9- to 12-pound hammer, until the leaves again spread to the edges. The leaves are removed again with the wooden pincers and placed on a leather cushion. They are now so thin that it takes only a breath from the worker to flatten them out, and a specially designed tool, called a "wagon," must be used to trim them. It has two adjustable blades of sharpened reed and looks like a small sled.

The 4-inch squares are again packed in a "mold" of goldbeater's skins about 5 inches square and beaten with hammers 7 to 10 pounds in weight for about 4 hours until they reach the edge of the skins. Then each square, now reduced to almost impalpable fineness, is trimmed down with a "wagon" to exactly 3⅜ inches and packed between protecting sheets, ready for sale.

To the 20th century mind this may seem like a slow and antiquated process, but the cost of inventing and building machinery to handle such delicate operations has until recently been considered too great for the volume of business. There are a few firms throughout the country manufacturing gold leaf by machinery, but, generally speaking, the hand-made product is preferred by the trade. A machine has no eyes to detect flaws, while in the hands of a careful workman every leaf is scrutinized and a more uniform product results.

THE ROMANCE OF THE ROEBLINGS

Bridges, cables and Roebling are as closely bound together as the wires in the cables that suspend such great bridges as the George Washington Bridge and the Golden Gate Bridge. For it was John A. Roebling who, in a small factory in Trenton, New Jersey, wove the first wire rope and developed an industry that has changed the history of transportation.

Roebling was not the first man to conceive or build suspension bridges. They were used in remote times in China, Japan, India and Tibet. The Aztecs of Mexico and the natives of Peru used this device for crossing chasms or swirling river currents. They used twisted vines or straps of hide fastened securely to strong trees or boulders to support the hanging foot bridges. The method is still employed in remote parts of the world; but these bridges are comparatively short and are not intended to carry great weight.

The first bridge hung on wire cables was over the Schuylkill River at Fairmount, Philadelphia, built in 1816 by Joseph White and Erskine Hazard, who owned a wire mill. The span was 408 feet long and provided a passageway of only 18 inches. With the first accumulation of ice and snow, the structure collapsed. In 1842 another hanging bridge over the Schuylkill was more successful. It remained in operation until 1872. But these bridges were mere toys in comparison to Roebling's projects. By spin-

ning wire into heavy cable he was the first one to suspend, successfully, bridges of 1,000 feet or more in span.

Roebling, son of a tobacco manufacturer, was born in 1806 in Mühlhausen, Germany. His mother had great ambition for this boy, her youngest son, and by many sacrifices managed to have him educated at the Royal University of Berlin. Roebling distinguished himself in engineering, architecture, bridge construction, hydraulics and philosophy. Shortly after his graduation he decided to join 60 or 70 others in migrating to the new land of promise—the United States.

On arriving here in August 1831, the group decided on farming for their future. Some turned to the Southland with its great plantations. Roebling, with others, because of their strong opinions against slavery, decided on the North and purchased 700 acres on the slope of the Allegheny ridge, about 25 miles from the then new town of Pittsburgh. There they founded the village of Germania, now called Saxonburg.

Those were the days when new transportation methods were being developed to carry goods to the ever-widening frontier. Railroads were in their infancy, but lumbering canal boats loaded with coal and merchandise were hauled along artificial waterways by mules and horses. This captured the interest of the engineer in Roebling, who had discovered that he had little talent for farming. In 1837 he got a job as assistant State engineer, and soon he was building dams and locks on the canals. The problem of sending the freight boats over mountains interested him immediately. At the base of a mountain these boats were floated into cradles that were hauled up by ropes to the next water stretch. Occasionally the rope, however stout, would break, and cradle, boat, cargo and passengers would go crashing down the mountain.

Roebling remembered having read that a German had twisted strands of wire into rope and decided to develop the idea. He purchased a quantity of steel wire, went back to his farm in Saxonburg and taught his friends and neighbors how to weave it into rope. His methods were crude but the result was startling; the wire rope held under great loads, and it was flexible enough to pass over the windlass. Soon this strong, tensile wire rope was replacing hemp rope for hauling towboat cradles and for towlines.

Canals sometimes had to cross natural rivers over which wooden aqueducts had to be built. These were costly and unsafe, for frequently their supporting piles and abutments would be crushed and destroyed by ice in the river. Roebling conceived the idea of a cross-river aqueduct suspended from wire cables anchored to the land. This, he argued, would be much safer because it would eliminate piers and posts in the river.

Learning that a new canal was to be built across the

Allegheny River at Pittsburgh, he laid his plans and calculations before the engineers. He frankly admitted that
what he was proposing had never been done bofere, and
he was staking his reputation on its success. He finally persuaded them that the advantage to be gained justified the
risk. The project proved so successful that Roebling received many commissions for similar cross-river aqueducts,
several of which are still in use.

It was but a step from a suspension aqueduct to a suspension bridge, but Roebling realized that he would need
larger shops, machinery and possibly mills to develop the
ideas that were taking shape in his mind. His friend Peter
Cooper had iron foundries in Trenton and urged him to
settle there. In 1848 he took about 20 trained men with
him to Trenton, where he designed and built his own
machinery to weave wire rope and cables.

Roebling's Early Bridges

From this plant came the massive cables that made the
bridge over Niagara Falls possible. And where could a
more dangerous and dazzling undertaking have been
found than spanning these hurling waters with a combination railroad and highway suspension bridge? But to
Roebling it was just another engineering problem. Many
engineers laughed at the idea of carrying a railroad train
over that turmoil of water, on a web apparently so frail.
Failure was freely predicted.

Roebling flew a kite across the gorge to get his first
wire over and from that single wire built up his cables.
The bridge was opened to the public in 1854. On March
16, 1855, the first railroad train in history crossed a suspension bridge, and to the amazement of the public the
bridge did not collapse.

This accomplishment demonstrated the soundness of Roebling's claims for giant wire structures and established him as one of the outstanding engineers of the age. Other contracts quickly followed. He built the Allegheny Bridge over the Monongahela River at Pittsburgh in 1856 and the Cincinnati-Covington Bridge over the Ohio in 1867.

In the meantime there was considerable agitation for a bridge over the East River connecting the cities of Brooklyn and New York. The idea still seemed to many like a wild dream, and most Brooklynites preferred the safety of their chugging ferries. Roebling, in the late fifties, had written to Abram S. Hewitt, distinguished engineer, later to become mayor of New York, suggesting a hanging bridge that would not interfere with navigation. But nothing had been done.

The winter of 1866-67 was the coldest, bitterest and longest New York had ever known. Huge drifts of ice surged and crackled around the keels of the ferries and tied up river traffic. Passengers from Albany, coming by train, reached New York before the Brooklynites could cross the river. Manhattan and Brooklyn looked across at each other and remembered Roebling and his dream of a bridge hanging on steel wire. The demand for the bridge rose to a clamor.

In May 1867 a charter was granted, and John Roebling was appointed chief engineer. But he was not to see the completion, or even the start of what he considered would be his crowning achievement. On June 28, 1869, Mr. Roebling was standing on a cluster of piles at the Fulton ferry slip, Brooklyn, fixing the site of the proposed tower. He failed to see a ferryboat before it crashed into the piling. One of his feet was crushed, necessitating the amputation of some of his toes. Tetanus set in and on July 22, as he neared his 63rd birthday, he died.

Colonel Washington Augustus Roebling, his son and associate, was appointed to succeed him. It was January 1870 before actual construction was started. A scow with a coil of ¾-inch wire rope was moored alongside the Brooklyn tower and the end of the coil hoisted to the top, passed down on the land side, then carried back. The scow was then towed to the New York side and the rope carried over that tower and wound on a huge drum till it hung above the river. A second wire rope was run in the same manner and the two were joined around huge driving wheels or pulleys at each end. An endless wire rope traveler, revolving by steam power, now stretched from city to city.

One day in August 1870 the hanging of the cable was started by a man on this slender aerial. In a "bosun's chair," he started in the traveler from the top of the Brooklyn tower down the long sag and up to the top of the New York tower while a million people gazed in wonder, bands played, and boat whistles shrieked.

The Brooklyn Bridge project introduced several innovations in construction. The foundations of the great towers were built by the caisson method. While the men working in the caisson dug out the earth underneath, others in the open air on top of the caisson laid the masonry of the towers. On the Brooklyn side the caisson was sunk about 50 feet. On the New York side it was necessary to go down about 90 feet to bedrock. More than a hundred men were affected, many fatally, by the dreaded caisson disease, or bends, during construction.

Washington Roebling spent much of his time in the caisson chambers. One day he was carried out unconscious from the effects of the bends. His speech was gone. After that he had to write his instructions to his assistants. By the end of 1872 he was an invalid and unable to visit the bridge. From that time until it was finished, except for six months abroad in an effort to regain his health, he directed the work from his home in Brooklyn.

With the aid of a telescope he could see the men at work and the dream taking shape—a symphony in steel, stone and concrete—the longest suspension bridge in the world. And then one day in 1883, with the sun shining, the waters of the river churned up by craft of all kinds, a group of dignitaries gathered in the middle of the bridge and the President of the United States, Chester A. Arthur, made the dedication address.

Washington Roebling sat in his window, the telescope held close to his eyes, watching the ceremonies. When the breeze shifted he could hear the excited tooting of the river craft and the blaring of the bands. At last! Brooklyn Bridge was a reality. Colonel Roebling remained partially paralyzed till he died in 1926 at the age of 84.

About 1900 Colonel Roebling and his brothers, Ferdinand and Charles, decided to withdraw from the competitive field of engineering contracts and concentrate all the energies of the firm on the perfection of its products.

While the name of Roebling is generally associated in the public mind with huge wire cables and wire rope, and it still continues to make these, the company also makes a wide variety of wire, covering almost every commercial and technical field, from the 4½-inch steel wire rope, down to the infinitesimal wire in the eyepiece of the telescope.

Wire can now be drawn so fine that it would take many strands to equal the thickness of a human hair. Perhaps the most amazing of the products of the industry are the cables of copper wire used in telephone service. For these the individual wires are covered with paper of various colors, which acts not only as a protection but enables men at the opposite ends of a long cable to identify the wires with which the connection is to be made. Steel wires about the size of the common lead pencil seem like a fragile substance from which to suspend great bridges. Yet these wires, when woven into cable, can support many times their own dead weight.

Modern Bridges

The ever-present question—which is the largest bridge—may be answered in several ways. If one judges by length of span, the distance between the towers, the new Golden Gate Bridge at San Francisco, with its main span of 4,200 feet and its total cable length of 7,640 feet from anchorage to anchorage, is the largest in the world. Measured in cable strength, the George Washington Bridge is the largest, even though the span is only 3,500 feet and the cable length from anchorage to anchorage is 4,200 feet. But its cable strength is 350,000 tons as compared to the 193,304 tons for the San Francisco Bridge. The George Washington Bridge is not yet complete. Its massive cables are designed to support a second roadway when required by increasing traffic.

Because of their great size, bridge cables are spun on the site. Every reach of the wire is laid flat and separate, and when all are in place they are bound together in strands. There are 61 strands in each of the four cables that support the George Washington Bridge. After being adjusted to a sag that would distribute the load, the strands were bound together into solid cylinders, each con-

George Washington Bridge

taining 26,474 wires. In addition to the cables there are 35 miles of suspender rope, representing about 10,000 miles of wire. Altogether the wires used in the George Washington Bridge would reach nearly five times around the world. Wire rope and parallel wire cables should not be confused. There is no twist in the cables that sustain bridges as there is in a wire rope.

The Roebling headquarters are in Trenton, where there are two great plants. The main one covers over 35 acres. The second lies a half mile farther south. At the turn of the century, when the company could crowd no more buildings on its Trenton acreage, it established about ten miles below Trenton the town of Roebling, where it owns over 200 acres. All together, there are more than a hundred buildings in the three plants, many of these of immense size and manufacturing capacity, all devoted to making one of the great necessities of this age—wire.

THE STORY OF LENOX POTTERY

Americans, who accept as a matter of course the out-standing achievements of their scientists and engineers, are sometimes surprised to learn that in the field of art, as well, they have achieved international importance.

Included in the permanent exhibition in the Ceramic Museum at Sèvres, France, among the rare and beautiful wares of Europe and Asia, are several examples of Lenox china. They are products of a factory in Trenton, New Jersey, and the result of long and patient effort on the part of a man who devoted his life to the accomplishment of an ideal, despite the handicaps of poverty and discouragement and the added burdens of blindness and paralysis.

Walter Lenox, as a schoolboy in Trenton, where he was born in 1859, used to stand for hours before a little pottery which he passed daily, fascinated by the transformation of the dull lumps of clay into beautiful shapes and forms as the rapidly spinning potter's wheel turned in the hands of the artisan. Young Lenox resolved that he would master this craft, one of the most ancient of mankind, and produce finer ware than any he had seen.

As an apprentice he learned how to make pottery. In his leisure hours he studied and experimented with design and color. Finally he became art director of the Ott and Brewer factory at Trenton and while there learned from Irish artisans, imported for the purpose, some of the processes of manufacturing Belleek—a particularly fine ware. But to accomplish his purpose it was necessary for Lenox to have his own plant. He was able to raise the money, but his backers were skeptical. They stipulated that the building should be designed as a tenement should the pottery fail.

The manufacture of cheap ware in large quantities would assure quick and large profits, while delicate and finely wrought ware would have a limited market. But Walter Lenox had one aim—quality. He was convinced that if he could produce something truly fine and beautiful the public would ultimately recognize it.

At this time unscrupulous china manufacturers in the United States were in the habit of marking their ware with English stamps in order to sell their goods. No one would believe that really fine china could be produced in America. Lenox was too proud and honorable to employ such unworthy methods, and he resolved to stand or fall on the merits of his products.

Failure followed failure before he produced the lovely, creamy, richly glazed china that proudly displays the Lenox stamp. In 1895, just as Walter Lenox was about to achieve his dream, he was stricken with paralysis and blindness. Burdened as he was with debt and physical handicaps, it looked as if his factory would have to be converted into a tenement. But the artist was not ready to surrender. He knew that his china was beautiful and that in time the public would learn to appreciate and buy it. Harry A. Brown, the secretary of the company, shared this faith. He became the eyes and legs of the stricken man. Together they worked to solve the monetary difficulties of the little industry.

The potter called his devoted friend "Dominie," some one to lean upon, some one to trust. Every day Lenox was taken to the pottery, and though he could not see, his sensitive fingers could trace the graceful forms and feel the glaze and texture of the china as it came from the kiln. "Dominie" took entire charge of the business and of the firm, and one memorable day he was able to announce that every note had been paid. A miniature kiln was built in the office; the canceled notes were placed in it and burned while Lenox stood by, tears streaming from his blinded eyes. Lenox addressed "his boys," as he called the workmen, and urged them never to abandon the ideal of creating beautiful china. Quality first—the money would come after.

The blind potter died in 1920, but his dream lives on in the modern plant built on the site of the first small factory, and in the finely textured product which his devotion and determination developed. Today the Lenox Pottery occupies more than seven acres of ground. The plant, constructed largely of glass to afford the maximum of light, has the best equipment for china making. The air is freed of dust by the latest ventilating devices. Yet here and there throughout the factory there are still reminders of the ancient potter's primitive methods.

Visitors from all over the world come to watch the evolution of dull clay and minerals into exquisite fragile china. It is a process requiring extreme precision and refinement.

The raw materials, clay, feldspar and flint, are selected by specialists. They are weighed and tested at every stage from mine to mixing room so that there will be no variance in the proportions. Even the water with which they are mixed is filtered and measured to the last ounce.

Several different kinds of clay are used in Lenox pottery. Feldspar is a crystallike rock formation which when crushed becomes a glistening white powder. New Eng-

land feldspar is used exclusively in Lenox pottery. When
the clay and rock powder have been properly mixed, they
are placed in a huge revolving cylinder containing water
and flint pebbles. This process is called pebble grinding.

After 50 hours the mixture, now of a thick, creamlike
consistency, is forced through a fine wire screen by air
pressure. This process, which lasts for two hours, eliminates all the large particles and results in a fine-textured
fluid called "slip." Electromagnets remove all iron atoms
from the "slip," and it is then allowed to age. No one
knows just why aging makes the clay easier to handle, but
from ancient times all potters have found it helpful to let
the "slip" stand for several days.

The clay is now ready to be shaped. This is the point
at which in the old days it would have been placed on the

LOADING SAG-
GERS IN A KILN

potter's wheel and molded by the craftsman's sensitive
fingers as the wheel spun. The modern equivalent of the
potter's wheel is called the jiggering machine. It is turned
by an electric motor, controlled by an operator whose
trained fingers guide the moist clay into a plaster mold.
He knows to the minute when the clay is in workable
condition. The work is so fine that an expert craftsman
can produce only a few pieces each day.

Not all pieces are formed on the jiggering machine.
Some intricate shapes are cast in plaster molds. When the
shapes are complete they are put aside to dry. They are

then carefully gone over with a camel's hair brush to make sure the surface is absolutely smooth.

When dry and ready for firing, the pieces are gently packed in coarse clay containers (called saggers) and carried to the kiln, which is 14 feet wide and more than 14 feet high. From time immemorial it has been the custom for workmen to carry saggers on their heads. This ancient method still prevails in the Lenox pottery.

One may catch his breath as he watches a workman climb the ladder with a load of saggers balanced on top of his head. But the artisans say that never has a single piece been lost by falling. When the great oven has been filled completely, the doors are sealed and the fires started. For 30 hours the delicate china is baked. The heat is increased gradually and carefully until it reaches 2,200 degrees Fahrenheit. Considering that it takes only 350 degrees to bake an ordinary cake, this gives an idea of the terrific heat used for these delicate vessels. In fact, the heat is so intense that if it were not for the steel bands with which the kilns are bound they would burst.

When the pieces are removed from the kiln they are carefully examined for any imperfection or warping. Imperfect specimens are immediately destroyed. Those that pass inspection are subjected to a fine sand blast to remove any clinging particles, bubbles or ridges.

The china next passes into the hands of the glaze dipper, who with remarkable dexterity immerses each piece in a glazing solution. It is then fired a second time, to fuse the glaze. If the glaze has been applied unevenly the whole piece will crack under the heat, which, for this operation, must reach a temperature of 2,100 degrees.

The piece is now ready for decorating with gold and colors. This work calls for unusual talent, and is one of the reasons for the high cost of production at the Lenox plant. Of the 325 employees, 39 are skilled craftsmen, with salaries as high as $90 a week.

Thousands of dollars' worth of 24-carat gold is used annually for embellishing the ware. No adulterated, so-called commercial gold is tolerated. In order to conserve every ounce of gold, all wiping cloths and utensils are burned to recover any clinging particles.

Color work is done in several ways. On some pieces the artist does the painting freehand, and on others he follows an outline design. Sometimes an elaborate design involving 14 or 15 colors is transferred and then supplemented by hand work.

At each stage of ornamentation the pieces must be fired in the decorating kiln. Color firing and gold firing require different degrees of heat, so that one piece may have to go into the decorating kiln several times before it is ready for final inspection. At every point experts pass upon each piece, and sooner or later the tiniest flaw is discovered. When a piece falls below standard it is immediately destroyed.

The insistence of Walter Lenox upon attaining nothing less than perfection and the devotion of his helpers have been amply justified. Today the lustrous Lenox china is in demand all over the world. There are 1,700 pieces in the White House dinner service, and sets have been ordered for the official banquet services of several other countries.

FROM PHONOGRAPH TO TELEVISION

The 20th century family accepts the victrola and the radio as part of the everyday equipment of the home, and yet only 60 years ago intelligent, wide awake men and women scoffed at the idea of permanently recording and reproducing the human voice or any other sound.

In 1877 Edison applied for a patent for the phonograph, and 10 years later Charles Summer Tainter and Alexander Graham Bell invented a new recording method and announced another sound-reproducing machine, which they christened the graphophone. These first machines were grotesque-looking contrivances. The records were cylindrical, and the sound was amplified through a large megaphone which, following the overornamental style of the period, took on fearful and wonderful shapes. The sounds were rasping and distorted, but listeners were grateful and enthusiastic.

The first great advance in the phonograph was made by Emile Berliner, who had aided Bell in the development of the telephone. Instead of a cylindrical record, Berliner used a disc. His instrument, called a gramophone, was marketed in 1896 through the Berliner Gramophone Company. Competition between the manufacturers of the two types of machine opened the field for new developments.

One day in 1895 Berliner brought his instrument to a young machinist in a shop back of a carriage facory on Front Street, in Camden, New Jersey. The machinist was

Eldridge R. Johnson, who had won a reputation as a maker of working models for inventors.

Johnson studied and experimented and finally perfected and patented a silent spring motor which ran with uniform speed and so did not distort the sound. This motor was so much superior to Berliner's model that Johnson received a contract to manufacture it for the Gramophone Company.

Johnson then turned to the improvement of the record itself. In 1898, by combining the flat disc with Bell and Tainter's method of recording, he turned out a record of exceptional merit which reproduced a popular song of the day sung by himself, *I Guess I'll Have to Telegraph My Baby*.

Then began a series of financial troubles. The Berliner Gramophone Company was operating at a loss, and Johnson was left without financial backing. Johnson finally took control of the company. He could continue production only because the employees in his little shop had faith in his invention and in him. Each week they turned back part of their wages and accepted in exchange a small interest in the business. The stock they bought made them rich.

Eventually Johnson triumphed over all business rivals, and some say that this fact prompted the choice of the name "Victor" for his machine and records. In 1901 he registered this name in the United States Patent Office, and later that year the Victor Talking Machine Company was organized. Johnson kept a controlling interest in the company, and the bulk of his stockholders were the faithful employees in his first little machine shop.

In the autumn of 1901 the Victor talking machine won its first gold medal over all competitors at the Pan-American Exposition at Buffalo, and within a year the company advertised that it had 10,000 dealers. Its business during this first year amounted to $2,000,000, and partly responsible was the support of the general musical firm of Lyon & Healy in Chicago.

A spurt of competitive production by the Columbia Gramophone Company, still using the cylinder recording principle of Edison and Tainter and Bell, caused the Victor Company to devise new methods for increasing sales. Johnson first gathered a roster of artists which included the great actress Sarah Bernhardt, Adelina Patti, Enrico Caruso and other great opera stars.

Then the company began research to improve phonograph construction, and out of the experiments came the "victrola." The general use of this name, coined by the company, testifies to the widespread popularity of the product. Up to that time the phonograph's sound delivery had been by means of tin or brass horns of all sizes and shapes. Johnson turned the horn downward into the cabinet of the machine itself, and the phonograph, for the first time, became an ornamental and attractive piece of household furniture. The handsomer models, priced at $200, had a brisk sale, and the Victor company had the phonograph field virtually to itself. Soon Columbia adopted a disc and cabinet machine, and seven years later Edison himself discarded his original cylinder for the disc. Following Johnson's example, he installed the new machine in a handsome cabinet.

Victor's purchase of a half interest in the Gramophone Company of London in 1920 opened the world markets of Europe, Asia, Africa and Australia, in addition to markets already controlled in North and South America. It was worth the $9,000,000 it cost.

When in 1924 the interest of the public shifted to radio,

Courtesy R. C. A.

"Putting It on the Wax" at Old Recording Studio, Camden

Nipper, the little fox terrier with his ear cocked for "His Master's Voice," the trade mark adopted by the Victor Company, seemed to be facing a dark future. But a new method of electric recording and reproduction developed in the research laboratories of the great communication companies brightened the outlook. In 1925 Victor began the manufacture of another sound-reproducing innovation which put the company on a full production schedule—the orthophonic victrola. Recordings could be made with such high fidelity that the great musical artists here and abroad flocked to the studios. Shortly afterward the company completed negotiations with the Radio Corporation of America for rights to combine the orthophonic victrola with the radio.

In 1929 RCA, which had been a subsidiary of the General Electric Company, separated from the mother corporation and planned to begin production of radios independently. The Victor company was purchased, and the plant in Camden was devoted mainly to the manufacture of radios. Though the popularity of phonographs dwindled, research in the reproduction of sound continued along with experiments in the field of radio.

The efficiency of the radio advanced rapidly, and the New Jersey company expanded until it was producing radio devices for almost every conceivable use. In addition to the transmission of sound, radio waves are used today in medicine, for industrial safeguards and in various other fields. A machine in a factory may be surrounded with waves so that if anyone approaches, the machine is automatically shut off.

In Camden, the capital of radio and the phonograph, more than 14,000 are employed in the 31 buildings during peak times to turn out the radios, phonographs and records that reach all parts of the world. From this same plant have come many of the developments that make talking pictures a successful reality. When the first sound movies appeared, the sound was reproduced from large phonograph records, but with this device there was a constant danger of breakage, and the records could not be cut and edited to synchronize with the films.

Finally a method was developed for converting sound into electrical impulses which are then reconverted into light waves. The light waves actuate a needle which scratches the film beside the pictures of the action. Thus a sound picture today is an actual photograph not only of

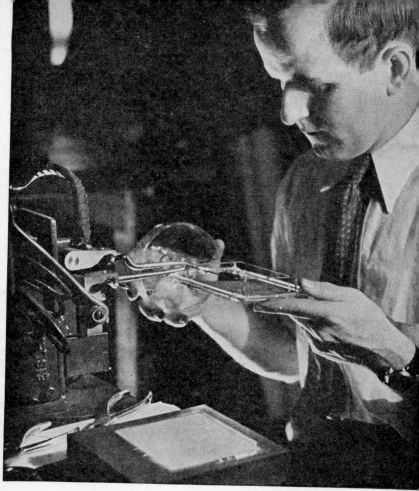

ASSEMBLING THE GRID OF AN ICONOSCOPE (TELEVISION
TUBE) IN THE R.C.A. RESEARCH LABORATORIES, CAMDEN

the actors but of their voices, which appear as zigzag lines.

Recently this technique was improved in the Camden
laboratories by the use of ultraviolet rays for the beam
instead of ordinary white light. Because it can be focused

more sharply, the ultraviolet beam produces a truer, clearer picture of the sound.

With this history of experimental success, it was only natural that RCA engineers should conduct one of the first successful demonstrations of television out of doors in the full brilliance of the midday sun. A special fire alarm was sounded, and, as the firemen rushed to the scene, the eye of a television camera was poked from a window to record the event, while a microphone picked up the clang of the bells and the scream of the siren. A mile away, across the city, a small group of spectators observed a greenish-hued picture of the action on a television apparatus, 5 by 7 inches. The ultimate home receiver may show a pale yellow picture.

Two new devices developed by Dr. Vladimir K. Zworykin, ace research man of the RCA laboratories, made this demonstration possible. He calls one of them an "iconoscope," which is the electric eye of the television camera. The other is the "kinescope," the receiving mechanism which projects the picture on the television screen.

Three major problems must be solved before television can come into general use. The size of the image transmitted is still too small for more than a limited gathering; the cost is prohibitive, and the television broadcasting radius is restricted to 30 miles. But research is yielding results, and engineers are rapidly achieving the goal of satisfactory reception regularly sustained.

DELAWARE BAY OYSTERS

The oyster was a favorite food of the Indians long before the coming of the white man. Over the Burlington Path and the Minnisink Trail, from the mountains to the New Jersey coast, the Indians made annual pilgrimages and held great oyster feasts. They, of course, knew nothing of oyster cultivation, but simply raked the oysters from the natural beds with pronged sticks. For the most part they ate them raw; but they also dried quantities of them for future use. Much of the wampum used for currency and decoration was made from the shells of oysters and clams.

The Indians taught the white settlers to appreciate the strange-looking bivalves, along with sweet corn, succotash, turkey and cranberries. As the years have passed, the State has improved the cultivation and marketing of this valuable article of diet, until the oyster industry has reached great proportions, representing an investment of $18,500,-000 and a gross annual business of more than $3,500,000. In New Jersey, which ranks fourth in the country's oyster production, about 2,000 people are employed in the industry in a variety of jobs: boatmen, planters, sorters, shuckers and packers.

New Jersey was a pioneer in scientific oyster propagation, just as it was in scientific agriculture. Under the direction of Dr. Julius Nelson of the New Jersey State Agricultural Experiment Station at Rutgers University, much was learned about the habits and peculiarities of this humble creature. One phase of the investigation carried on by the scientists was protection of the growing oyster from contamination. Almost every oyster-producing State, through the Federal and State Boards of Health and its State Board of Fisheries, has established rules governing the planting and dredging of oysters and the packing and shipping of them to market. Oysters may be handled only by workers who have passed a health examination, and they may not be harvested from waters that have been polluted.

In New Jersey, oysters used to be produced mainly from Raritan Bay, the Shrewsbury River and Barnegat Bay. The first two of these are now impractical for breeding. Barnegat Bay is still a rich oyster field, but the industry now centers around Delaware Bay near the outlet of the Maurice River at Bivalve, at Port Norris and at several other points in that vicinity. The Maurice River Cove has over 31,000 acres of oyster beds, possibly the largest single acreage in the world. Owned by the State, the beds are under the control of the State Board of Shell Fisheries and are leased to operators upon certain conditions. In other words, a man may not actually own an oyster bed. But he is given the privilege of gathering oysters year after year from the same spot as long as he pays his lease fee of 50 cents an acre.

The average plot of ground leased for oystering measures from 25 to 30 acres. An operator may obtain several leases if grounds are available. He recognizes his own acreage by stakes planted at the corner boundaries. These may be marked by a feed bag, a tin can, a splash of paint or any other distinguishing mark. All lessees are protected in their rights to the stock on their grounds, and this protection is enforced by guard boats which are provided, manned and operated by the State. Oystermen must also pay a dredging fee for each boat they use.

From Colonial days until recently the oyster beds in Delaware Bay were a battleground for warring oystermen from the two states bordering the bay. There were violent disputes calling for police interference. But on October 9, 1933, the U. S. Supreme Court settled the controversy by decreeing that the oyster beds of Delaware Bay lying east of the main ship channel belonged to the State of New Jersey. This decision added $1,250,000 to the value of the State's oyster industry, and there has been no trouble since.

The cultivation and gathering of oysters are rigidly controlled by the Board of Shell Fisheries, which employs a director who must be an experienced oysterman. Operations are conducted very much as in farming. The grounds are planted and the crop is harvested; but instead of horses and reapers, schooners and dredges are used. The insects which are so destructive to plant life have their counterparts in undersea pests which molest the oysters. Drumfish weighing 40 to 50 pounds crack or crush the oystershells with their powerful jaws and eat the meat. Starfish have for the most part been eliminated by local action, but drills are still the most vicious of the oyster's enemies. They are conical-shaped mollusks that drill through the shell, discharging a fluid that dissolves the oyster. The drill than sucks out the liquefied oyster.

Recently a successful method of exterminating drills has been put into operation by the Works Progress Administration. Basketlike traps, made of open mesh wire and containing young oysters, are placed on the borders of the seedbeds to attract the drills. The numerous traps are connected by subordinate ropes to master ropes which are kept on the surface by floats. Once a week men visit the baskets, shake off the drills into their skiffs and reset the traps for further catches. The drills are taken ashore by the millions and destroyed.

Sometimes storms carry mud or sand over the beds and suffocate the oysters. Another enemy of the oyster is polluted water. Against this nature has provided its own protection. Around the oyster is a membrane called a mantle, through which all water must pass. This mantle strains out any foreign substance and is so sensitive that it detects any dangerous matter in the water. Automatically the oystershell closes up before too much harmful water has entered. When the water is too cold (48 degrees Fahrenheit or less) the shell closes and the oyster hibernates, just as does a bear or a frog, and remains in this state until the water has become warm again.

The oyster beds of Delaware Bay extend halfway across the Bay from Cape May to Oyster Cove, just south of Stow Creek in Salem County. Midway between these points are the natural or seed grounds provided by nature. Here conditions of wind, tide and shore line provide ideal conditions for development of the seed oysters. To the north and south of these natural grounds are the planted grounds where oysters dredged from the natural beds are planted.

Oysters multiply by spawning. During the summer months, when the water reaches 70 degrees, female oysters on the planted grounds eject microscopic eggs by the million. The eggs, rising to the surface of the water in a cloudy mass, are fertilized by contacting the more abundant floating sperm of the male oysters. During this free-swimming period these potential oysters have the power to submerge or raise themselves in the water. In strong tides they sink to the bottom, where they remain until the danger of being swept out to sea has passed. Normally their drift is toward the natural seed grounds. When, at length, shells begin to form, the young oysters or "spats" sink permanently and attach themselves to whatever clean surface is available. Since the bottom of the bay is either sandy or muddy, and the young oyster can only attach itself to a clean surface, the State periodically spreads old oystershells over the bottom of the natural grounds, and to these the tiny organisms cling as they grow. From then on they are known as sets.

The natural or seed grounds, owned and controlled by the State, are a common property from which all licensed oystermen may gather seed, or sets, for their own licensed planting grounds. Each oysterman's license fee depends upon the tonnage of his boat, and, in the months of May and June only, each man may gather as many seed oysters from the natural grounds as his skill permits. During the other ten months the natural grounds are left to replenish themselves.

Seeking seed for planting, on May 1 the fleet of graceful white-sailed and freshly painted ships sets off for the natural seed grounds. From the Maurice River alone more than 100 boats leave at one time, necessitating expert seamanship to avoid collision. All propeller wheels are removed as required by law, for in shallow water a propellor would disturb the seed, and waste oils would endanger the young oysters.

At the seed grounds the oystermen cruise around, dragging dredges hung from both sides of the boats, slowly scraping from the bottom the old shells on which the spats have grown to the average size of a 25¢ piece. As soon as a catch has been hauled on deck the crew sets to work culling out those shells to which no seed oysters are attached.

OYSTER FLEET

Shells without attached seed are shoveled back into the water as required by law. State guards keep a sharp eye on the oyster boats to see that the unseeded shells are thrown back. Even the most hardened oystermen use rubber finger stalls in this work to avoid being cut by the sharp edges of the shells.

When he has gathered a load the captain hastens to his individual oyster ground to plant the new seed over bottom that he has dredged clean the previous year. Each oysterman divides his plot into sections marked off by stakes, each section containing oysters in different stages of development from the newly planted spats to mature oysters ready for market.

Harvesting begins in September. On the planted grounds the scene is not so picturesque as at the natural beds. The white sails—and sometimes the masts as well—have been removed, and powerful motors propel the schooners and work the winches. The captain, usually the owner, stands in the stern, handling the wheel and the ropes that apply the power to lower and raise the two dredges amidship. The deck crew of four or five men, often relatives of the owner, stand by to handle the dredges after the winches have drawn them to deck level.

These dredges are large, heavy bags made of iron rings. Holding open the mouth of each dredge is an iron frame edged with teeth on the under side. When the engine has lowered the dredges to the bottom they trail behind the schooner, like hand rakes on a lawn, gathering in oysters. When the dredges are raised to the rail the members of the crew hook the teeth of the dredges to a deck bar. The frames of the dredges now being locked in position, the oystermen seize the lower ends of the iron-mesh bags and, upending them, spill the contents on the deck. The dredges are then lowered again and the process is repeated. Vertical and horizontal rollers on the sides of the boats keep the dredges and chains from cutting into woodwork. When the ship is finally loaded, it turns either to the storage floats, to the wharves where the oysters are sorted for market, or to the shucking house. Then it chugs out for another load.

At the shucking houses the oysters are removed from the shells. The people who do this work are called shuckers, and they become so expert that they can open oysters as fast as a hungry oyster-eater can devour them. The shuckers grade oysters according to sizes, small, medium or very large. Opened oysters are placed in cans which are packed in cracked ice to be sent long distances.

Shellpile, opposite Port Norris on Maurice River, where oysters are shucked and shipped, derives its name from the immense piles of shells that accumulate in the process of shucking. The empty shells find a ready market. Some are converted into agricultural lime for fertilizer, some are rough-ground for use on poultry farms to provide a stronger growth of eggshell, and the rest are purchased by the State to spread on the natural seed grounds.

Recently there has been established at Port Norris a packing plant where oysters are vacuum packed in eight-ounce enamel-lined tins. Oysters are edible at any time, even in the R-less months; but since May to August is the spawning season, they are not dredged for market so as to enable the stock to multiply.

The possibility of finding a pearl in a New Jersey oyster is very remote. Certain chemicals and warm water are needed to create pearls. Therefore the waters of the Pacific and Indian Oceans are more friendly to the development of these valuable gems.

Oystermen in Delaware Bay are the stalwart, supple, weather-bronzed descendants of the pioneer Swedes and English who settled the Delaware Basin and began the oyster industry. While ashore in the idle months they apply themselves to fixing up their boats and houses. Being skillful seamen, they are in demand for taking out summer fishing parties. From a curious stranger they may withdraw into silence, but to overtures of friendly interest they respond with cordiality. Theirs is a simple, closely knit community life. They like their work and encourage their children to follow them in it.

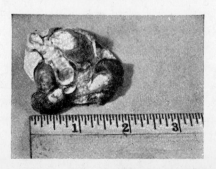

OYSTER
"SETS"

THE AGE OF PLASTICS

Webster's dictionary defines plastic as "capable of being molded or modeled." Quite recently the term plastics has been adopted to cover a great new industry that is fast entering every corner of modern life, from kitchen to office, from factory to palace.

Celluloid, Bakelite, Pyralin, Catalin, Lucite, Plastacele and many other substances belonging to this vast group of new products have become indispensable to 20th century civilization. In the interiors of buildings and ships plastics have replaced iron and wood. In homes they insulate electric appliances and supply heatproof handles for pots and kettles. Combs and buttons are made of plastic; father smokes a pipe with a plastic mouthpiece, and uses a plastic ashtray when mother watches him; and the windows in the car are safe only because a thin sheet of a cellulose plastic cemented between two sheets of glass makes them shatterproof. In fact, a list of all the products made of plastic material would make a sizable book.

Since 1873, when the Celluloid Manufacturing Company moved to Newark from Albany, New Jersey has been active in the production of plastics. In 1936 the value of plastics produced in New Jersey was $15,000,000, about one-third of the output of the entire Nation. Large producers that have followed the lead of the Celluloid Corporation in manufacturing various types of plastics are the Du Pont Company in Arlington, the Luzerne Rubber Company at Trenton, the Naugatuck Chemical Division of the United States Rubber Company, Passaic, the Richardson Company, New Brunswick, and the Bakelite Corporation, which in 1910 set up a factory at Perth Amboy and now has two large plants, one in Bound Brook and another in Bloomfield.

Civilization has progressed as man has learned to adapt to his needs materials of the three natural kingdoms: animal, vegetable and mineral. Down through the centuries he learned to till the fields, domesticate animals, utilize metals, the power of the wind and the water. More recently, in the 19th century, man's ingenuity enabled him to turn the wheels of great engines by harnessing steam, electricity, oil and gas.

All this had been done with the materials supplied by nature. The metals came from the earth. Water was a gift. Fire burned only because of oxygen in the air.

In the middle of the 19th century, however, there developed a shortage of certain natural products. There was not enough amber for combs and ornaments, bone for buttons, ivory for piano keys and billiard balls, to supply the increasing demand. Scientists and chemists began to look for substitutes. Here, indeed, was a new kingdom to be conquered. In this, which is coming to be called the fourth kingdom, men were seeking by formulas and scientific experiment to supplement the materials made in nature's laboratory.

To spur research a $10,000 prize was offered about 1860 for an ivory substitute in the making of billiard balls. John Wesley Hyatt, born in Starkey, New York, November 28, 1837, was working as a journeyman printer in Albany when he decided to try to produce the much-needed material and win the prize. He had little knowledge of chemistry, but he started conducting his experiments in his spare time, at night and on Sundays. Although he discovered several compositions, none was good enough to replace ivory billiard balls.

With the help of his two brothers Hyatt set up a factory to make checkers and dominoes out of pressed wood. Meanwhile he continued his search for an ivory substitute. Finally, about 1868, he mixed flakes of paper, shellac and collodion (a cottonlike substance mixed with alcohol and ether). Together these materials hardened into a new product. Billiard balls made from it sold by the thousands.

Inspired by success, Hyatt continued his experiments. He treated ordinary cotton with acids to form what is called cellulose nitrate or pyroxylin, added camphor and produced a plastic that would take any shape and harden quickly. It was a new product and must, therefore, have a new name. Hyatt's brother, Isaiah, an editor, chose "celluloid," a combination of the word "cellulose" and "oid" (from the Greek word meaning *like*).

Dentists were the first to make use of this new product to replace the dental plates of hard rubber then in use. The Hyatt brothers organized the Albany Dental Plate Company and prospered.

In 1871 they established the Celluloid Manufacturing Company and began making knife handles, piano keys, brushes and novelties. Two years later the factory was moved to Newark. Celluloid entered the political picture in 1872 when the first campaign buttons of that material were used in the contest between Grant and Greeley. Toward the end of the century, collars made of celluloid, which could be kept eternally fresh with a damp cloth, were a popular innovation.

The successful development of celluloid accelerated plastic research throughout the world. In Newark the

Reverend Hannibal Goodwin was handicapped by the continual breaking of the glass stereopticon plates he used to illustrate his Sunday School lectures. The minister saw that the celluloid developed by the Hyatt brothers might be used to replace the glass plates which were so easily broken. His problem was to make celluloid as clear as glass.

In his parsonage attic Goodwin went to work. Occasionally his wife and family downstairs were disturbed by explosions. The walls of the old house, still standing on Broad Street, bear the stains and scars of the experiments; but by 1887 he had succeeded in making and patenting a transparent film that was flexible enough to be wound on spools. This was the beginning of the motion picture.

In Germany, too, the search for newer and better plastics was continuing. In 1890 Dr. Adolph Spitteler, a Hamburg teacher, tried to make a white writing board as a substitute for the blackboard. He was experimenting with various chemicals with poor results, when one day he mixed ordinary sour milk with formaldehyde, a colorless gas. The result was a hard shiny substance that resembled the cow's horn rather than its milk. This material, known as casein plastic, is made into buckles, buttons and novelties.

About this time a new adventurer, Dr. Leo Baekeland, a Belgian chemist, entered the field. He had just perfected and sold to the Eastman Kodak Company his patent for Velox photographic printing paper and was looking for new fields of endeavor. He decided that if he could find a substitute for expensive shellac used in varnishes and insulating materials he would have answered a problem that had been facing chemists for years. Dr. Baekeland's

Courtesy Bakelite Corp'n

first work was to check the attempts of his colleagues to find out where they had failed.

He proceeded slowly and carefully, observing the reactions between various materials he was using. As he watched the changes taking place in the test tubes and retorts, he saw a promise of an entirely new material—something far beyond a substitute for natural resins.

In 1907 he was successful in obtaining a hard substance by combining phenol and formaldehyde. This new material had many of the properties of amber, but it was much stronger and harder, and it was almost impervious to heat. Once it had taken form under terrific heat, nothing could melt it. The new substance was called Bakelite resinoid after its inventor.

At the time of its invention, Dr. Baekeland estimated

Courtesy Bakelite Corp'n.

that this new product could be used in 43 industries.
Today Bakelite is used in hundreds of different ways.
Bakelite was first introduced to industry when the Boonton Rubber Company, Boonton, New Jersey, molded it
for use as insulating material at the request of an electrical company.

Generally speaking, there are two forms of plastics in
use today: thermoplastics and thermosetting plastics.
Thermoplastics, to which group celluloid belongs, may be
softened and remolded after they are formed; but the
thermosetting plastics can never be recast or remolded.
Bakelite is a member of the thermosetting plastic family.

Modern plastics, made from a soft mass, are cast and
molded into various shapes. In the production of molded
materials the liquid resinoid is allowed to harden. Then
it is pulverized and mixed with a filler such as wood,

Courtesy Du Pont & Co.

LUCITE

flour or asbestos. Under heat and pressure the substance becomes soft enough to be formed by dies into any desired shape. After it is shaped in this manner it is again allowed to harden. Molded Bakelite is a plastic of this kind.

Plastics for casting are poured while in a liquid state into forms where they harden. The product is furnished to the trade in sheets, rods and tubes which are cut as if they were wood or steel. Decorative and colorful plastics are made by the casting process.

When plastics enter into the construction of laminated sheets for use in radio cabinets, wallboards, electrical instrument panels, gear wheels and kindred products, a slightly different process is used. Instead of forming sheets of the plastic by molding or stamping, the resinoid is made in the form of a varnish. Into this liquid is dipped either paper or cloth. When many coats have been applied and dried, the stiffened cloth or paper is cut to the required size, and placed in layers one on top of the other. These are pressed together under terrific pressure and heat, and the whole mass solidifies into one sheet. This is called a laminated plastic because it is built of layers. It is much tougher than a plain plastic sheet would be, because the cloth or paper acts as a reinforcement.

Strangely enough, the plastic industry got its greatest stimulus during the business depression. Manufacturers everywhere were losing money and needed new products to stimulate sales. Newer, more durable and more beautiful plastics made their appearance in almost every conceivable shape. The "gadget" industry called on the plastic chemists to find new materials for ashtrays, cigarette holders, automobile accessories, ornamental jewelry, scuffless heels and countless other small items that are bought in great quantities.

Industries that had existed for years without using plastics began to employ them in an effort to brighten their wares. A large manufacturer of grocery scales found that his salesmen had to be brawny as well as brainy to demonstrate their ware. Some of the counter scales weighed as much as 165 pounds. A new plastic called Plaskon, one of the ureaformaldehyde resins, was invented to take the place of metal. Besides cutting the weight of the scales from 165 pounds to 55 pounds, Plaskon, which is made in bright colors, has been extended to include poker chips, buttons, boxes, radio cabinets and frames.

Other recent plastic products are: Catalin, a phenol-formaldehyde resin made in many colors for buckles, beads, chessmen, etc.; Lumarith, a cellulose acetate used in making noninflammable motion picture film; and Lucite, a methyl methacrylate plastic recently perfected by the E. I. Du Pont de Nemours Company which is carrying the industry into still another field.

This highly transparent and nonshattering plastic is so strong that it can be readily carved for ornamental use. Because it retains transparency and can be more accurately molded than glass, Lucite has been introduced in reflectors for highway lighting. Placed at regular intervals on either side of the road, these reflectors pick up the light from oncoming automobiles and illuminate the roadway so effectively that much of the glare from headlights is eliminated. This is a long step toward overcoming the dangers of night driving.

In Washington, the new Library of Congress contains $100,000 worth of Bakelite laminated plastics, used both for decoration and utility. A comparable sum was spent on plastics for the de luxe staterooms on the new British liner *Queen Mary*.

The work of improving and inventing plastics goes on. The field is almost unlimited. Even the inventors cannot foresee all of the new uses to be found for their products. It is possible that plastic houses will be built before many years; or that some article, hitherto undreamed of, will be placed on the market and revolutionize modern life.

CEDAR MINING IN NEW JERSEY'S SUNKEN FOREST

Mining and lumbering, two industries that seem to bear little relation to one another, have been combined uniquely in the swamplands of southern New Jersey in a district that looks as if it would yield nothing but mud and mosquitoes. A century or more ago a sunken forest of white cedar was discovered in the Great Cedar Swamp which stretches for seven miles across the neck of Cape May peninsula, following the shores of Dennis Creek and Cedar Creek, that drain the swamp's overflow.

Early settlers of the region dug into the thick muck of the swamp and brought up great trees that had lain for centuries covered more and more by the accumulation of swamp ooze. From these they cut logs and shingles for their homes.

Cedar mining was an important industry in South Jersey until about 50 years ago. Then, as cheaper lumber was brought in from the northwest, the industry fell into a decline. Recently a small company of men engaged in removing peat for fertilizer from the swamplands near Haleyville in Cumberland County discovered another sunken forest. Logs buried from 4 to 20 feet deep are now being mined and sent to the sawmill at Dennisville to be made into planks. Cedar is valuable for use as shingles, siding for boats, and for other purposes where it will be called on to resist water.

It is this quality of resistance to dampness that has pre-

SEARCHING FOR CEDAR LOGS

served the buried cedar logs. Lumber cut from them is as usable as that made from living cedar and gives off the same fragrance as if it had been cut yesterday in the green forests.

It is not uncommon to find buried cedar logs in swampy places throughout the United States; but there are few places where men have troubled to dig for the hidden treasure. No one can estimate how long these logs have lain in their mucky bed. The count of the annual ring growths on one of the logs recently mined showed that the tree was 500 years old when it fell. There is a tradition of a log found a century ago with more than 1,000 rings.

The submergence of these cedar trees is explained in several ways—none of which has been proved conclusively. One school of thought has it that the land on which the trees stood sank gradually. As water began to stand around the trees the earth softened, the trees lost their hold, and overturned. The land continued to sink and eventually the growth was entirely buried beneath the silt. Another theory maintains that a great hurricane once leveled the entire forest of about 12 square miles.

The felled giants then slowly sank beneath the ooze. Among the many legends of South Jersey is one that attributes the submergence of the cedar forest to the flood that prompted the building of Noah's Ark.

The surface of the swamp is largely covered with brush and a few stunted trees surrounded by pools of water. There are higher spots, however, where the ground is dry and where farming has been made possible by the use of dykes that keep out floods.

That South Jersey land is sinking has been well known for a century or more. Commodore Stephen Decatur when a guest at Cape May Point measured the loss each year from 1804 to 1820 and found that the coast had receded about 160 feet in that time. The State geologist 70 years ago reported the sea still advancing. The silt that has buried the trees has also filled some of the streams. There are records and pictures of large ships built along Dennis Creek where only motorboats now run. There are great areas of salt marsh on the coast of Delaware Bay once said to have been farm land.

When the first white settlers came to southern New Jersey they found themselves much hampered in their explorations of the interior by the Great Swamp, which prevented their building roads across the land, and they had to use boats to travel. It is not certain how or when they discoverd the sunken forest, but it probably was very early in the State's history. There is a cabin made of hand-hewn cedar timber on the grounds of the Hancock House, at Hancock's Bridge near Salem, that is said to have been built by the Swedes more than 200 years ago with cedar mined from the swamps of New Jersey. In 1740, when Independence Hall needed a roof, hand-split shingles from the Great Cedar Swamp's logs were used, and about

30 years ago the Hall was reshingled with Cape May cedar.

For many years there has been at Dennisville a saw-mill that cuts the logs into planks and shingles. Captain Ogden Gandy, now 90 years old, runs the sawmill. He remembers the days when ships of 200 to 1,000 tons were built along Dennis Creek. At that time most of the men in this neighborhood were seafarers. Between voyages young Gandy used to mine the cedar logs and help to cut them into boards and shingles.

It is said by some people that shingles made from these cedar logs will last for 100 years, although Mr. Gandy does not claim a longer life for them than 60 or 65 years. One of the customers of the Dennisville sawmill was a water tank builder. One day he told Mr. Gandy that he would buy no more of his material, because it was too good. "Tanks built of your cedar last a lifetime," he said, "and I never get repeat orders. I can build a tank of soft Southern pine and in a few years my customer will need another tank." The tank builder never bought another foot of cedar.

The cedar wood is used in boatbuilding, although it is not tough enough for the hulls of large ships. It is used for the center boards of boats and for parts of motorboats and other small craft.

The men who go out into the swamps to mine the sub-merged cedar are called "swampers." Armed with progues, which are iron rods about 12 feet long, pointed at one end with a ring or loop at the other, the swampers poke around in the deep muck until one of them strikes a sound log. With his progue the swamper finds out just how the log lies; then he and his helpers shovel off the muck until the log is in view.

LONG CEDAR PLANKS CUT FOR BOAT BUILDING

With log saws, very much like those used to cut ice from lakes and rivers, the logs are cut into six-foot lengths. While the men are cutting the logs the water flows into the hole made by taking off the muck. In many instances the water will be deep enough to allow the sawed-off section to float to the surface. This, of course, is a help to the swamper, for then all he has to do is attach a rope to the section, place a couple of skids under it, and haul it to solid footing.

When the logs do not float to the surface the swampers are obliged to fasten a rope or chain around the section, pull it to the surface, and then lift it with skids and man power.

In the last few years a tractor, or perhaps an old automobile engine, or, if conditions permit, a truck has been used to haul the logs out after they are cut. The logs are dragged to a point where the ground is solid enough to enable them to be loaded on trucks and hauled to the sawmill.

They have to lie in the sun for some time to dry out. Then the outside slabs are cut off, either thick or thin, according to the quality of the log. The balance of the log is cut into strips for the manufacture of shingles. Some of the board lengths are kept for use in boatbuilding.

Because of the inaccessibility of the swamplands and the difficulty and expense of extracting the logs from their ancient burial place, it is not likely that cedar mining will ever be a major industry. But those who have made use of this prehistoric cedar value it for its lasting quality.

TRANSPORTATION

JOHN FITCH AND HIS STEAMBOAT

Whistles from tugboats, ferries and factories salute the arrival of every new transatlantic liner on her maiden voyage to New York Harbor. Streams of water are sprayed from a municipal fireboat, planes wheel overhead with newsreel cameramen, excursion boats and small craft of every kind cluster about the giant vessel, while trim gray patrol boats of the Coast Guard regulate the harbor traffic. From the skyscrapers of Manhattan and from the shores of Brooklyn and Staten Island thousands of people watch the new liner as she noses her way up the channel, past the Statue of Liberty and into a berth on the Hudson River.

There were no whistles, planes or skyscrapers on an August day in 1807 when an awkward little boat with a tall smokestack churned steadily up the river toward Albany at the then amazing speed of four miles an hour. No photographers recorded the scene, but there were thousands of watchers on both shores of the river to shout and cheer with a fervor that is unknown to the placid throngs who turn out these days to see a new ship come in.

The little steamboat, the *Clermont*, built by Robert Fulton, was hailed as one of the wonders of the world. Back of the demonstration that brought permanent fame to Fulton was the story of another man's struggle, discouragement and tragic death; a story that has been almost lost in the crowded record of America's progress.

Nine years before the triumphal voyage of the *Cler-*

mont, Colonel John Stevens, at his home in Hoboken, New Jersey (now the site of Stevens' Institute of Technology), had perfected a steamboat which he tried out on a run from Belleville to New York. This boat he called the *Little Juliana.* In 1807 he applied for a lease to operate his second boat, the *Phoenix,* as a steam ferry between Hoboken and New York. This was the first steam ferry in the world, but it had a short career, for Robert Fulton had obtained from New York a monopoly to operate boats on the Hudson, and Stevens was ordered to take his boat out of service.

Nothing daunted, the *Phoenix* steamed jauntily down the bay to the open sea and headed for the Delaware River, thus making a record as the first ocean-going steam vessel.

But 20 years before the sensational voyage of the *Clermont,* another boat on another river had dazzled the imagination of a group of prominent American citizens, members of the convention gathered in Philadelphia to frame a Federal Constitution. This was the first boat in America to be propelled by steam for any distance, the invention of John Fitch, an obscure clockmaker and silversmith, born in Connecticut in 1743.

At the outbreak of the Revolution Fitch had been made a lieutenant in the Colonial Army. It soon became apparent that he would be of more service to the cause as a gunsmith and armorer, and Washington ordered him to Trenton. He worked long hours on weekdays and even Sundays in his gun shop, making arms for the fighting men. His few spare moments were devoted to study. Books were rare in those days, but Fitch read every one he could find. When the British entered Trenton in 1776, Fitch fled with what belongings he could gather to Bucks

County, Pennsylvania, where he buried part of his little hoard of savings. The English had heard of his activities as a gunsmith and destroyed his little shop on King Street.

At the close of the Revolution Fitch sought an appointment as a surveyor in the western country soon to be opened up to settlers. He had traveled as far west as Kentucky. There he had invested some of his savings in land.

Soon after this fresh start he had been captured by savages while on a voyage down the Ohio and had been marched by them through the wilderness as far west as Detroit. From his experience with the Indians he retained a vision of the vast opportunities that were offered in the unexplored country; great rivers, and miles of woodland ready for the hand of the enterprising white man. So far the only means of reaching this new treasure-land was by horse- or mule-drawn wagons, or hand-propelled boats.

One day after his return to Pennsylvania, Fitch was walking along the street in Neshaminy. His progress somewhat slowed by rheumatism contracted during his wilderness journeys, he looked rather enviously at a dashing horse-drawn carriage that sped by him. Speed—that was what was wanted in this new country—and power that would draw heavy loads.

He had read of the Englishman, James Watt, who had discovered the power of steam. To Fitch and others the idea had occurred that steam might be used to propel wagons. Although he had never seen a drawing of a steam engine, he began to design an engine for wagons. After working with the idea enthusiastically for a week, he decided it would be impractical to operate a heavy vehicle over the rough roads.

But he did think that a steam engine might move a boat against tide and wind and at greater speed than was possible with sail or oars. Afire with his new idea, he set to work on drawings for a boat with an engine. Three weeks later he took his drawings to a friend, the Reverend Nathaniel Irwin, who was much interested in the young inventor's idea. The minister took from his shelves a book with a description and drawing of a stationary steam engine. This was the first that Fitch knew of an engine in operation, although one had been used for pumping at the copper mine in Arlington, New Jersey, since 1753. News traveled slowly in those days, but ideas for inventions were developed in all parts of the civilized world among people who had no communication with one another—ideas born of the necessity for improving man's mode of life.

When Fitch saw that a practical use had been found for steam, he set to work with renewed enthusiasm to carry out his plan. Like all inventors and men of genius who can see into the future beyond the actual accomplishment of their own hands and brain, Fitch visioned steamboats traveling up and down the rivers of the new country, carrying food and clothing to the new settlers in the wilderness, bringing back wood, furs and other products to

JOHN FITCH'S STEAMBOAT OF 1786, 1787

the cities on the coast. He gathered all available literature on the steam engine and saturated his mind with it. His first model, built of brass, had wooden side paddle wheels; but he later abandoned these in favor of a row of oars or paddles suspended from a frame.

Fitch Seeks Aid

He traveled to Mount Vernon to see General Washington to enlist his interest in presenting his idea to Congress —not only to protect his patent rights but to secure financial aid. He interviewed the members of the legislatures of Virginia, Pennsylvania, Delaware, New York and New Jersey. The last-named State was the first to grant him exclusive rights to construct and operate steamboats on the rivers and streams under its jurisdiction. This was in March 1786. The other states followed New Jersey's example shortly, but Congress still withheld its support.

From Virginia came a rival claim, made by a young man named James Rumsey, who said that he had invented a steamboat. Fitch refuted his claim by proving that the boat was propelled only by a stream of water sucked in at the bow and forced out at the stern by a steam engine. Rumsey's boat, moreover, moved at only two miles an hour and never traveled more than 400 yards.

But Fitch needed more than legal rights to carry out his plan successfully. Money was necessary to build models, and money was one thing that John Fitch did not have. He has come down in history as "Poor John Fitch." Although the "poor" probably refers to the unjust treatment he received and the chain of unfortunate circumstances that thwarted his ambition, it is probably true that, if John Fitch had been able to command enough money to work out his experiments, his sad story would have had a very different ending.

He tried to enlist the support of the American Philosophical Society of Philadelphia, of which Benjamin Franklin was president. But Franklin, whose many inventions were already being widely used in America and Europe, was merely amused at Fitch's efforts. Having seen the plans and the first working model, Franklin remarked: "The amount of room taken up in the hull by the engine and fuel and the excessive cost of upkeep makes this type of navigation unfeasible. I do not believe it will ever prove practical."

Fitch's enthusiasm and many letters of appeal gained him enough backing to organize "The Steam Boat Company," as fantastic a title in those days as would be "The Mars Transportation Company" today. When the company had accumulated $300 in subscriptions the intrepid inventor started to work to build his boat. He had managed to secure the aid of a young watchmaker named Henry Voigt. Together they labored hours over models and plans until on July 27, 1786, they announced that they were ready to demonstrate the successful operation of a boat by steam.

The boat was about 45 feet long, with a row of paddles on either side attached to an endless chain. Not much larger than a fisherman's dory, most of the space in the hull was taken up by the bulky engine, and what little room remained was occupied by the piles of wood required for fuel.

The noise and confusion caused by the crude engine scared many of the onlookers, who expected it to explode at any minute. Not a few of the crowd moved away before the tiny vessel had a fair trial. One person, however, had faith in the future of Fitch's ideas. He was the Spanish Ambassador to this country, who wanted the rights to the invention for his own country. Fitch refused his offers of financial aid, preferring to keep his invention for the improvement of America's commerce.

The Steamboat Runs

The inventor returned to his workshop, determined to improve on his first attempt. On August 22, 1787, with all members of the Constitutional Convention except General Washington present, John Fitch's second steamboat, its engine chugging steadily, moved sedately up the Delaware River against the tide, its paddles swinging rhythmically on either side. Despite the success of the demonstration, people could not see that steam would ever operate a boat as quickly or cheaply as sails or oars. Moreover,

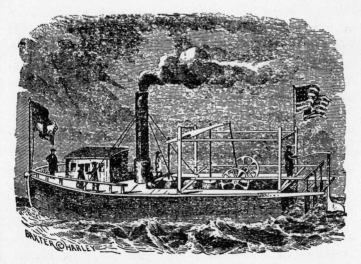

JOHN FITCH'S STEAMBOAT—1788, 1789, 1790

they looked askance at the snorting little demon that furnished the uncanny power, and expected the whole contraption to blow up.

There were, however, a number of people, inspired by Fitch's enthusiasm, willing to finance further experiments in overcoming defects in the engine. Once more the inventor and his mechanic went to work. By July 1788 they were ready to launch another boat on the Delaware. The new model had a row of paddles, shaped somewhat like snow shovels, at the stern. The whole countryside turned out for the exhibition. Both shores of the river were lined with cheering spectators as the little craft plowed against the current up to Bordentown, making eight miles an hour.

Just before reaching the dock the boiler sprang a leak so that the engine would not work. They had to cast anchor and wait for the next tide to float them ashore. Nevertheless, John Fitch's boat had done what had never been done in the world before. It had been impelled for twenty miles by steam against the tide. This little accident was of the sort that turns enthusiasts into scoffers. But to a man like John Fitch, who had faith in his ideas and determination to succeed, it acted only as an incentive.

Fitch and Voigt returned to their workshop and by October had completely redeemed themselves. Two successful trips with boatloads of passengers were made to Burlington in 190 minutes.

Fitch's crowning achievement was his commercial steamboat of 1790. All that summer the boat carried passengers and freight to and from various points along the Delaware and Schuylkill. It was operated on a schedule, just as are the steamboats of today. But it was not a financial success. The public did not patronize it, for they saw no practical use for steamboats. Time meant very little in those easy-going days, and it was hard to convince them that coal and wood would ever be more effective than wind.

Fitch was eager to present the Nation with his precious gift. He was sure that steam navigation would play a great part in the opening up of the west by conquering the waters of the mighty Mississippi; but his pleadings fell upon deaf ears, and he was consistently ignored by the Federal Government.

Money for further experiments was hard to find. One boat, built for use on the Ohio River, ran aground in a storm and was wrecked. There were constant accidents that discouraged his backers, while powerful friends of Rumsey did all they could to balk his efforts.

Fitch Goes to Europe

The various uses to which the new steam power could be put was a subject that was occupying the attention of inventors and scientists the world over. Considerable experimentation was going on in England, France, Holland and other European countries at this time. Discouraged by the attitude of his fellow countrymen and anxious to see what could be gained by further investigation, Fitch managed to secure the aid of a few faithful friends to finance a trip abroad.

With the idea of exploiting his plans in some of the continental countries, he took into his confidence Aaron Vail, the U. S. consul at l'Orient, France. Unfortunately, Fitch had chosen an inopportune time to promote his idea in France. This was the year 1793, and the turmoil of the French Revolution put an end to his plans. Leaving his drawings and specifications with Vail in France, Fitch traveled to England. Perhaps another reason for his failure to get a hearing was that among the number of people in Europe at the time studying the problem of steam navigation was Robert Fulton. Fulton had what Fitch had not—a rich, enthusiastic, liberal and influential patron, Chancellor Robert Livingston of New York. He also had at his disposal the very best machinery that could be made in Europe, whereas Fitch had made his own with the help of an ordinary blacksmith. There seems little doubt that Fulton had access to Fitch's drawings while they were in the hands of Aaron Vail, for when the *Clermont* sailed up the Hudson in 1807 her engine was designed from plans that had originated and been patiently worked out by the obscure and forgotten genius.

In the depths of his discouragement, two years before, Fitch had said one day, when he was 48 years old, "The day will come when some more powerful man will get fame and riches from my invention; but nobody will believe that poor John Fitch can do anything worthy of attention."

Return to America

Wearied and discouraged, and completely out of money, Fitch shipped for home as a common sailor. For a while he wandered about Philadelphia, trying desperately to gain the backing he so badly needed. Frantic at the blindness of Congress, utterly powerless to obtain recognition that was justly his, hungry and poorly clad and half-demented from discouragement, he turned his back on the scene of his disappointment and proceeded to his land in Kentucky. He found it occupied by squatters whom he had to eject.

He tried to gain the support of his Congressman from

Kentucky, but met with the usual rebuff. Heartbroken, penniless and tired of the long struggle, Fitch committed suicide during the spring of 1798. He was buried in a pauper's grave in the churchyard at Bardstown, Kentucky.

His death went unnoticed, and by the time Fulton launched his *Clermont* in 1807 Fitch was no longer even a memory. The success of Fulton's vessel struck the world like a bombshell, and credit for the invention of the steamboat went to Fulton on a sweeping tide of public admiration.

In 1887, exactly 100 years after Fitch's first steamboat was launched on the Delaware River, the Legislature of Connecticut, the State in which he was born, placed a bronze tablet to his memory on the east wall of the State Capitol. The memorial reads: "First in world's history to invent and apply steam propulsion of vessels through water." The tablet was dedicated with appropriate ceremonies.

The citizens of Kentucky, Fitch's adopted State, were spurred into action as a result of the Connecticut memorial. The inventor's body was removed from its obscure burial place to the Bardstown Public Square. A fund of $15,000 was obtained from Congress to erect a suitable memorial to Fitch's memory, and the body of the illustrious pioneer in steam navigation was placed in a sarcophagus.

At Trenton, along the banks of the Delaware on John Fitch Way, a memorial boulder, placed in 1921, honors the man whose crude engine was the first to disturb the placid waters of the river.

THE FIRST RAILROAD IN NEW JERSEY

James Watt, a studious lad, seated in his mother's kitchen in Greenock, Scotland, watched the lid of the teakettle rise from the pressure of the steam within. He realized then that steam was power. This discovery, and the boy's ability to apply it in the first stationary steam engine, brought about the railroad.

In 1788, at his home in Hoboken, Colonel John Stevens, engineer, read of the invention of the young Scot in an English journal and ordered one of the Watt stationary engines shipped to him. Stevens was one of the forward-looking men of the country. He had served as an officer in the Revolution and at the age of 27 was appointed State Treasurer. He realized that transportation was to play a great part in the development of the country that he loved, and he saw in the Watt steam engine promise of a solution of this problem. At first he devoted his experiments to applying steam to navigation, although there were many others working in this same field.

When the adaptation of steam power to boats was assured by the successes of John Fitch, Robert Fulton and Stevens' own *Little Juliana* (the first regularly operated steam ferry in the world), the indefatigable engineer turned his attention to the development of a steam-propelled wagon.

This was a period when a change in the method of hauling freight from one part of the State to the other was under consideration. Canals, expensive as they were to build and to maintain, seemed to be the only alternative to the horse-drawn wagons traveling the almost impassable roads.

As early as 1812 Stevens had urged De Witt Clinton, later Governor of New York, to abandon plans for the proposed Erie Canal and to substitute a railroad. He claimed that a speed of 20 to 30 miles an hour could be attained with railroad cars and declared that 100 miles an hour might be achieved. He had traveled in vain to New York, Pennsylvania and even as far as North Carolina, trying to have the legislatures appropriate funds for his railroad-building plan. But he was considered a visionary, and Chancellor Robert Livingston of New York bade him try out his railroad himself in order to see whether there was really anything practical in his plan.

The colonel was an old man well in his seventies, but he was indomitable. In 1824 he completed construction of an experimental "steam waggon," as he called it, and built a circular track on the grounds of his Hoboken estate (now occupied by the athletic field of Stevens' Institute). He invited the members of the Society for Internal Improvement, of which he was the founder, to witness the result of his years of study and experiment. The engine was mounted on a platform with ordinary wagon wheels which were geared to the track by casters placed at the end of vertical posts on each corner of the frame. The fire was built, the water connected with the tubes from a barrel, steam generated in confinement, just as the steam had been generated in the kettle in Greenock, the throttle was opened, and the wheels of the "steam waggon" turned. Around and around the wooden track at 12 miles an hour traveled the first locomotive built and operated in this country. The boiler and steam valve used that momentous day are now in the Smithsonian Institution in Washington.

John Stevens, 76 years old when he accomplished this marvel, could not expect to realize his dream of wide railroad development. But he had made the initial step, and his sons would carry on for him.

In 1830 the two sons, Robert Livingston and Edwin, became president and treasurer respectively of the Camden and Amboy Railroad, chartered by the New Jersey Legislature. The cars were to be horse-drawn and used primarily for freight. Despite the successful performance in England of a locomotive made by George Stephenson called the *Rocket*, few people considered steam locomotives seriously. Nevertheless, Robert L. Stevens, following in the path laid out by his father, sailed for England to investigate the new engine, authorized to order one should it appear practicable.

Stevens had been studying the problem of rails and on the way over whittled out in wood the model of a design for T-rails, which are the standard rails in use on all American railroads today. Arriving in England, he had considerable difficulty in finding a firm that would manufacture the iron rails according to his specifications. Finally, by placing a generous deposit against the possible breakdown of the machinery, he persuaded a mill operator to undertake the job.

An improvement on the *Rocket* called the *Planet* gave so satisfactory a demonstration that Stevens decided to order one engine for the new American railroad. Pending the arrival of the new engine, Robert and Edwin Stevens had the roadbed laid at Bordentown. Rock was transported from the quarries at Sing Sing, New York, and laid much as a cobblestone road would be spread, the spikes to hold the rails down being driven between the stones. But the failure of a shipment of rock caused the road builders to try wooden ties, which were found to be far more satisfactory.

The *John Bull*, as the locomotive was called, with all its component parts and the six and one-half miles of rail, reached Bordentown in 24 shiploads during 1831. The arrival caused considerable excitement; but to young Isaac Dripps, the mechanic who had undertaken to assemble the engine, it was a matter of deep concern. The parts were uncrated and laid on the ground. Then it was discovered that Stephenson and Company, the English makers of the engine, had neglected to send the drawings by which it could be assembled. Here was a picture puzzle in iron that would have dismayed most mechanics, but it did not deter Isaac Dripps. He had never seen a locomotive, but he set to work doggedly, fitting one part to the other, and by trial and error the *John Bull* finally took shape after several weeks of hard labor.

The locomotive was fitted on its wooden platform and to this was attached the tender, another wooden platform which carried pinewood for fuel and a whisky barrel filled with water. The barrel and the engine were connected by a leather pipe made by a local cobbler. Behind the tender were two carriages with flanged wheels to fit the tracks and with benches for the passengers. The engine had been tried out several times to see whether Dripps had managed to get all the parts just in the right places, and now, on November 12, 1831, all was ready for the final test. Invitations had been sent to members of the legislature at Trenton. All Bordentown and vicinity turned out for a gala day. In the gathering were many

A PIECE OF CAMDEN & AMBOY R. R. TRACK SHOWING
STONE TIES

farmers ready to celebrate the failure of the experiment, for if this newfangled thing worked they stood to lose the business of supplying horses and their feed to the railroads. They could not foresee that success would help every Jerseyman who had anything to sell to the great outside world.

When Ben Higgins, assistant to Dripps, stoked the boiler with pinewood, and the great plumes of black smoke shot from the funnel, the people backed away. It must have been a fearsome sight. The visitors were reluctant to accept invitations to ride. But there was one in the crowd who was not afraid, Madame Murat, wife of Prince Murat, exiled French nobleman who was living in Bordentown at the time. She tucked her bonnet down tightly, drew her billowing skirts close to her legs, and was helped

Courtesy D. Appleton-Century Co.

THE JOHN BULL

up to a seat in one of the carriages. Following her example, the rest of the company stepped gingerly on board; Robert Stevens gave the word to the faithful Dripps, and the throttle was pulled open. The wheels spun ineffectually for a while but finally gripped the tracks, and the Camden and Amboy Railroad was functioning. Later, their clothes strewn with ashes and their eyes filled with smoke, the group of dignitaries and their friends made their way triumphantly to Arnell's Hotel, where a gala luncheon was served.

Following the demonstration the *John Bull* waited patiently in a shed while the railroad was finished between Bordentown and South Amboy. In September of the following year it was placed in regular service.

In 1891 the Pennsylvania Railroad, which had leased

the Camden and Amboy 20 years previously, erected a monument at Bordentown in honor of the *John Bull*. Sunk in a granite slab is a bronze tablet with this inscription:

> First movement by steam on a railroad in the State of New Jersey, November 12, 1831, by the original locomotive "John Bull," now deposited in the United States National Museum in Washington. The first piece of track in New Jersey was laid by the Camden and Amboy Railroad between this point and the stone 3500 feet eastward, in 1831.

The Camden and Amboy, however, cannot claim the honor of being the first American railroad with locomotive power. The Baltimore and Ohio Railroad, the oldest company in continuous service in the United States, sent out its first train from Baltimore on August 28, 1830. It ran to Ellicott's Mills, a distance of 13 miles, drawn by an engine called the *Tom Thumb*, built by Peter Cooper. There was also the Carbondale and Honesdale Railroad in Pennsylvania, which made a trial run with an English engine, the *Stourbridge Lion*, August 8, 1829.

The railroads developed so rapidly that the little *John Bull* was soon out of date. It was stowed away in the care of the Smithsonian Institution along with the boiler and steam valve of Colonel John Stevens' earlier locomotive that had raced around his circular track at Stevens' Castle.

After 62 years, in 1893, the iron picture puzzle that Isaac Dripps had so laboriously put together for Robert and Edwin Stevens was run out of the Museum and given another opportunity to display its prowess. Beside a modern locomotive, it looked like a beetle. It was taken to New York and there hitched to the old carriages that it had first drawn. There had been a long search to find them. One was being used as a chicken coop; the feathered passengers had to be dispossessed. The *John Bull* and its ancient tender and carriages were put on the railroad tracks and pointed due west. The boiler was stoked, water fed the tubes, steam generated once more in the old engine, and with a snort the train was under way for Chicago, 930 miles distant. The journey was made without breakdown or accident. In every city and village along the way it was hailed by enthusiastic crowds. Its holiday ended, the antique locomotive was taken back to Washington, there to remain as a symbol of great American achievements.

THE MORRIS CANAL

In the 1820's America was expanding, and there was great enthusiasm for artificial waterways to transport heavy materials such as coal and iron from the isolated interior to the growing manufacturing centers along the Atlantic seaboard. There were vast stretches of country rich in iron and coal that were forced to depend for transportation on the slow-moving horse- or mule-drawn wagons traveling the often impassable roads.

One day in 1822 a Morristown, New Jersey, man named George P. McCulloch was fishing at Great Pond, or Lake Hopatcong as it is now called. It occurred to him that the amount of water spilling out of that lake would be enough to maintain a canal running from Hopatcong east to Newark and west to the Delaware. At that time coal from the mines in the vicinity of Easton, Pennsylvania, had to be transported to eastern cities by the long water route down the Delaware and up the New Jersey coast, or by wagons which could haul only a ton. Fox Hill, between Denville and Parsippany, was a grade of almost 30 percent. It took powerful horses and oxen to haul even a small load over the hill.

Following the discovery of iron ore all over Morris County, forges had sprung up before the Revolution. In a single stretch of the proposed canal between Rockaway and Andover, a distance of 15 miles, there were 56 forges, most of which had been forced to shut down because they had practically exhausted the local supply of wood fuel.

Large shipments of coal through the canal would mean the rebirth of this industry.

McCulloch's idea gained in popularity, and a bill was introduced in the 1824 session of the New Jersey Legislature in an attempt to obtain State funds for building the canal. The legislature did nothing about it. The canal backers, however, got a charter authorizing them to build a canal with private funds, if the money could be raised. Under the name of the Morris Canal and Banking Company the corporation was launched in a spirit of speculative enthusiasm. The charter was so liberal that it permitted the company to issue its own currency. Years later the company was forced into bankruptcy as a result of the privileges which seemed so desirable when it began.

The original charter provided for a capital stock of $2,500,000. The right to condemn land for canal purposes was granted. The State retained the right to take over the canal at a fair valuation after 99 years or to extend the charter 50 years, after which ownership would pass to the State without payment. Another provision granted the heirs of the original owners the right to repossess the land that they had given or sold in case the canal was abandoned. Some of the land was given outright. Some was bought for the nominal sum of 6¢ an acre, and some was seized without due process of law.

Interest in the Morris Canal and great expectations for its money-making possibilities were stimulated by the success of the Erie Canal in New York, completed in 1825. But the New Jersey route offered serious obstacles for the engineers. In order to traverse the 55 miles from the Hudson to the Delaware the canal would have to wind for almost twice that distance through the hills, climb to

a height of 1,000 feet, and descend more than 700 feet over the humpbacked ridge of New Jersey.

The only solution was to build planes, or inclined tracks, connecting one level of water with another. A boat was floated onto a cradle that ran under the water on tracks. When the boat had settled securely on the cradle, both were dragged uphill by chains wound on drums. Power was supplied by the overflow of water from the upper to the lower levels. When the cradle reached the top it was run into a lock; water was admitted, and the boat floated off the cradle again. From there the boat proceeded by mule power to the next plane, where the operation was repeated. In this way the boats were literally carried over the mountains. For gentler changes in elevation, ordinary locks were used without planes. When the canal was completed it had 23 planes and 23 locks.

Construction of the Morris Canal began in 1825, soon

THE CANAL
CROSSES THE PAS-
SAIC RIVER ON AN
AQUEDUCT

after the first money had been raised. Six years later the waterway was opened to traffic between Newark and Phillipsburg. Hand labor was the backbone of the construction job. Concrete, as used today, was unknown. All masonry had to be of stone construction, held together by lime mortar. There were no compressed-air drills or dynamite, no steam shovels or motor trucks, no iron girders or "I" beams. A working day was from sunrise to sunset. The wages were 90 cents a day or even less.

Rocks were blasted by drilling holes with hand drills and then filling the holes with black powder. After tamping them with clay and dropping a glowing coal on the clay, the blaster ran for cover. Practically every foot of earth and stone was removed from the canal excavation by hand. Even wheelbarrows were scarce. Horses and oxen were needed for farm work and were grudgingly loaned or leased for canal construction.

The organizers of the canal company, more interested in the project as a stock-selling proposition than as a useful enterprise, were short-sighted in making their plans. The canal was built only 52 feet wide at the top, 20 feet wide at the bottom and 4 feet deep. Compared with the other canals of that day, it was far too small. The 70-ton barges in use on the Lehigh Canal in Pennsylvania were too large for the new canal. This meant that the coal, instead of being carried direct from the mines in Pennsylvania, had to be transferred from the large boats to smaller ones carrying only 25 tons.

Although the canal was designed primarily for commerce, people were so delighted with the picturesque waterway that a packet boat drawn by three horses made daily excursions between Newark and Paterson. Fares were 25¢ to Bloomfield and 50¢ to Passaic. This was a favorite holiday trip for Newarkers.

From Phillipsburg on the Delaware, opposite Easton, the canal ascended Pohatcong Mountain, came down again, and idled past Port Murray, Rockport and Hackettstown. Passing Saxton Falls, it edged along Sussex County at Waterloo and Stanhope and then touched Lake Hopatcong, its water source, and came into Morris County. Here it made a snakelike way to the east, passing Morris Landing, Kenvil, Wharton, Dover, Rockaway, Boonton, Towaco, Mountain View. At Little Falls it crossed the Passaic River in a wooden aqueduct, finally turning southward through Belleville and Newark to Newark Bay.

The inclined planes, which had delighted visiting legislators and other observers when they were first tested, sometimes provided unexpected thrills. Upon one occasion a car carrying the barge *Electa* was beginning the descent of the Boonton plane when the sprocket chain broke. Laden with iron, the boat tore down the track at terrific speed, striking the water at the bottom with such force that it ricocheted over a 20-foot embankment into a clump of trees. The captain's wife, extricating herself from the branches, "allowed" she had come down pretty fast, but thought "that was the way the thing worked." After more serious accidents, hemp ropes were substituted for chains, and damage to boats, canal equipment and human beings was somewhat reduced. Eventually the hemp ropes were replaced by wire cables.

Although it was doomed to financial failure and decay, the new waterway brought prosperity to the adjoining country during its comparatively brief existence. Before the barges came with coal from the Pennsylvania mines, Boonton was a village with grass-grown streets. It sprang into life with a blast furnace, four forges and a mill for manufacturing iron sheets. The machinery and expert workers were brought from England, and soon 200 people were employed by the East Jersey Iron Manufacturing Co. Forges and iron works flourished throughout the northern part of the State. Little towns such as Port Murray, Port Colden, Pequannock, Pompton and Rockaway were developed. The canal proved an industrial godsend to Newark, where factories eagerly awaited cheap coal. The city doubled its population between 1830 and 1835.

In 1836 there was a wave of national prosperity; Morris Canal stock, which had sold at 32 in 1834, rose to 188 in a year. The dirctors purchased $6,000,000 worth of improvement bonds of Indiana and Michigan, then young and struggling States. After selling these to the public, some of the money was used to extend the Morris Canal to Jersey City, but most of it was dissipated. Then the canal was mortgaged for nearly $1,000,000, but the stockholders' interests were not protected. The company went bankrupt and thousands of investors lost everything.

Out of the proceedings, however, came a reorganized canal company. In 1844 the canal was enlarged, enabling the heavier Lehigh boats to come directly from the mines through the Lehigh Canal, across the Delaware and through the Morris Canal. These were made in two sections hinged together, to enable them to pass up and over the steep inclines of the planes. From then on the canal begun to prosper. At the peak of its prosperity in 1866 there were as many as 1,200 boats in operation, an average of 12 boats a mile.

But the reorganization came too late. Whereas the usual time for the trip between Phillipsburg and Jersey City was five days, railroads were now able to haul coal between the two points in eight hours. Each car, carrying almost as much as a canal boat, continued to draw tighter and tighter the noose that was slowly but surely choking life from the canal.

Besides the railroad competition, which alone was enough to kill the canal traffic, there were other forces at work. The canal basin in Jersey City had become enormously valuable for other purposes. The Lehigh Valley Railroad, which had leased the canal in 1871, had found it a burden to carry. The revenue was not sufficient to pay for the upkeep, but under the terms of the lease the railroad company was obliged to keep the canal navigable. When traffic had dwindled to little or nothing the company demanded that the State take over the property. This was in 1903. Finally no craft were seen along the quiet waterway except a few canoes or motorboats on pleasure voyages to and from Lake Hopatcong.

Probably the most insistent demand for abandonment came from Hudson Maxim, one of the inventors of smokeless powder, who owned many hundreds of acres at Lake Hopatcong, the primary source of water for the canal. Under the charter the canal company had been permitted to construct a 6-foot dam to hold the water of the lake in time of flood and heavy rainfall, thus ensuring a sufficient supply for operation in abnormally dry seasons. As a result the surface area of the lake, already the largest in New Jersey, was more than doubled in size. But if, as permitted by law, this 6-foot supply was drawn off, parts of Lake Hopatcong would become a mudflat, reeking with decaying vegetation.

While it was conceded that the canal was worthless for transportation and that in the cities the sluggish waters were a menace to health, there were many who fought strenuously to preserve its rural sections as beauty spots. The Morris Canal Parkway Association was formed to champion the cause of the derelict. It was not concerned with the sections of the canal that ran through cities. The members were willing to compromise with Maxim and guarantee that only the overflow waters of Lake Hopatcong would be used. They pointed out that with the discontinuance of canal boat traffic the enormous amount of water needed to work the locks and planes would be saved.

But the State Assemblymen, in whose hands the fate of the canal rested in 1924, thought otherwise. During the countless hearings that took place they heard the old canal referred to as "an open sewer" and "a man-made octopus sapping northern New Jersey of its water." And so it was that the old Morris Canal, doomed from its birth, was finally abandoned officially.

The canal is now dead, a dried ditch, its towpaths overgrown with brush and weeds, its locks, planes and bridges obliterated. Only here and there remain shallow stretches of stagnant water.

There are many who remember it in its day of good service when tired mules tugged and pulled the clumsy barges; when man and beast rested while a spinning water wheel dragged the boat and cargo uphill to the next level; when the air resounded with shouts and cracking whips.

Mules were driven not by lines but by shouted commands. "Gee" meant go to the right, "Haw," left. Those words were and are still used in driving oxen. But another, doubtless of French origin, "petitwhoa," meant, in mule, not to "whoa" at all but to "dig in your toes." This was used when a boat loaded with 70 tons of coal or ore had to be started out of a lock. A too sudden surge or yank would break the towline. This would have meant an outburst of profanity and possibly a beating with the huge blacksnake whip that the driver always carried. So the mules soon learned that "petitwhoa" meant just that— "whoa, a little."

When an old mule had outlived his usefulness, he went to his reward. He was led to the nearest canal-mule cemetery, knocked over the head with the dull end of an axe and buried in a shallow grave. One of these canal-mule burying grounds is a part of the seventh hole of Rockaway River Golf Course at Denville.

Canal boats had to be steered, otherwise they would run "spang" into the bank as the mules towed them along. The boatman, usually the captain, did the steering while his hand drove the mules.

One of the few pieces of poetry originating on the Morris Canal was sung to the tune of *Climbing Up the Golden Stairs*. A verse went something like this:

Old Bill Miller
Ridin' on the tiller
Steering 'round the Browertown Bend;
Old Davy Ross
With a ten dollar hoss
Comin' up the Pompton Plane.

The "canaller's" life was a sort of gypsy, vagabond existence, out in the open with little hard work. When it once got into a man's blood it stayed with him. There are many cases where "canalling" was the chosen occupation of entire families through generations.

The number of people who sometimes lived in a small boat cabin was almost unbelievable. There were no toilet accommodations of any kind. Bathing was done with a tin basin on deck. When washday came the clothes were strung from the towline posts.

Aside from the boatmen, the workmen were mostly lock tenders, plane tenders and towpath walkers. The last were just what the name implies. They walked the towpaths, covering a beat of from 6 to 10 miles, on a sharp lookout for possible leaks which might flood an entire area. The chief enemies of the towpath walker were muskrats who burrowed into the banks to make their nests. A colony would almost honeycomb a bank in a few days if not prevented.

In Newark there are several living reminders of the waterway. Plane Street is the site of one of the planes on the canal. On Orange Street, just below First Street, is one of the old drums used to pull the boats up the rise and over Orange Street. The Newark subway is built on the old canal bed where it ran under Broad Street between the old post office and Kresge's Department Store and under the old Center Market, as far as Mulberry Street. Here the boatmen were forced to pole the barges through the dark, damp tunnel, ill smelling and alive with rats. Near Waterloo, in Sussex County, there is a small section preserved by the State, the only part of the 109 miles that is still usable.

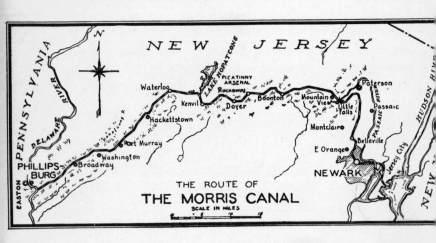

THE ROUTE OF
THE MORRIS CANAL
SCALE IN MILES

THE LINCOLN TUNNEL

The Lincoln Tunnel, latest vehicular traffic link between New York and New Jersey, is buried 20 feet or more under the mud bed of Hudson River. Built in four years by the Port of New York Authority, at a cost for the south tube of about $45,000,000 and 15 lives, the Lincoln Tunnel provides direct access from Weehawken, New Jersey, to 39th Street, Manhattan, lessening the congestion of the Holland Tunnel in rush hours and the necessity of traveling the crowded downtown area of New York City. It will connect by means of Manhattan's non-parking crosstown streets with the New York-Queens Midtown Tunnel now being constructed under the East River to form a direct route from New Jersey to Long Island. Completion of the twin or north tube has been deferred, and meantime the south tube is operated on a two-way traffic basis.

It must have been close to this spot that Colonel John Stevens, the Hoboken inventor and engineer, planned to lay his vehicular tunnel under the Hudson in 1806. But the site and the idea are the only similarities. The iron and concrete of the Lincoln Tunnel do not bear much relationship to the wooden tube that John Stevens proposed to lay on the Hudson River bed. The colonel drew plans for a tunnel with an eight-foot diameter to be constructed in sections and sunk to the river bottom. He even took depth soundings to show that his project would not interfere with river shipping. One thing he did not count on: the difficulty of getting American capitalists to invest in so novel and fantastic a scheme. He never got the money.

Technical advances made a tunnel beneath the Hudson a reality in 1908 when the Morton Street tubes of the Hudson and Manhattan Railroad were put into service. The facilities for individual vehicles, which John Stevens dreamed of, were not provided, however, until 1927, when the Holland Tunnel was finished.

The Lincoln Tunnel was projected shortly after completion of the Holland Tunnel, but because of the 1929 crash construction was postponed until the Federal Government came to the Port Authority's aid with a loan of $37,500,000 on September 1, 1933. A loan of $26,000,000 was made available four years later. All Federal advances subsequently were repaid. The Government also provided outright grants of $4,700,000 to construct certain westward extensions of the approaches, and $3,100,000 to be applied to labor cost.

Early in the spring of 1934 a shaft 30 by 40 feet was dug 55 feet deep at the base of the Palisades. At the bottom of the shaft the 400-ton "shield" was constructed, and the actual work of boring the tunnel began. The shield, a British invention first used in a simple form in 1825, is substantially a large steel pipe with a sharp edge at the front to cut through the earth. A short distance behind this cutting edge is a heavily braced steel bulkhead with openings which can be closed when necessary. Inside this "pipe" and protected by the bulkhead the men work. As the shield was shoved forward by a ring of 28 hydraulic jacks operating under a pressure which could be raised to as much as 8,000 pounds per square inch, the tunnel builders, or "sandhogs," put together cast-iron and steel rings which form the skeleton of the tunnel.

Each of the rings, two and one-half feet wide and 31 feet in outside diameter, is composed of 14 segments and a key piece. The sections were lifted into place by a giant mechanical arm called an erector, and bolted together by a newly invented hydraulic wrench which permitted construction of 45 feet of tunnel shell in one day. The previous record had been 24 feet.

The work of constructing these rings went on inside the shield, which fitted like a thimble over the first several feet of the tunnel. Where passing through rock at each end of the tunnel, the space between the outside of the tunnel rings and the rock was filled with cement and sand forced through holes in the segments under 90 pounds of pressure. This is known as "grouting" and serves to protect the tunnel by filling the voids.

Operations were started in solid ground at each side of the river. Here solid rock was encountered, which the

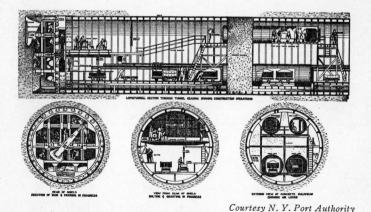

Courtesy N. Y. Port Authority

CHART OF TUNNELING OPERATION

men had to blast away. As the work progressed, test holes were drilled diagonally upward so that the point at which soft ground began could be determined. Once water-bearing material was reached, a concrete bulkhead, 10 feet thick, was built so that the forward part of the tunnel could be sealed airtight to allow the use of compressed air.

Now began the most dangerous part of the work. Erection of the tunnel rings proceeded in the same manner, but under entirely different conditions. Air under pressure was forced into the area in front of the concrete bulkhead to counteract the inward pressure of the water and the river mud. Instead of solid rock, the shield now encountered soft mud through which it could force its way without blasting. All the front openings of the shield except two were sealed, and these were equipped with hydraulically operated steel doors which could be opened to allow silt to ooze into the tube. Some of the silt was retained in the tunnel as ballast; the rest was removed by small cars such as are used in mines. The mud ballast deposited along the floor served to weigh the tunnel down until it was ready for concreting.

In general, there was a tendency for the tube to rise, because the weight of the hollow, air-filled shell was less than the weight of the greenish-gray mud which it displaced. For the same reason, an empty milk bottle will spring to the surface once the weight which keeps it under water is removed.

The driving of the shield along its intended line was directed by the engineers, and its position constantly checked by precise survey methods. Any tendency of the shield to deviate from its true course was corrected by applying the force of the jacks *unequally* to bring it back to its true course.

A finished tunnel passing (as does this one) through Hudson River silt has been found to move imperceptibly with the tides of the river and with the changing seasons. In the case of a previously built tunnel, the rise and fall with the tide was found to be only one-eighth of an inch; each year it rises and falls one-quarter of an inch. Over a period of years the structure also settled slightly. No such figures are yet available for the Lincoln Tunnel. Compared with the George Washington Bridge, the deck of which is 6 feet lower in hot weather than in cold, the tunnel movement is inconsequential.

In the confined tube, sweating in the high temperature and constantly exposed to threats of explosion and inundation, the sandhogs worked under air pressures that ranged between 8 and 45 pounds above normal. They were not allowed to smoke because of the danger of fire; in the higher pressures they could not whistle because the compressed air was too heavy to put into vibration. Air pressure was the tyrant which ruled their work; it determined their wages and working hours, protected them against flood or threatened them with illness and fire.

The hours and pay for these "human moles" are regulated by the amount of pressure under which they work. Up to 18 pounds of pressure, they receive a minimum of $10 for an eight-hour day. The wages increase and the number of hours they may work decreases until a man gets a minimum of $13 for a day consisting of two periods, each of one-half hour, at 48 to 50 pounds of pressure.

Unless great care is taken, the change from compressed air to normal air pressure causes a painful and dangerous illness known as caisson disease or the "bends." The nitrogen forming part of the air breathed in while under compression is not freed immediately when pressure is removed but, for a time, remains in the blood stream and tissues. When the individual returns suddenly to a normal atmosphere, the internal pressure of the compressed nitrogen is not counterbalanced by an external pressure, hence it forms gas bubbles that cause agonizing pains in the joints of the body, distention of the heart and loss of the sense of balance. In extreme cases it may even cause death.

To guard against this disease, the sandhogs enter and leave the tunnel through large boilerlike tanks or airlocks which are built in the concrete bulkhead. There were four such locks in the Lincoln Tunnel bulkhead—two for men and two for materials. The locks are equipped to increase or decrease the air pressure gradually.

Shifts of 20 to 30 men, on entering the tunnel, stay in the airlock only a few minutes until the pressure equals that in the working area. When they leave, they are required to remain in the lock for a period which depends upon the working pressure and ranges up to 50 minutes, so that the body has ample time to lose all the high-pressure nitrogen. Sandhogs must be served coffee on reaching a normal atmosphere.

A newspaper reporter once went down into a tunnel to observe operations and carried with him a bottle of whisky. While there, he took a drink and recapped the bottle. Later, in the airlock as the air pressure was being reduced, the bottle exploded. The high air pressure in the partly empty bottle had enough power to shatter the glass when the external pressure did not offer resistance. This is an exaggerated example of what happens to sandhogs with the bends.

Although cases of the bends have been greatly reduced today, the Lincoln Tunnel diggers had to wear badges bearing the notice: "Compressed air employee. If ill rush by ambulance to hospital lock at 38th Street and Eleventh Avenue or south of Pier K at Hudson River, Wee-hawken."

At one period during the progress of the work, in 25 working days 1,040 feet, or approximately one-fourth of the underriver section of the tunnel, was bored. This was a record in underwater tunneling. At the start, however, progress was much slower because of the rock. At times the upper part of the shield was cutting through muck while the lower part encountered rock. In this area it was particularly necessary to drill for a distance in front of the shield to discover soft spots. If the shield should cut into the soft spot unexpectedly, the compressed air might force its way through to the surface, allowing the water and muck to enter the tunnel and, incidentally, causing a violent disturbance in the water above. This is known as a "blow."

The two sections of the tunnel were to meet at the New York wharf line. A huge steel box, 52 by 45 by 100 feet, with cutting edges along its open bottom, was lowered into the river. The sandhogs worked in the bottom of this caisson in pressures up to 45 pounds and high temperatures, digging out the muck and rock. As they dug, the caisson sank while the air pressure kept out the river.

In December 1934, after six months of work, the caisson was brought down to final position at a depth of 100 feet, the bottom paved with concrete and the compressed air removed. The structure awaited the shields approaching from either side. On August 2, 1935, about a year and a half after digging had begun, the first tube of the Lincoln Tunnel was "holed through." The shields, which had finished their job, were taken apart, and the two sections met inside the caisson, the centers within one-quarter of an inch of each other!

When the two sections of the 8,215-foot tube had been joined, the bulkheads and compressed air were no longer necessary. The interior was lined with 16 inches of concrete and faced with tile, the brick roadway (21½ feet wide) was laid, and telephone, telegraph, electricity and ventilating systems were installed. The caisson, concreted permanently in place, served as the foundation for one of the ventilating plants; the others were built at the shafts in Manhattan and Weehawken, where the work began.

The white tiled walls with blue borders went up, and the ceiling of glass tiles, stippled to reduce glare from lights, was placed. This is the largest glass ceiling in the world. If one man alone could have built the Lincoln Tunnel, he would have had to work more than 720 years. If he could also have manufactured and transported all the materials, he would have spent an additional 17 centuries! Fifty thousand tons of iron and steel alone were used for the tunnel skeleton, which was fastened together with 346,000 bolts, each weighing 10 pounds with nuts and washers.

Ex-President Herbert Hoover was present at the ceremonies in the tunnel on October 15, 1937, to celebrate its completion. The formal dedication took place the following December 21 in the presence of Governors Herbert Lehman of New York and Harold Hoffman of New Jersey, Mayor Fiorello La Guardia of New York City and Secretary of the Interior Harold Ickes.

Meanwhile, work had begun on the second tube of the tunnel, which was holed through in the spring of 1938. At that time the Port of New York Authority decided to postpone completion of the second tube until connecting links with New Jersey's major highways had been finished. The north tube, like the one already in use, will measure 4,600 feet under the river, but will be only 7,400 feet from portal to portal.

The ventilation system, which in general follows the plan developed for the Holland Tunnel, changes the air in the tunnel completely every one and one-half minutes. The intakes are spaced along the curbs near the tunnel floor; the vitiated air, lighter than the fresh air because of the presence of the heated gases of automobile exhausts, rises and is sucked out through ducts placed about 15 feet apart along the ceiling. The system is so planned that even if a considerable number of the 32 gigantic fans which keep the air flow regular were to break down, traffic could continue uninterrupted.

Traffic in the tunnel is planned and controlled with the same care. Vehicles with Diesel engines, trucks carrying gasoline and explosives, or any vehicle over five tons with a speed less than 20 miles per hour are forbidden. Service trucks maintained by the Port of New York Authority make necessary tire repairs and provide towing facilities free of charge. The policemen on duty alternate two hours in the tunnel and two hours on the plaza to keep the cars spaced 75 feet apart and moving steadily at 30 miles an hour.

In addition to the Lincoln Tunnel, the Port of New York Authority owns and operates the Holland Tunnel, George Washington Bridge, Bayonne Bridge, Goethals Bridge, Outerbridge Crossing and the Port Authority Commerce Building. Created in 1921 by an agreement between New York and New Jersey with the approval of Congress, the Authority is a nonprofit public agency, the purpose of which is to develop the Port of New York area—the commercial, industrial and financial center of the Nation. The 12 commissioners, six from each State, are appointed for a six-year period. They serve without pay.

The Port Authority obtains its funds by borrowing on its credit. It sells bonds, which are promises to pay a certain amount of money with interest. Those who buy the bonds do so because they believe that the Port Authority will be able to pay back this money with its income from the revenues collected from its facilities. In this the Port Authority is unlike other government agencies, which are supported by taxes. By the Port Authority method, the various facilities are paid for by those who use them. Residents of New Jersey and New York who do not use the tunnels or bridges therefore do not contribute one cent to their support.

Motor traffic over the Hudson doubled between 1925 and 1931, when 26,000,000 vehicles crossed the river. Some estimates indicate that within the next 25 years 280,000 vehicles will travel across the Hudson daily. The Lincoln Tunnel is the latest step in planning for this future.